Best of
Cold Foods

Foreword by Mable Hoffman

HPBooks®

ANOTHER BEST-SELLING VOLUME FROM HPBooks®

Publisher: Rick Bailey
Editorial Director: Retha M. Davis
Editor: Carroll P. Latham
Art Director: Don Burton
Book Assembly: Kathleen Koopman, Barry Myers
Book Manufacture: Anthony B. Narducci
Recipe testing by International Cookbook Services: Barbara Bloch, President; Rita Barrett, Director of Testing; Nancy Strada, Testing Assistant

Published by HPBooks, Inc.
P.O. Box 5367, Tucson, AZ 85703   602/888-2150
ISBN 0-89586-336-7
Library of Congress Catalog Card Number 85-60201
©1985 HPBooks, Inc.   Printed in West Germany
1st Printing

First published under the title *Die beste Dr. Oetker Kalte Küche*
©1982 by Ceres-Verlag Rudolf-August Oetker KG, Bielefeld

Contents

Salads _____ 60-77

Crisp Summer Salad, page 77.

Aspics & Mousses _____ 78-91

Green-Vegetable Aspic, page 86.

Fish & Shellfish 92-107

Gravlax with Dill Sauce, page 95.

Steak Tartare, page 110.

Filled French Loaf, page 146.

Salmon & Caviar Sandwiches, page 150.

Tequila Splash, page 206.

Caviar Appetizer, page 37

Live Lobster with Truffles.

Foreword

Mable Hoffman is author of the classic *Crockery Cookery, Crepe Cookery* and five other best-selling cookbooks. Together, Hoffman cookbooks have won five Tastemaker Awards, the coveted "Oscar" for cookbooks, and have sold over 8 million copies worldwide.

Gone are the days when most of our meals consisted of family recipes handed down from our mothers and grandmothers. Our food horizons and interests have expanded drastically. Every year, more of us who travel to Europe or other parts of the world are introduced to new and exciting foods. We return home with an appreciation for new ingredients, new flavors and new methods of food preparation. We want to duplicate these new-found dishes in our own kitchens. Local supermarkets, in an effort to satisfy our desires, offer an increasing selection of foods.

Best of Cold Foods is a cookbook that is born out of this new awareness. It includes everything from unusual appetizers and nibblers to impress your friends, to luscious make-ahead desserts that wait in your refrigerator or freezer until you are ready to serve them. Originally developed in Germany, the recipes have been kitchen-tested by International Cookbook Services, an experienced U.S. recipe-testing firm and carefully edited by the exacting staff at HPBooks.

When I heard about *Best of Cold Foods,* my first thought was that the book would have wonderful suggestions that would enable me to serve delicious food without spending hours in a hot kitchen. And my expectations were fulfilled. The book contains dozens of main-dish salads and fruit platters that hit the spot on a sweltering summer evening. But even more helpful are the many other recipes that fit into our busy lives throughout the year. Take a look at some of the breads or sandwiches and you'll see what I mean. Sesame-Seed Bread, page 130, or French Luncheon Loaf, page 142, present a pleasant way to break the monotonous lunch-box syndrome. Stuffed Greek Aspic, page 88, is equally good at Easter or New Years. Special-Occasion Breakfast, page 106, is excellent for any occasion.

America's obsession with outdoor eating—whether it is a family picnic in the park or a tailgate get-together before the big game—calls for foods that are packable and good to eat. A quick look at the recipes in this book will reveal ideas that fit into your particular outdoor activity.

For home entertaining, all of us prefer to spend time with our guests instead of preparing last-minute dishes in the kitchen. What could be more relaxing than a menu where foods are prepared ahead, giving you time to enjoy your own party? There's a wide range of picture-perfect, make-ahead aspics and terrines featuring various kinds of seafood, poultry and vegetables accented with fresh or dried herbs. Many of these impressive dishes, made with fresh ingredients, fit into our current interest in healthy foods that are low in cholesterol and calories.

Speaking of picture-perfect dishes, there is at least one beautiful color photograph on almost every page. These clear and appetizing reproductions of the food look so appealing that you want to rush right out to the kitchen to begin creating. It's much more fun to try a new recipe when you're inspired by a beautiful photograph of the finished food.

The recipes in this book are written in an easy-to-follow style with details on final preparation and garnishing. The photos complete the picture by showing finished foods in their proper serving dishes and give you excellent examples to duplicate. Garnishing details—such as a feathery sprig of fresh dill on a shrimp appetizer, a thin twist of lemon peel curled around tender green beans or a swirl of whipped cream and shaved chocolate over a cherry dessert—increase appetite appeal and show you quick ways to dress up these dishes.

Most dramatic of all are the larger-than-life, double-page photos that separate the chapters. They provide unbelievable impact as you leaf through the book. I think you'll find this book a most impressive as well as informative addition to your cookbook collection. It certainly presents "cold foods at their best."

Mabel Hoffman

Appetizers

Lobster-Pineapple Appetizer

Seafood Appetizer

1/4 cup dry white wine or dry vermouth
1/4 cup water
4 black peppercorns
1 lemon wedge
1/4 teaspoon salt
1/2 lb. sole or flounder fillets
1/4 lb. mushrooms
1 (8-3/4-oz.) can mussels, drained
1 (7-oz.) can shrimp, drained
1 (8-oz.) can cut white or green asparagus, drained
2 tablespoons mayonnaise
2 tablespoons dairy sour cream
2 tablespoons orange juice
1 tablespoon ketchup
1 teaspoon prepared horseradish
1 tablespoon brandy, if desired
Salt and freshly ground pepper
Lettuce leaves
Dill sprigs

In a medium skillet, combine white wine or vermouth, water, peppercorns, lemon and 1/4 teaspoon salt. Add fish fillets. Bring to a simmer; simmer until fish flakes easily, about 5 minutes. Use a wide spatula to remove poached fish from liquid; set aside to cool. Slice mushrooms. In a medium bowl, combine mussels, shrimp, asparagus and sliced mushrooms. Cut cooled fish into 3/4-inch pieces; add to shrimp mixture, tossing gently to distribute. In a small bowl, combine mayonnaise, sour cream, orange juice, ketchup, horseradish and brandy, if desired. Stir in salt and pepper to taste.
To serve, line 4 to 6 cocktail glasses with lettuce. Spoon seafood mixture into lettuce-lined glasses. Top each cocktail with a dollop of dressing. Garnish with dill sprigs. Serve cold. Makes 4 to 6 servings.

Lobster-Pineapple Appetizer

1 egg yolk
1 tablespoon vinegar or lemon juice
2 teaspoons prepared mustard
1 teaspoon sugar
Pinch of salt
Pinch of freshly ground pepper
1/2 cup olive oil or vegetable oil
1/4 cup whipping cream
1 tablespoon dry sherry
1/4 lb. mushrooms
1 (8-oz.) can lobster, drained
1 (8-oz.) can pineapple chunks, drained
4 lettuce leaves
4 parsley sprigs

Beat egg yolk in a 2-cup measure. Stir in vinegar or lemon juice, mustard, sugar, salt and pepper. Pour oil into cup very slowly, beating constantly with a small whisk. Beat in cream and sherry. Slice mushrooms. Set 4 lobster pieces aside for garnish. In a medium bowl, combine remaining lobster, pineapple and sliced mushrooms.
To serve, spoon into 4 cocktail glasses. Pour dressing over each. Garnish each cocktail with 1 reserved lobster piece, lettuce leaf and parsley sprig. Serve cold. Makes 4 servings.

Seafood Appetizer

On previous pages: Steamed Shrimp, page 33

Broccoli Appetizer

1 lb. broccoli
3 tomatoes
4 oz. Camembert cheese, diced (about 1 cup)
1/2 cup mayonnaise
1/2 cup dairy sour cream
1 tablespoon finely chopped fresh tarragon or
   1 tablespoon Pernod
Salt and freshly ground pepper
Lettuce leaves
Chopped pistachios, if desired

Break broccoli into short flowerets. Cook in lightly salted water until crisp-tender, about 7 minutes. Drain in a colander; rinse with cold water to stop cooking. Reserve 8 to 12 flowerets for garnish. Place remaining cooked flowerets in a medium bowl. Peel and dice tomatoes. Add diced tomatoes and cheese to cooked broccoli; toss gently. In a small bowl, combine mayonnaise, sour cream and tarragon or Pernod. Stir in salt and pepper to taste.

To serve, line 4 to 6 cocktail glasses with lettuce. Spoon vegetable mixture into lettuce-lined glasses; pour dressing over each. Garnish with reserved broccoli flowerets and pistachios, if desired. Serve cold. Makes 4 to 6 servings.

Broccoli Appetizer

Lobster Cocktail

2 tomatoes
1 lb. cooked lobster
1/2 cup plain yogurt
1 tablespoon Italian seasoning
Salt and freshly ground pepper
1 (8-1/2-oz.) can whole-kernel corn, drained
12 pimento-stuffed green olives, sliced
Dill sprigs

Cut tomatoes into wedges. Remove seeds; cut tomato wedges into strips. Cut lobster into 3/4-inch pieces. Set tomato strips and lobster pieces aside. Spoon yogurt into a small bowl; stir until smooth. Stir in Italian seasoning. Add salt and pepper to taste. In a medium bowl, combine tomato strips, lobster pieces, corn and olives; toss gently to distribute.

To serve, spoon into 4 cocktail glasses. Top each with a dollop of dressing; garnish each with a dill sprig. Serve cold. Makes 4 servings.

Lobster Cocktail

Asparagus-Shrimp Cocktail in Orange Cups

Asparagus-Shrimp Cocktail in Orange Cups

1 qt. water (4 cups)
1 bay leaf
1 tablespoon mustard seeds
1/4 teaspoon dill seeds
1/4 teaspoon salt
4 black peppercorns
1/2 lb. large unshelled shrimp (8 to 12)
1 (14-1/2-oz.) can cut white or green asparagus, drained
5 tablespoons mayonnaise
2 tablespoons whipping cream
2 tablespoons dry sherry
2 teaspoons lemon juice
Salt and freshly ground pepper
2 large oranges

In a large saucepan, combine water, bay leaf, mustard seeds, dill seeds, salt and peppercorns. Bring to a boil; simmer about 4 minutes. Add shrimp; simmer 2 to 4 minutes or until shrimp become firm and turn pink. Drain, discarding liquid, bay leaf, seeds and peppercorns. Shell and devein cooked shrimp; set aside. In a medium bowl, combine asparagus and shelled shrimp; set aside. In a small bowl, combine mayonnaise, cream, sherry and lemon juice. Stir in salt and pepper to taste. Spoon over shrimp mixture; stir gently. Cut oranges in half; scoop out fruit. Remove seeds and white pith from fruit; cut fruit into small pieces. Stir fruit pieces into shrimp mixture.

To serve, place orange shells on individual plates; fill with shrimp mixture. Serve cold. Makes 4 servings.

Tomato-Filled Zucchini Boats

4 zucchini, each about 6 inches long
3/4 cup bottled Italian dressing
3 tomatoes
1/2 cup diced green bell pepper
1/2 cup diced celery
1/4 cup chopped ripe olives
1 teaspoon Italian seasoning
1 garlic clove, if desired, minced
Salt and freshly ground black pepper
Lettuce
Finely chopped fresh parsley

Trim ends off zucchini. Cook trimmed zucchini in lightly salted water until crisp-tender, about 8 minutes. Cut each cooked zucchini in half lengthwise; scoop out seeds. Place zucchini boats in a shallow glass dish, cut-side up. Reserve 1/4 cup Italian dressing. Sprinkle 1/2 cup Italian dressing over zucchini boats. Refrigerate at least 2 hours.

To complete, peel and finely chop tomatoes. In a medium bowl, combine chopped tomatoes, bell pepper, celery, olives, Italian seasoning and garlic, if desired. Stir in salt and black pepper to taste and reserved 1/4 cup Italian dressing. Line 4 individual plates with lettuce. Drain marinated zucchini boats.

To serve, place 2 marinated zucchini boats on each lettuce-lined plate. Spoon tomato mixture into boats; garnish with chopped parsley. Serve cold. Makes 4 servings.

Avocado-Crabmeat Cocktail

Smoked-Trout Appetizer

Avocado-Crabmeat Cocktail

2 ripe avocados
Lemon juice
1 (6-1/2-oz.) can crabmeat or
  1 (6-oz.) pkg. frozen crabmeat, thawed
1/4 lb. mushrooms
3/4 cup dairy sour cream
3 tablespoons ketchup
1 teaspoon prepared horseradish
1 tablespoon Italian seasoning
1 tablespoon brandy, if desired
Salt and freshly ground pepper
4 dill sprigs

Cut avocados in half lengthwise; remove pits. Scoop out flesh, leaving about 1/4 inch of flesh in shells. Dice scooped-out avocado flesh; place in a medium bowl. Sprinkle with lemon juice. Sprinkle lemon juice on flesh remaining in shells. Drain and flake crabmeat; add to diced avocado. Slice mushrooms; add to avocado mixture. Toss gently to distribute. In a small bowl, combine sour cream, ketchup, horseradish, Italian seasoning and brandy, if desired. Stir in salt and pepper to taste.
To serve, spoon salad into reserved avocado shells. Top each with a dollop of dressing; garnish each with a dill sprig. Serve cold. Makes 4 servings.

Smoked-Trout Appetizer

1 (10-oz.) pkg. frozen smoked-trout fillets (4 fillets), thawed
Lemon juice
4 escarole leaves
4 endive leaves
4 orange slices
4 teaspoons prepared horseradish

Sour-Cream & Dill Dressing:
1/4 cup dairy sour cream
4 teaspoons freshly chopped dill
1 teaspoon lemon juice
Salt and white pepper

Sprinkle trout fillets with lemon juice. Arrange escarole and endive on 4 individual plates. Place 1 fillet on each plate; garnish each with an orange slice and 1 teaspoon horseradish.
To make dressing, in a small bowl, combine sour cream, dill and lemon juice. Stir in salt and white pepper to taste. Serve trout cold with dressing. Makes 4 servings.

Top to bottom: Herbed Yogurt Dip, page 161, Cheesy Scotch Eggs

Cheesy Scotch Eggs

1/2 cup milk
1 tablespoon butter or margarine
1/2 cup sifted all-purpose flour
2 eggs
1/3 cup grated Parmesan cheese (1 oz.)
1/4 teaspoon ground nutmeg
Salt and freshly ground pepper
Dry bread crumbs or cracker meal
5 hard-cooked eggs
Vegetable oil for deep-frying
Radish sprouts
Herbed Yogurt Dressing, page 161

Cover a small plate with waxed paper; set aside. In a medium saucepan, combine milk and butter or margarine. Stirring occasionally, bring to a boil over medium heat. Remove saucepan from heat; immediately add flour. Stir until batter is smooth; beat 1 minute. Beat in 2 eggs, 1 at a time, until mixture is blended. Beat in Parmesan cheese and nutmeg. Season with salt and pepper. Pour bread crumbs or cracker meal into a small bowl. Dip hard-cooked eggs in batter, then in crumbs; place on paper-covered plate. Refrigerate 30 minutes.
To complete, heat oil in a wok, deep-fryer or large saucepan to 350F (175C) or until a 1-inch bread cube turns golden brown in 60 seconds. Deep-fry eggs, 1 or 2 at a time, until golden brown. Drain on paper towels; set aside to cool.
To serve, cut cooled eggs in half crosswise. Arrange on a platter around radish sprouts. Serve with Herbed Yogurt Dressing. Makes 10 appetizers.

Cheese Platter

Assorted cheeses, such as Swiss, St. Marcellin (goat),
    Tilsit, Camembert, provolone, Roquefort and Gouda
Purple or green grapes
Cocktail bread
Assorted plain crackers

Remove cheese from refrigerator at least 30 minutes before serving. Arrange on cheese boards or platters; decorate with grapes. Serve with cocktail bread and assorted plain crackers. Cheeses in photo will make 10 to 15 servings.

Note: Almost any assortment of cheeses is appropriate. Provide a balance between hard cheese, semi-soft cheese and soft cheese. Be sure to include both strong and mild cheese. Serve with any fresh fruit in season.

Cheese Platter

Cheese-Stuffed Pepper Slices

Cheese-Stuffed Pepper Slices

1 large green bell pepper
1 large yellow bell pepper
1 (8-oz.) pkg. cream cheese, room temperature
1/4 cup butter or margarine, room temperature
1/2 pint dairy sour cream (1 cup)
3 hard-cooked eggs
1 teaspoon prepared mustard
1 teaspoon paprika
Salt and freshly ground pepper

Cut tops off bell peppers; remove seeds. Rinse under cold running water; invert on paper towels to drain. In a large bowl, combine cream cheese, butter or margarine and sour cream; stir until blended. Press hard-cooked eggs through a sieve into cream-cheese mixture. Stir in mustard and paprika. Stir in salt and pepper to taste. Spoon mixture into drained bell peppers, packing tightly. Cover; refrigerate overnight.
To serve, cut into 1/3- to 1/2-inch-thick slices. Makes 16 to 20 slices.

Marinated-Mushroom & Ham Appetizer

3/4 lb. mushrooms
1 cup thinly sliced green onions
Lemon juice
1/3 cup olive oil
Salt and freshly ground pepper
1/4 lb. cooked ham
Finely chopped fresh parsley

Thinly slice mushrooms. In a medium bowl, combine sliced mushrooms and green onions. Sprinkle with lemon juice; then sprinkle olive oil over top. Season with salt and pepper; toss gently. Cover; refrigerate at least 2 hours. Cut ham in julienne strips.
To serve, spoon refrigerated mushroom mixture into 4 individual dishes. Arrange ham strips over tops; garnish with parsley. Serve cold. Makes 4 servings.

Caviar Slices

Caviar Slices

1 (2-oz.) jar black lumpfish caviar
5 tablespoons cream cheese, room temperature
8 slices French bread
4 lime slices
1 red onion, cut in rings
4 dill sprigs

In a small bowl, mash 1/2 of caviar; stir in cream cheese until smooth. Spoon mixture into a pastry bag fitted with an open-star tip. Pipe in a circle onto bread slices, turning pastry bag as mixture is piped. Spoon remaining caviar evenly into centers of piped cheese mixture. Place 2 caviar-topped bread slices on each of 4 individual plates. Garnish each with a lime slice, several onion rings and a dill sprig. Makes 4 servings.

Celeriac-Chive Appetizer

3/4 lb. celeriac
1/2 cup mayonnaise
1/4 cup dairy sour cream
1 tablespoon Dijon-style mustard
1 to 2 tablespoons snipped chives
Salt and freshly ground pepper
1 bunch watercress
Pimento strips

Peel celeriac; cut into julienne strips. In a medium saucepan, cook celeriac strips in lightly salted water until crisp-tender, about 5 minutes. Drain in a colander; rinse in cold water to stop cooking. Place cooked celeriac in a medium bowl; set aside. In a small bowl, combine mayonnaise, sour cream, mustard and chives. Stir in salt and pepper to taste. Spoon over cooked celeriac; toss gently to coat.
To serve, spoon coated celeriac into 4 individual dishes. Place watercress around edge of each dish; garnish celeriac with pimento strips. Serve cold. Makes 4 servings.

Smoked Salmon with Dilly Beans

1/2 lb. fresh whole green beans
1 small onion, diced
2 tablespoons vegetable oil
2 tablespoons lemon juice
1 teaspoon sugar
2 tablespoons chopped dill sprigs
Salt and freshly ground pepper
1/4 cup dairy sour cream
1/4 cup mayonnaise
2 teaspoons prepared horseradish
4 large smoked-salmon slices
4 thin lemon slices
Dill sprigs
4 thin lemon-peel strips

Cook beans in lightly salted water until crisp-tender; drain. Place drained beans in a medium glass dish. In a small bowl, combine onion, oil, lemon juice, sugar and chopped dill. Stir in salt and pepper to taste; pour over beans. Stir well; refrigerate until thoroughly chilled. In a small bowl, blend sour cream, mayonnaise and horseradish.
To serve, place 1 salmon slice and several green beans on each of 4 individual plates. Cut lemon slices in half. Curve each half into a circle; place 2 halves on or near salmon on each plate. Spoon a dollop of dressing into each circle. Garnish beans with dill sprigs and lemon-peel strips. Makes 4 servings.

Smoked Salmon with Dilly Beans

Melon & Chicken Appetizer

Melon & Chicken Appetizer

1 Persian melon
1/2 lb. mushrooms
2 cups diced cooked chicken
1/3 cup bottled vinaigrette dressing
Lemon juice
Salt and freshly ground pepper
Parsley sprigs

Cut melon into 4 wedges. Discard seeds; scoop out some flesh, leaving a thick layer of flesh in shells. Dice scooped-out flesh; place in a large bowl. Thinly slice mushrooms; add to melon. Add chicken and vinaigrette dressing. Season with lemon juice, salt and pepper. Toss to distribute.
To serve, spoon mixture onto melon quarters. Garnish with parsley sprigs. Makes 4 servings.

Variation

Add a few drops hot-pepper sauce or Worcestershire sauce to vinaigrette dressing.

Caviar-Cheese Ring

Caviar-Cheese Ring

1 (8-inch) Brie cheese wheel (about 2 lbs.)
2 (3-1/2-oz.) jars red lumpfish caviar
1/2 cup whipping cream
1 (8-oz.) carton whipped cream cheese
Salt and freshly ground pepper
1/2 cup walnut halves

Using a 2-inch biscuit cutter, cut center from Brie. Set center aside for another use. Cut ring in half horizontally, making 2 rings. Reserve 2 tablespoons caviar for garnish. Spread remaining caviar over bottom ring. Beat cream until stiff peaks form; fold into cream cheese. Season with salt and pepper. Spoon 1/2 cream-cheese mixture into a pastry bag fitted with a medium open-star tip. Spread remaining cream-cheese mixture over caviar filling. Place other half of ring on top. Press walnut halves onto side of ring.

To serve, pipe reserved cream-cheese mixture decoratively on top of ring. Garnish with reserved caviar. Makes 1 cheese ring.

Indian Shrimp Cocktail

1 qt. water (4 cups)
1 bay leaf
1 tablespoon mustard seeds
1 teaspoon dill seeds
1 lemon slice
1/4 teaspoon salt
2 black peppercorns
1/2 lb. large unshelled shrimp (8 to 12)
2 bananas
2 apples, peeled, cored, diced
Lemon juice

Curry-Ginger Dressing:
1/2 pint dairy sour cream (1 cup)
2 teaspoons chopped hazelnuts, walnuts, pecans
  or almonds
1 teaspoon curry powder
1 teaspoon ground ginger
1 teaspoon sugar
Salt
Parsley sprigs

In a large saucepan, combine water, bay leaf, mustard seeds, dill seeds, salt and peppercorns. Bring to a boil; simmer about 4 minutes. Add shrimp; simmer 2 to 4 minutes or until shrimp become firm and turn pink. Drain, discarding liquid, bay leaf, seeds and peppercorns. Refrigerate shrimp until chilled. Shell and devein cooked shrimp; set aside. Slice bananas. In a medium bowl, combine apples, sliced bananas and shelled shrimp. Sprinkle with lemon juice.

To make dressing, in a small bowl combine sour cream, nuts, curry powder, ginger, sugar and salt to taste. Spoon over fruit mixture; toss gently.

To serve, spoon fruit mixture into 4 cocktail glasses; garnish each with a parsley sprig. Serve cold. Makes 4 servings.

Salami & Glazed Onions

Shrimp-Topped Eggs

Photo on pages 24 and 25.

1 qt. water (4 cups)
1 bay leaf
1 tablespoon mustard seeds
1/4 teaspoon dill seeds
1/4 teaspoon salt
2 black peppercorns
8 large unshelled shrimp
4 hard-cooked eggs
1/2 (8-oz.) carton whipped cream cheese
1 to 2 tablespoons whipping cream
1 teaspoon paprika
1 teaspoon curry powder
Salt and freshly ground pepper
2 lemon slices, quartered
Dill sprigs

In a large saucepan, combine water, bay leaf, mustard seeds, dill seeds, salt and peppercorns. Bring to a boil; simmer about 4 minutes. Add shrimp; simmer 2 to 4 minutes or until shrimp become firm and turn pink. Drain, discarding liquid, bay leaf, seeds and peppercorns. Refrigerate shrimp until chilled. Shell and devein cooked shrimp; set aside. Cut eggs in half lengthwise. Remove yolks; set egg whites aside. Mash yolks or press through a sieve into a medium bowl. Stir in cream cheese, 1 tablespoon whipping cream, paprika and curry powder until mixture is creamy. Stir in salt and pepper to taste. Add more cream, if necessary. Spoon into a pastry bag fitted with a closed-star tip.
To serve, pipe mixture evenly into reserved egg whites. Place shelled shrimp on top of filling; garnish with lemon quarters and dill sprigs. Serve cold. Makes 8 appetizers.

Salami & Glazed Onions

2 tablespoons olive oil
1/2 lb. pearl onions
2 tablespoons sugar
Salt and freshly ground pepper
1/2 cup dry white wine
2 tablespoons lemon juice
1 tablespoon tarragon vinegar
1/4 lb. Genoa salami, very thinly sliced
Mint sprigs
4 tomato wedges
French bread

Heat olive oil in a small skillet. Add onions; sauté about 4 minutes, stirring constantly. Sprinkle with sugar; season with salt and pepper. Cook until onions are lightly browned, stirring constantly. Add wine, lemon juice and vinegar. Cook over low heat 10 to 15 minutes. Set aside until cool. Drain well.
To serve, arrange salami, cooked onions with dressing, mint and tomato wedges on 4 individual plates. Serve with French bread. Makes 4 servings.

Shrimp-Filled Avocado

Shrimp-Filled Avocados

1 qt. water (4 cups)
1 bay leaf
1 tablespoon mustard seeds
1/4 teaspoon dill seeds
1/4 teaspoon salt
2 black peppercorns
1/2 lb. small unshelled shrimp (about 35)
2 ripe avocados
Lemon juice
3 medium tomatoes

Creamy Dill Sauce:
1/2 cup dairy sour cream
1/4 cup half and half
2 tablespoons finely chopped fresh dill
1 teaspoon Worcestershire sauce
Salt and freshly ground pepper
Lemon juice
Hot-pepper sauce
Lettuce leaves
4 lemon slices
4 dill sprigs

In a large saucepan, combine water, bay leaf, mustard seeds, dill seeds, salt and peppercorns. Bring to a boil; simmer about 4 minutes. Add shrimp; simmer 2 to 4 minutes or until shrimp become firm and turn pink. Drain, discarding liquid, bay leaf, seeds and peppercorns. Refrigerate shrimp until chilled. Shell and devein cooked shrimp; set aside. Cut avocados in half lengthwise; remove pits. Scoop out flesh, leaving about 1/4 inch of flesh in shells. Sprinkle lemon juice on flesh remaining in shells. Dice scooped-out avocado flesh; place in a medium bowl. Sprinkle lightly with lemon juice. Dice tomatoes. Add diced tomatoes and shelled shrimp to diced avocado; toss to distribute. Fill avocado shells with shrimp mixture.
To make sauce, in a small bowl, combine sour cream, half and half, chopped dill and Worcestershire sauce. Season to taste with salt, pepper, lemon juice and hot-pepper sauce. Spoon over shrimp mixture.
To serve, arrange lettuce leaves on 4 individual plates. Place 1 filled avocado half on each plate. Garnish each with a lemon slice and dill sprig. Makes 4 servings.

Ham-Stuffed Tomatoes

4 large tomatoes
2 tablespoons mayonnaise
2 tablespoons plain yogurt
1 tablespoon vinegar
Pinch of paprika
Salt and freshly ground black pepper
1/2 small green bell pepper
3/4 lb. cooked ham
Lettuce leaves
4 parsley sprigs

On stem end, cut off about 1/4 of each tomato; remove seeds and juice from tomatoes, leaving shells intact. Invert on paper towels to drain. In a small bowl, combine mayonnaise, yogurt, vinegar and paprika. Stir in salt and black pepper to taste. Dice bell pepper; cut ham in julienne strips. Stir diced bell pepper and ham strips into mayonnaise mixture.
To serve, spoon mixture evenly into drained tomato shells. Garnish with parsley sprigs. Line a small platter with lettuce leaves. Arrange stuffed tomatoes on a lettuce-lined platter. Serve cold. Makes 4 servings

On previous pages, from left: Filled Artichoke Bottoms, page 27; Shrimp-Topped Eggs, page 23; Pâté-Topped Veal Medallions, page 28; Firm Aspic, page 84.

Leeks with Vinaigrette

Leeks with Vinaigrette

8 to 12 leeks
1 garlic clove
3 tablespoons vegetable oil
2 tablespoons white-wine vinegar
1 tablespoon prepared mustard
2 tablespoons finely chopped chives
Salt and freshly ground pepper
1 hard-cooked egg

Wash leeks thoroughly to remove sand. Trim off green ends. Place trimmed leeks in a large saucepan; add garlic. Cover with lightly salted water; bring to a boil. Simmer about 15 minutes or until leeks are tender. Drain; discard garlic. Set cooked leeks aside to cool. In a small bowl, combine oil, vinegar, mustard and chives. Stir in salt and pepper to taste. Place cooled leeks on a platter; pour dressing over top. Refrigerate 1 to 2 hours.
To serve, chop hard-cooked egg. Sprinkle chopped egg over leeks; serve cold. Makes 4 servings.

Filled Artichoke Bottoms

Photo on pages 24 and 25.

8 canned artichoke bottoms, drained
1/3 lb. liver pâté
About 2 tablespoons dairy sour cream
1 tablespoon brandy
2 kiwifruit slices, quartered
Fresh herbs

Drain artichoke bottoms; set aside. In a medium bowl, combine pâté, 2 tablespoons sour cream and brandy; stir until smooth. Add more sour cream, if necessary. Spoon into a pastry bag fitted with an open-star tip; pipe mixture evenly onto artichoke bottoms. Garnish each with a piece of kiwifruit and fresh herbs. Makes 8 appetizers.

Celery with Creamed Roquefort

4 large celery stalks
8 oz. Roquefort cheese, crumbled, room temperature
2 to 3 tablespoons whipping cream
Hot-pepper sauce

Rinse celery stalks; arrange on a platter. Press cheese through a sieve into a small bowl. Blend in cream and hot-pepper sauce to taste, stirring until smooth. Spoon cheese mixture into a pastry bag fitted with an open-star tip. Pipe cheese into celery stalks. Refrigerate until ready to serve. Makes 4 servings.

Quick & Easy Pâté

1 (8-oz.) pkg. cream cheese, room temperature
1/2 lb. liverwurst
1 teaspoon Worcestershire sauce
1/3 cup finely chopped walnuts, pecans or hazelnuts
Parsley sprigs
Cocktail bread
Assorted crackers

In a blender or food processor fitted with a metal blade, process cream cheese and liverwurst until smooth. Stir in Worcestershire sauce and nuts. Spoon into a serving dish; refrigerate until ready to serve.
To serve, garnish with parsley sprigs. Serve with cocktail bread and assorted crackers. Makes about 2 cups.

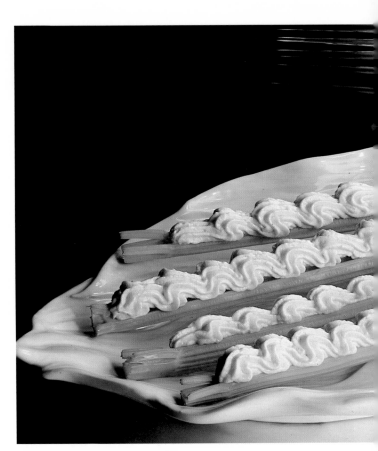

Celery with Creamed Roquefort

Pâté-Topped Veal Medallions

Photo on pages 24 and 25.

2 to 3 tablespoons butter or margarine
1 lb. boneless veal-loin roast, cut in 8 slices
Salt and freshly ground pepper
2 tablespoons brandy
1/3 lb. liver pâté
About 2 tablespoons dairy sour cream
Sliced maraschino cherries
Mandarin-orange sections
Thyme leaves
Firm Aspic cubes, page 84, if desired

In a large skillet, melt butter or margarine. Add veal; sauté about 3 minutes on each side. Remove from skillet; season with salt and pepper. Sprinkle 1 tablespoon brandy over sautéed veal; set aside to cool. In a small bowl, combine liver pâté, sour cream and remaining brandy; stir until smooth. Spoon pâté mixture into a pastry bag fitted with an open-star tip.
To serve, pipe pâté mixture onto each sautéed veal slice. Garnish with cherries, orange sections and thyme leaves. Garnish with Firm Aspic cubes, if desired. Makes 8 appetizers

Unbaked Savory Cheese Pie

1 cup salted-soda-cracker crumbs
3 tablespoons butter or margarine, melted
1 (8-oz.) pkg. cream cheese, room temperature
1/2 pint dairy sour cream (1 cup)
1 tablespoon Worcestershire sauce
1/2 cup chopped celery
1/2 cup chopped ripe olives
1/4 cup chopped red bell pepper
1/4 cup chopped green bell pepper
2 tablespoons snipped chives
3 or 4 drops hot-pepper sauce
Salt
Pimento strips
Ripe-olive halves
Fresh fruit
Assorted crackers

Lightly grease bottom and side of an 8-inch springform pan. Place cracker crumbs in a small bowl. Stir in butter or margarine until blended. Press over bottom of greased pan. Refrigerate until chilled. In a medium bowl, stir cream cheese until smooth. Stir in sour cream and Worcestershire sauce. Stir in celery, chopped olives, bell peppers and chives. Season with hot-pepper sauce and salt. Spread over chilled crust; smooth top. Cover with plastic wrap; refrigerate 2 to 3 hours or until thoroughly chilled and firm.

To serve, run tip of a knife around edge of pan; remove pan side. Leaving pie on pan base, place pie on a serving plate. Garnish with pimento strips and ripe-olive halves. Serve with fresh fruit and assorted crackers. Makes 1 pie.

Avocados with Roquefort Cream

2 ripe avocados
Lemon juice
1/2 pint dairy sour cream (1 cup)
1 small onion, diced
3 oz. Roquefort cheese, crumbled, room temperature
2 tablespoons whipping cream
Salt and freshly ground pepper
Ripe olives
Lettuce leaves

Cut avocados in half lengthwise; remove pits. Scoop out flesh, leaving about 1/4 inch of flesh in shells. Sprinkle lemon juice on flesh remaining in shells. Place scooped-out avocado flesh in a blender or food processor fitted with a metal blade. Add sour cream, onion, Roquefort cheese and whipping cream; process until smooth. Stir in salt and pepper to taste. Spoon mixture into a pastry bag fitted with an open-star tip. Pipe into avocado shells. Refrigerate 1 hour or until thoroughly chilled.

To serve, arrange filled avocado shells on a platter; garnish with olives and lettuce leaves. Makes 4 servings.

Avocados with Roquefort Cream

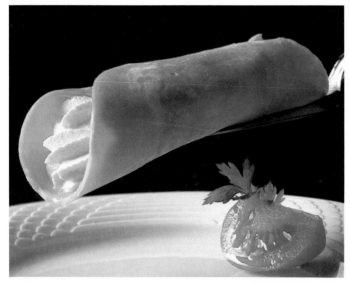

Ricotta-Filled Ham Rolls

Stuffed Salmon Cones

Ricotta-Filled Ham Rolls

8 oz. ricotta cheese (1 cup)
1 tablespoon prepared horseradish
1 tablespoon lemon juice
1 teaspoon sugar
Salt and freshly ground pepper
1/2 pint whipping cream (1 cup)
8 large slices boiled ham
4 tomato wedges
4 parsley sprigs

In a medium bowl, combine ricotta cheese, horseradish, lemon juice and sugar. Stir in salt and pepper to taste. Whip cream until stiff peaks form; fold into cheese mixture. Spread mixture evenly on ham slices; roll up ham and filling.
To serve, place 2 ham rolls and 1 tomato wedge on each of 4 individual plates. Garnish each with a parsley sprig. Makes 4 servings.

Stuffed Salmon Cones

10 thin slices smoked salmon
Lemon juice
1/2 pint whipping cream (1 cup)
1/4 cup prepared horseradish
1 teaspoon sugar
Salt
10 dill sprigs

Sprinkle salmon with lemon juice. Roll each salmon slice into a cone. In a small bowl, whip cream until stiff peaks form. Stir in horseradish, sugar and salt to taste. Spoon mixture into salmon cones. Or, spoon cream mixture into a pastry bag fitted with a plain tip; pipe into salmon cones.
To serve, arrange on a platter; garnish each salmon cone with a dill sprig. Serve cold with any remaining cream mixture. Makes 10 servings.

Mushroom-Salami Tartlets

Tomatoes & Mozzarella

Mushroom-Salami Tartlets

1/2 lb. mushrooms
3 tablespoons lemon juice
1 teaspoon Italian seasoning
Salt and freshly ground pepper
1 (12-oz.) box frozen tartlet shells (12 shells), thawed
12 small slices salami
2 to 3 tablespoons dairy sour cream
Fresh herbs

Thinly slice mushrooms; place in a medium glass dish. Sprinkle with lemon juice; season with Italian seasoning. Season with salt and pepper. Refrigerate at least 2 hours. Preheat oven to 425F (220C). Separate tartlet shells; prick bottoms. Place 4 empty tartlet tins inside 4 pricked shells; place on an un-greased baking sheet. Bake 5 minutes. Remove empty tins; bake shells 8 minutes longer. Repeat with remaining tartlets. Cool on a wire rack. Using a 3-1/2-inch round cutter, cut salami slices into rounds. Set salami slices aside; dice salami trimmings. Add diced trimmings to mushroom mixture; stir in sour cream.
To serve, line cooled tart shells with salami slices; fill with mushroom mixture. Garnish with fresh herbs. Makes 12 tartlets.

Tomatoes & Mozzarella

2 large tomatoes
8 oz. mozzarella cheese
1/4 cup olive oil
2 tablespoons wine vinegar
Salt
Freshly ground pepper
3 to 4 fresh basil sprigs
French bread, sliced

Slice tomatoes and cheese. Overlap tomato and cheese slices on a platter or on individual plates. Combine olive oil, vinegar and salt to taste. Sprinkle over tomatoes and cheese. Sprinkle with pepper; garnish with basil. Serve cold with bread. Makes 4 servings

White Asparagus with Sour-Cream Sauce

White Asparagus with Sour-Cream Sauce

Lettuce leaves
4 slices white bread, toasted, buttered
1 (15-oz.) can white asparagus spears, drained

Sour-Cream Sauce:
1/3 cup dairy sour cream
1/3 cup mayonnaise
2 teaspoons vinegar
Salt and freshly ground pepper
2 slices cooked ham, slivered
About 2 tablespoons chopped fresh parsley

Arrange lettuce leaves and toast on 4 individual plates. Place 1/4 of asparagus spears over toast on each plate.
To make sauce, in a small bowl, combine sour cream, mayonnaise and vinegar. Stir in salt and pepper to taste; stir until blended. Spoon dressing over asparagus. Sprinkle with ham; garnish with parsley. Makes 4 servings.

Scallop-Filled Avocados

3/4 lb. bay scallops
2/3 cup lime juice
1 tomato
1/2 cup minced shallots
2 tablespoons chopped fresh dill
1-1/2 tablespoons olive oil
Salt and freshly ground pepper
2 ripe avocados
Lemon juice
Dill sprigs

Cook scallops in gently boiling water 1 to 2 minutes or until firm and opaque. Use a slotted spoon to remove scallops from water; drain on paper towels. Place cooked scallops in a glass dish; pour lime juice over top. Stir well; cover. Refrigerate at least 4 hours. Peel and dice tomato. Stir diced tomato, shallots, chopped dill and olive oil into marinated scallops. Stir in salt and pepper to taste; set aside. Cut avocados in half lengthwise; remove pits. Sprinkle avocados with lemon juice.
To serve, place 1 avocado half on each of 4 individual plates. Spoon scallop mixture into avocado centers; garnish with dill sprigs. Serve cold. Makes 4 servings.

Steamed Shrimp

Photo on pages 12 and 13.

1 lb. large unshelled shrimp (16 to 25)
1 bay leaf
1 garlic clove
5 thick lemon slices
6 black peppercorns
1/2 teaspoon salt

Cocktail Sauce:
1 cup ketchup
3 tablespoons prepared horseradish
Juice of 1 lemon
Hot-pepper sauce

Place shrimp in a large saucepan. Cover with water; add bay leaf, garlic, 1 lemon slice, peppercorns and salt. Cover pan, leaving cover slightly ajar. Bring to a boil. Turn off heat as soon as steam begins to come from saucepan. Hold cover in place to keep steam in saucepan as you drain off water. Cover tightly; set aside. Let shrimp steam 15 minutes. Discard seasonings from pan. Shell and devein shrimp. Cover and refrigerate shelled shrimp until chilled.

To make sauce, in a small bowl, blend ketchup, horseradish, lemon juice and hot-pepper sauce. Cover and refrigerate until chilled.

To serve, garnish shrimp with remaining lemon slices; serve with Cocktail Sauce. Makes 4 servings.

Asparagus & Proscuitto

Asparagus & Prosciutto

1 to 1-1/2 lbs. fresh white or green asparagus
8 prosciutto slices
Chopped fresh parsley

White-Wine Dressing:
2 egg yolks
1/2 cup dry white wine
Salt and freshly ground pepper
1/2 cup whipping cream

Wash and trim asparagus. In a large saucepan, cook asparagus in lightly salted water 10 to 15 minutes or until crisp-tender. Drain; set aside to cool. Arrange cooked asparagus on 4 individual plates. Roll prosciutto slices; place 2 rolled prosciutto slices on each plate. Garnish asparagus with parsley.

To make dressing, in a medium bowl, beat egg yolks until blended. Beat in wine until smooth; stir in salt and pepper to taste. In a small bowl, whip cream until stiff peaks form; fold into egg-yolk mixture. Serve dressing in a separate bowl. Makes 4 servings.

Steamed Shrimp

Spiced Cheese on Crackers

Spiced Cheese on Crackers

1 (8-oz.) carton whipped cream cheese
8 oz. dairy sour cream (1 cup)
Salt
Paprika
2 teaspoons Italian seasoning
Crackers
Pimento-stuffed olives, halved
Capers
Radish slices
Dill sprigs
Tiny onion rings dipped in paprika
Cucumber slices
Parsley sprigs
Small red peppers

In a medium bowl, combine cream cheese and sour cream; stir until blended. Season with salt and paprika. Stir in Italian seasoning.
To serve, spoon into a pastry bag fitted with a medium open-star tip; pipe onto crackers. Garnish with olives, capers, radish slices, dill sprigs, onion rings, cucumber slices, parsley sprigs or small red peppers. Makes about 30 appetizers.

Shrimp & Artichoke Appetizer

1 qt. water (4 cups)
1 bay leaf
1 tablespoon mustard seeds
1/4 teaspoon dill seeds
1/4 teaspoon salt
2 black peppercorns
1 lb. large unshelled shrimp (16 to 25)
Lettuce leaves
2 (6-oz.) jars artichoke hearts, drained
4 to 5 tablespoons ketchup
3 tablespoons half and half
1 teaspoon sugar
1 tablespoon brandy, if desired
Salt and freshly ground pepper
Pimento-stuffed green olives, sliced

In a large saucepan, combine water, bay leaf, mustard seeds, dill seeds, salt and peppercorns. Bring to a boil; simmer about 4 minutes. Add shrimp; simmer 2 to 4 minutes or until shrimp become firm and turn pink. Drain, discarding liquid, bay leaf, seeds and peppercorns. Refrigerate shrimp until chilled. Shell and devein cooked shrimp; set aside. Line a platter with lettuce leaves. Arrange artichoke hearts over lettuce. Arrange shrimp over artichokes. In a small bowl, combine ketchup, half and half, sugar and brandy, if desired. Stir in salt and pepper to taste.
To serve, pour dressing over shrimp and artichokes. Garnish with olives; serve cold. Makes 4 servings.

On previous pages: Fresh Figs with Ham, page 39

Cheese Mounds

1 (8-oz.) carton whipped cream cheese
1 tablespoon half and half or milk
1/4 teaspoon celery salt
3 drops hot-pepper sauce
1 hard-cooked egg yolk
Crackers
Carrot slices
Parsley sprigs
Pimento-stuffed green olives, halved
Black lumpfish caviar
Truffle strips or ripe-olive strips
Sweet-pickle fans
Chopped red and green bell pepper
Small red peppers

In a medium bowl, combine cream cheese, half and half or milk, celery salt and hot-pepper sauce; stir until blended. Press hard-cooked egg yolk through a sieve into cheese mixture. Stir to distribute.

To serve, spoon cheese mixture into a pastry bag fitted with a medium open-star tip. Pipe in mounds on crackers. Garnish with carrot slices, parsley sprigs, olives, caviar, truffle strips or ripe-olive strips, pickle fans, bell peppers, small red peppers or another cracker. Makes 15 to 18 appetizers.

Cheese Mounds

Liptauer

1 (8-oz.) pkg. cream cheese, room temperature
1/4 cup butter or margarine, room temperature
2 tablespoons finely chopped onion
1-1/2 teaspoons anchovy paste
1 teaspoon Dijon-style mustard
About 1 teaspoon paprika
1 teaspoon caraway seeds
Cocktail bread
Assorted crackers

In a blender or food processor fitted with a metal blade, process cream cheese, butter or margarine, onion, anchovy paste, mustard and 1 teaspoon paprika until smooth. Add caraway seeds; process briefly.

To serve, spoon into a small serving bowl; sprinkle with additional paprika. Serve with cocktail bread and assorted crackers. Makes about 1-1/2 cups.

Caviar Appetizer

Photo on pages 212 and 213.

2 hard-cooked egg yolks
2 (3-1/2-oz.) jars black lumpfish caviar
1 small onion, minced
Melba-toast rounds
Lemon slices

Press egg yolks through a sieve into a small serving dish. Place caviar and onion in separate small serving dishes. Place dishes on a large platter; surround with Melba toast and lemon slices. Serve chilled. Makes 4 to 6 servings.

Basil-Cheese Ball

Walnut-Cheese Ball

2 (8-oz.) pkgs. cream cheese, room temperature
2 cups shredded Cheddar cheese (8 oz.)
1/2 cup finely chopped ripe olives
2 tablespoons snipped chives
1 tablespoon Worcestershire sauce
Finely chopped walnuts
Assorted crackers

In a medium bowl, combine cream cheese and Cheddar cheese; stir until blended. Add olives, chives and Worcestershire sauce; stir until blended. Refrigerate until firm.
To serve, shape into a large ball; roll in chopped nuts. Refrigerate until ready to serve. Serve with assorted crackers. Makes 1 cheese ball.

Basil-Cheese Ball

1/2 lb. goat cheese, such as chèvre Valençay or
   St. Marcellin, room temperature
3/4 cup butter or margarine, room temperature
1/4 cup grated Parmesan cheese (3/4 oz.)
1/2 cup half and half
1/2 cup chopped fresh basil
1/4 cup ground pine nuts
1/4 cup toasted pine nuts
French or Italian bread

In a medium bowl, combine goat cheese, butter or margarine, Parmesan cheese and half and half; stir until blended. Stir in basil and ground pine nuts until blended. Refrigerate until firm.
To serve, shape into a ball; roll in toasted pine nuts. Place on a serving plate. Serve with French or Italian bread. Makes 1 cheese ball.

Rosy Mushrooms

Roquefort Balls

1/4 cup butter, room temperature
4 oz. Roquefort cheese, room temperature
1 teaspoon minced capers
1 teaspoon brandy
Freshly ground pepper
Chopped fresh parsley
Assorted crackers

In a medium bowl, combine butter and cheese; beat until blended. Stir in capers and brandy. Season with pepper. Refrigerate until firm. Shape into 12 small balls; roll cheese balls in parsley. Refrigerate until ready to serve. Serve with assorted crackers. Makes 12 cheese balls.

Layered Caviar

1 medium onion
2 hard-cooked eggs
1 (3-1/2-oz.) jar salmon caviar
1 (3-1/2-oz.) jar black lumpfish caviar
1 (3-1/2-oz.) jar golden lumpfish caviar
Melba toast

Finely dice onion and hard-cooked eggs. Spoon 1/2 of salmon caviar in bottom of a small glass serving bowl. Cover with 1/2 of diced onion and 1/2 of diced hard-cooked eggs. Top with 1/2 of black caviar and all of golden caviar. Cover with remaining diced onion and eggs. Top with remaining black caviar, then with remaining salmon caviar. Refrigerate until thoroughly chilled.

To serve, place bowl on a serving dish; surround with ice. Serve with Melba toast. Makes 6 to 8 servings.

Layered Caviar

Rosy Mushrooms

1/2 cup white wine
1 to 2 tablespoons tomato paste
1/4 cup olive oil
1 onion, diced
2 teaspoons dried leaf thyme
1 teaspoon sugar
1 bay leaf
Salt and freshly ground pepper
1 lb. mushrooms, sliced
1 tablespoon chopped fresh parsley

In a medium saucepan, stir wine into tomato paste until blended. Stir in olive oil, onion, thyme, sugar and bay leaf. Season with salt and pepper. Bring to a boil over medium heat. Add mushrooms; simmer 6 minutes, stirring occasionally. Spoon into a serving dish; refrigerate until chilled.

To serve, remove and discard bay leaf. Garnish with parsley. Makes 4 to 6 servings.

Prosciutto & Peaches

4 ripe, firm peaches
2 cups dry vermouth
1/4 cup packed light-brown sugar
1/4 teaspoon ground cinnamon
1/8 teaspoon ground cloves
4 prosciutto slices
Mint leaves

Peel peaches; cut each in half. Remove and discard pits. In a medium saucepan, combine vermouth, brown sugar, cinnamon and cloves. Bring to a boil; reduce heat. Add peach halves; simmer about 10 minutes or until peaches are slightly tender. Remove peaches with a slotted spoon; drain on paper towels until cool. Cut prosciutto slices in half. Wrap 1/2 slice prosciutto around each cooked peach half.

To serve, place 2 prosciutto-peach rolls on each of 4 individual plates; garnish with mint leaves. Refrigerate until well chilled. Makes 4 servings.

Fresh Figs with Ham

Photo on pages 34 and 35.

4 fresh figs
8 slices Westphalian ham
Buttered toast

Rinse figs in cold water. Pat dry with paper towels; cut each in half lengthwise. Arrange 2 fig halves and 2 slices ham on individual plates. Cut toast diagonally into quarters. Serve toast points with figs and ham. Makes 4 servings.

Nibblers

Filled Pastry Rings & Miniature Cream Puffs

Choux Paste:
1/4 cup butter or margarine
1/4 teaspoon salt
1/2 cup water
1/2 cup all-purpose flour
2 eggs
1/2 teaspoon baking powder
Vegetable oil for deep-frying

Filling:
4 oz. blue cheese or Roquefort cheese, crumbled
1/2 cup butter or margarine, room temperature
1/2 cup whipping cream

Garnish:
Chopped fresh parsley
Caraway seeds
Poppy seeds
Paprika

Grease baking sheets; set aside. Preheat oven to 400F (205C).

To prepare choux paste, in a medium saucepan, combine butter or margarine, salt and water. Over medium heat, bring to a boil, stirring until butter or margarine melts. Remove from heat; immediately add flour all at once. Stir vigorously with a wooden spoon until mixture forms a ball and comes away from side of pan. Cool slightly. Add eggs, 1 at a time, beating well after each addition.

To make miniature cream puffs, spoon half of dough into a pastry bag fitted with a large star tip. Pipe dough in 20 walnut-size mounds, 1 inch apart, on greased baking sheets. Bake in preheated oven 18 to 20 minutes or until puffed and golden brown. Remove from baking sheets; cool on wire racks.

To make pastry rings, cut 20 (4-inch) squares of parchment paper. Grease squares; set aside. Stir baking powder into remaining choux paste. Spoon dough into a large pastry bag fitted with a 5/8-inch star tip. Pipe dough in small rings, 1-1/2 inches in diameter, onto greased parchment paper. Pour oil 2 inches deep into a deep-fat fryer, large skillet or saucepan. Heat oil to 370F (190C) or until a 1-inch bread cube turns golden brown in 50 seconds. Leaving paper attached, invert 3 or 4 circles of dough into hot oil, paper-side up. Deep-fry until paper releases from pastry. Use tongs to remove and discard paper. Deep-fry pastry until golden on both sides, 1 to 2 minutes. Use a slotted spoon to remove rings from hot oil; drain on paper towels. Repeat with remaining rings. When cool, cut rings and cream puffs in half crosswise.

Filled Pastry Rings & Miniature Cream Puffs

On previous pages: Puff-Pastry Salt Sticks, page 45

To prepare filling, in a small bowl, mash cheese. Add butter or margarine; beat until smooth. In a small bowl, whip cream until stiff peaks form; fold into cheese mixture. Reserve 2 tablespoons cheese filling. Spoon remaining filling into a pastry bag fitted with a small star tip. Pipe filling into bottom of pastry rings and cream puffs. Replace tops; spread a thin layer of reserved filling over tops. Sprinkle with parsley, caraway seeds, poppy seeds or paprika. Refrigerate until ready to serve. Makes 32 to 40 appetizers.

Herb Tidbits

1 (1/4-oz.) pkg. active dry yeast (1 tablespoon)
1 teaspoon sugar
1/2 cup warm water (110F, 45C)
3 tablespoons butter or margarine, melted
1/2 teaspoon salt
1-3/4 cups all-purpose flour
2 teaspoons Herbs de Provence or Italian seasoning
Milk
Coarse salt

In a medium bowl, combine yeast, sugar and water. Let stand until foamy, 5 to 10 minutes. Stir in butter or margarine and 1/2 teaspoon salt. Stir in 1-1/4 cups flour; beat well. Stir in herbs and enough remaining flour to make stiff dough. Turn out dough onto a lightly floured surface. Knead until dough is smooth and elastic, 6 to 8 minutes. Clean and grease bowl. Place dough in greased bowl, turning to coat all sides. Cover; let rise in a warm place, free from drafts, until doubled in bulk. Grease baking sheets. Punch down dough.
To shape dough, divide into 4 equal pieces. Cut each piece into 9 equal pieces. Shape each piece into a small ball, pinching and tucking ends under. Place balls, 1-1/2 inches apart, on greased baking sheets. Cover; let rise until almost doubled in bulk.
To complete, preheat oven to 375F (190C). Brush raised dough with milk; sprinkle with coarse salt. Bake in preheated oven 12 to 15 minutes or until golden brown. Remove from baking sheets; cool on wire racks. Makes 36 appetizers.

Mexican Cheese Puffs

1-3/4 cups all-purpose flour
1 teaspoon salt
1/2 teaspoon chili powder
1/8 teaspoon red (cayenne) pepper
1/2 cup butter or margarine
1/2 cup dairy sour cream
1 cup finely shredded Monterey Jack cheese (4 oz.)
1 (4-oz.) can chopped green chilies, well drained
Paprika

In a medium bowl, blend flour, salt, chili powder and red pepper. Use a pastry blender or 2 knives to cut in butter or margarine until mixture resembles coarse crumbs. Stir in sour cream, cheese and chilies until blended. Shape dough into a flat ball. Wrap in waxed paper; refrigerate 2 hours.
To complete, preheat oven to 375F (190C). On a lightly floured surface, roll out dough until 1/4 inch thick. Cut dough with a 1-inch scalloped cutter or small aspic cutters. Place on ungreased baking sheets; sprinkle tops with paprika. Bake in preheated oven 15 to 18 minutes or until puffed and golden brown. Remove from baking sheets; cool on wire racks. Makes 54 to 60 puffs.

Herb Tidbits

Sesame-Cheese Sticks

1/2 (8-oz.) pkg. cream cheese, room temperature
3 tablespoons milk
3 tablespoons vegetable oil
1 egg
1 egg white
1-3/4 cups all-purpose flour
2 tablespoons grated Parmesan cheese
2-1/2 teaspoons baking powder
3 tablespoons sesame seeds
1 teaspoon salt
1 egg yolk beaten with 1 tablespoon milk for glaze

In a medium bowl, beat cream cheese, milk, oil, whole egg and egg white until smooth. In another medium bowl, blend flour, Parmesan cheese, baking powder, sesame seeds and salt. Add flour mixture to cream-cheese mixture. Stir with a fork until blended and mixture begins to bind together. Knead dough in bowl 8 to 10 strokes. Wrap dough in waxed paper; refrigerate 30 minutes.

To complete, preheat oven to 375F (190C). Grease baking sheets. On a lightly floured surface, roll out dough to a 13'' x 10'' rectangle. Cut dough in half lengthwise. Cut each half into 5'' x 3/4'' strips. Using a long, narrow spatula, lift strips and place 1 inch apart on greased baking sheets. Brush with egg-yolk glaze. Bake in preheated oven 13 to 15 minutes or until golden brown. Remove from baking sheets; cool on wire racks. Makes about 32 sticks.

Sesame-Cheese Sticks

Spiced Almonds

1 tablespoon granulated sugar
1 tablespoon brown sugar
1/4 teaspoon ground mace
1/2 teaspoon ground cinnamon
1/4 teaspoon ground allspice
3 tablespoons butter or margarine, melted
2 cups whole unblanched almond

Preheat oven to 350F (175C). In a 13'' x 9'' baking pan, combine sugars, mace, cinnamon, allspice and butter or margarine. Stir to blend. Add almonds; toss to coat. Spread in a single layer in baking pan. Bake in preheated oven about 10 minutes, stirring occasionally. Spoon onto paper towels to cool. Makes 2 cups.

Stacked Cheese Triangles

2/3 cup butter or margarine, room temperature
1 (8-oz.) pkg. cream cheese, room temperature
3 tablespoons half and half or milk
2 tablespoons Italian seasoning
1 tablespoon tomato paste
1 teaspoon paprika
1 tablespoon anchovy paste
12 thin slices pumpernickel bread

In a medium bowl, combine butter or margarine, cream cheese and half and half or milk; stir until blended. Divide mixture among 3 small bowls. Add Italian seasoning to 1 of bowls, tomato paste and paprika to another bowl and anchovy paste to remaining bowl. Stir each to blend. Trim crusts from bread, if desired. Spread each mixture on 3 bread slices. Arrange in 3 stacks, spread-side up, with 1 of each spread in each stack. Top each stack with a plain bread slice. Wrap each stack in plastic wrap; refrigerate 2 to 3 hours.

To serve, cut each stack into 4 triangles. Makes 12 sandwiches.

Caraway-Cheese Squares

1/2 (17-1/4-oz.) pkg. frozen puff pastry (1 sheet),
  thawed
1 egg yolk beaten with 1 tablespoon milk for glaze
Salt and freshly ground pepper
Paprika
1 tablespoon caraway seeds
1 cup finely shredded Gouda, Swiss or
  Gruyère cheese (4 oz.)

Preheat oven to 400F (205C). On a lightly floured surface, unfold pastry. Roll out pastry to a 12-inch square. Using a sharp knife or pastry wheel, cut rolled pastry into 1-1/2-inch squares. Place squares, 1 inch apart, on ungreased baking sheets. Brush squares with egg-yolk glaze. Do not let glaze run over edges. Sprinkle with salt, pepper, paprika and caraway seeds. Top each square with a little cheese. Bake in preheated oven 15 to 18 minutes or until puffed and golden. Remove from baking sheets; cool on wire racks. Makes 64 squares.

Caraway-Cheese Squares

Puff-Pastry Salt Sticks

Photo on pages 40 and 41.

1 (17-1/4-oz.) pkg. frozen puff pastry (2 sheets),
  thawed
1 egg yolk beaten with 1 tablespoon milk for glaze
Coarse salt

Preheat oven to 400F (205C). On a lightly floured surface, unfold 1 pastry sheet. Brush with egg-yolk glaze; sprinkle with coarse salt. Cut in half crosswise; then cut in 5'' x 1/2'' strips. Twisting ends in opposite directions, twist each strip into a spiral. Place spirals, 1 inch apart, on ungreased baking sheets. Repeat with remaining pastry sheet. Bake in preheated oven 12 to 15 minutes or until puffed and golden brown. Remove from baking sheets; cool on wire racks. Makes 80 sticks.

Variation

Puff-Pastry Cheese Sticks: Omit coarse salt. Brush pastry with egg-yolk glaze; then sprinkle with grated Parmesan cheese or finely shredded Swiss cheese. Twist and bake as directed above.

Curried Almonds

3 cups whole blanched almonds (1 lb.)
3 tablespoons butter or margarine, melted
1-1/2 tablespoons curry powder
1 tablespoon salt

Preheat oven to 300F (150C). Spread almonds in a single layer in a shallow roasting pan. Drizzle butter or margarine over almonds; toss to coat. Toast in oven 30 to 40 minutes, shaking pan occasionally. In a small bowl, blend curry powder and salt. Sprinkle over nuts; shake pan to coat almonds thoroughly. Return coated almonds to oven. Bake in preheated oven 20 to 30 minutes or until almonds are golden brown, shaking pan occasionally. Drain nuts on paper towels. Serve warm or cold. Makes 3 cups.

Cheddar-Cheese Sticks

3/4 cup butter or margarine, room temperature
2 cups finely shredded Cheddar or Colby cheese (8 oz.)
2 cups all-purpose flour
1 teaspoon baking powder
3/4 teaspoon paprika
1 teaspoon salt

Preheat oven to 375F (190C). In a medium bowl, beat butter or margarine until fluffy. Stir in cheese. In a medium bowl, blend flour, baking powder, paprika and salt. Stir into cheese mixture until blended and mixture forms a dough. Spoon dough into a large pastry bag fitted with a large star tip. Pipe in 4-inch strips, 1 inch apart, on ungreased baking sheets. Bake in preheated oven 10 to 12 minutes or until golden. Remove from baking sheets; cool on wire racks. Makes 28 to 30 sticks.

Cottage-Cheese & Chive Bites

8 oz. small-curd cottage cheese (1 cup)
1 cup all-purpose flour
1 teaspoon salt
1/2 teaspoon baking powder
1/2 cup butter or margarine, room temperature
2 tablespoons chopped fresh chives
Hot-pepper sauce
1 egg beaten with 1 tablespoon milk for glaze

In a blender or food processor fitted with a metal blade, process cottage cheese until smooth; set aside. In a medium bowl, blend flour, salt and baking powder. Add pureed cottage cheese, butter or margarine, chives and hot-pepper sauce. Stir with a wooden spoon until blended. Knead dough in bowl 8 to 10 strokes. Grease baking sheets; set aside. Preheat oven to 400F (205C).

To complete, on a lightly floured surface, roll out dough until 1/2 inch thick. Cut dough with a 1-inch scalloped cutter or small aspic cutters. Place cut dough, 1 inch apart, on greased baking sheets; brush tops with egg glaze. Bake in preheated oven 12 to 15 minutes or until golden. Remove from baking sheets; cool on wire racks. Makes 26 to 30 appetizers.

Cheddar-Cheese Sticks

Viennese Bacon Rounds

1/2 lb. bacon, diced
1 onion, finely chopped
1 egg, separated
2 tablespoons water
2 cups all-purpose flour
1 teaspoon baking powder
1 tablespoon milk
Caraway seeds
Coarse salt, if desired
Grated Parmesan cheese, if desired

In a medium skillet, sauté bacon over medium heat until partially cooked. Add onion; sauté until onion is transparent and bacon is crisp; set aside. In a small bowl, beat egg white and water until blended. In a medium bowl, blend flour and baking powder. Stir in egg-white mixture and bacon mixture with pan drippings. Stir with a fork until mixture forms a ball. Divide dough in half. Shape each piece into a 1-1/2-inch-thick log. Wrap logs in waxed paper; refrigerate until firm, about 1 hour.
To complete, preheat oven to 375F (190C). Remove 1 log from refrigerator; cut into 1/4-inch slices. Place slices, 1 inch apart, on ungreased baking sheets. Repeat with remaining refrigerated log. Beat egg yolk with milk; brush over slices. Sprinkle with caraway seeds. Or, if desired, sprinkle with coarse salt or Parmesan cheese. Bake in preheated oven 15 to 18 minutes or until golden brown. Remove from baking sheets; cool on wire racks. Makes 48 to 52 rounds.

Note: Coarse salt and cheese will increase salty flavor.

Viennese Bacon Rounds

Cheese-Stuffed Pecans

1/2 (3-oz.) pkg. cream cheese
1/2 teaspoon prepared mustard
2 tablespoons grated Parmesan cheese
Dash of hot-pepper sauce
About 2 cups pecan halves

In a small bowl, beat cream cheese, mustard, Parmesan cheese and hot-pepper sauce until fluffy. Spread mixture on flat surface of 1/2 of pecans. Top with remaining pecan halves, placing flat sides together. Makes about 2 cups.

Cheese Snails

Cheese Snails

1 cup all-purpose flour
1 cup finely shredded Swiss or Gruyère cheese (4 oz.)
1/4 cup ground almonds
1 teaspoon baking powder
1/2 cup butter or margarine
1 egg, separated
1 tablespoon water
1 tablespoon milk
1/4 cup grated Parmesan cheese (3/4 oz.)

In a medium bowl, combine flour, Swiss or Gruyère cheese, almonds and baking powder; toss until blended. Use a pastry blender or 2 knives to cut in butter or margarine until mixture resembles coarse crumbs. Beat egg white with water. Add to flour mixture; toss with a fork until dough begins to bind together. With your hands, gather dough and shape into a flat ball. Divide dough in half; wrap each half in waxed paper. Refrigerate 30 minutes.
To shape dough, on a lightly floured surface, roll out 1 piece of dough to an 11'' x 9'' rectangle. Beat egg yolk with milk until blended; brush over dough. Sprinkle coated pastry with 2 tablespoons Parmesan cheese. Starting on a short end, roll up dough jelly-roll style. Repeat with remaining dough. Wrap rolls separately in waxed paper; refrigerate 1 hour.
To complete, preheat oven to 375F (190C). Grease baking sheets. Cut each refrigerated roll into 1/4-inch slices. Place slices, 1 inch apart, on greased baking sheets. Bake in preheated oven 12 to 15 minutes or until golden. Remove from baking sheets; cool on wire racks. Makes 72 snails.

Honeyed Walnuts

1/4 cup butter or margarine
2 tablespoons honey
1/4 teaspoon grated lemon peel
2 cups walnut halves

Preheat oven to 300F (150C). In a medium skillet, melt butter or margarine. Stir in honey and lemon peel. Add walnuts; stir to coat evenly. Spread walnut mixture in a 9-inch-square baking pan. Bake in preheated oven 15 minutes, stirring once or twice during baking. Stir occasionally as walnuts cool to prevent sticking. Drain on paper towels, if desired. Serve in a small decorative bowl. Makes 1 cup.

Cheesy Nuts

1 tablespoon butter or margarine
1 tablespoon vegetable oil
1 cup whole unblanched almonds
1/4 cup grated Parmesan cheese (3/4 oz.)
1/8 teaspoon garlic powder
1/4 teaspoon salt, if desired

In a medium saucepan, melt butter or margarine. Add oil. When hot, add almonds; toss to coat. Over medium-high heat, sauté almonds, stirring constantly, until heated through. In a small bowl, combine cheese, garlic powder and salt, if desired. Add sautéed almonds, tossing to coat. Drain on paper towels, if desired. Cool before serving. Serve in a small decorative bowl. Makes 1 cup.

Cheese Triangles

1 cup all-purpose flour
2/3 cup grated Parmesan cheese or
   finely shredded Swiss cheese (2 to 3 oz.)
3/4 teaspoon paprika
1/2 teaspoon dry mustard
1/2 teaspoon salt
1/2 cup butter or margarine
1 egg
About 5 tablespoons milk
Paprika

In a medium bowl, blend flour, cheese, 3/4 teaspoon paprika, dry mustard and salt. Use a pastry blender or 2 knives to cut in butter or margarine until mixture resembles coarse crumbs. In a small bowl, beat egg and 3 tablespoons milk until blended. Sprinkle over flour mixture; stir with a fork until dough begins to bind together. Shape into a flat ball; wrap in waxed paper. Refrigerate 30 minutes.

To complete, preheat oven to 375F (190C). Grease baking sheets. On a lightly floured surface, roll out dough to a 12" x 10" rectangle. Cut dough into 2-inch squares. Cut each square in half diagonally, making triangles. Place triangles, 1 inch apart, on greased baking sheets. Brush with milk; sprinkle with paprika. Bake in preheated oven 12 to 15 minutes or until golden. Remove from baking sheets; cool on wire racks. Makes 60 triangles.

Cheese Triangles

Fried Walnuts

2 cups water
2 cups walnut halves
4 to 5 tablespoons sugar
Vegetable oil for deep-frying
Salt

In a medium saucepan, bring water to a boil. Place walnuts in a sieve. Plunge walnuts into boiling water; boil rapidly 1 minute. Drain well. In a medium bowl, sprinkle boiled walnuts with sugar; toss until thoroughly coated. Pour oil 2 inches deep in a deep-fryer, large skillet or saucepan. Heat oil to 370F (190C) or until a 1-inch bread cube turns golden brown in 50 seconds. Deep-fry walnuts 4 to 5 minutes, stirring several times during cooking. Remove with a slotted spoon; place in a strainer. Sprinkle with salt; shake strainer to coat walnuts. Drain on paper towels, if desired. Serve in a small decorative bowl. Makes 2 cups.

Glazed Pecan Halves

2 tablespoons sugar
2 tablespoons butter
1 cup pecan halves

In a medium skillet, heat sugar until caramelized and lightly browned, stirring constantly. Add butter; stir until melted. Add pecans. Shake pan, or stir until evenly glazed and heated through. Stir occasionally as pecans cool to prevent sticking. Drain on paper towels, if desired. Serve in a small decorative bowl. Makes 1 cup.

Soups

Wine Soup with Figs

Wine Soup with Figs

1 (17-oz.) can figs with syrup
Water
2 lemon slices
1 (3-inch) cinnamon stick
1/8 teaspoon ground cardamom
1 to 2 tablespoons sugar
2 tablespoons quick-cooking tapioca
2 cups dry white wine

Drain syrup from figs into a 2-cup measure; set figs aside. Add enough water to fig syrup to make 2 cups. Pour into a medium saucepan. Add lemon slices, cinnamon, cardamom, sugar and tapioca. Bring to a boil; reduce heat. Simmer about 30 minutes, stirring occasionally. Discard lemon slices and cinnamon stick. Pour syrup mixture into a large bowl; stir in wine. Slice reserved figs; add to soup. Refrigerate until thoroughly chilled.

To serve, ladle into individual bowls or serve in a chilled soup tureen. Makes 4 servings.

Cold Fruit Soup

1/2 cup dried apricot halves
1/3 cup raisins
3 tablespoons sugar
1 (3-inch) cinnamon stick
2 whole cloves
5 cups water
2 tablespoons cornstarch
2 tablespoons water
1 (20-oz.) pkg. frozen mixed fruit, partially thawed

Cut each apricot half into 2 pieces. In a large saucepan, combine apricot pieces, raisins, sugar, cinnamon and cloves. Stir in 5 cups water; bring to a boil. Reduce heat. Cover; simmer 10 minutes or until fruit is tender. Dissolve cornstarch in 2 tablespoons water; stir into soup. Stirring constantly, cook until mixture boils and is slightly thickened. Discard cinnamon and cloves; cool mixture slightly. Pour into a large bowl; stir in mixed fruit. Refrigerate until thoroughly chilled.

To serve, ladle into individual bowls or serve in a chilled soup tureen. Makes 6 servings.

On previous pages: Chilled Broccoli Soup, page 59

Cold Blueberry Soup

1 (16-oz.) pkg. frozen blueberries or
    1-1/2 pints fresh blueberries (3 cups)
3 cups water
1/2 cup sugar
2 tablespoons lemon juice
1/4 teaspoon ground nutmeg
1 (3-inch) cinnamon stick
1/8 teaspoon salt
1 pint plain or blueberry-flavored yogurt (2 cups)
4 thin lemon slices

In a large saucepan, combine blueberries, water, sugar, lemon juice, nutmeg, cinnamon and salt. Bring to a boil; reduce heat. Cover and simmer 10 minutes. Discard cinnamon; pour blueberry mixture into a blender or food processor fitted with a metal blade. Process until smooth. Pour into a large bowl. Cover; refrigerate until thoroughly chilled.

To serve, stir yogurt; then stir into soup. Ladle into individual bowls or serve in a chilled soup tureen. Garnish with lemon slices. Makes 4 servings.

Danish Cherry Soup

1 lb. dark sweet cherries, pitted
2 cups water
1 cup dry red wine
1 lemon, quartered
1/4 teaspoon ground cinnamon
1/8 teaspoon ground cloves
1/4 cup sugar
2 tablespoons cornstarch
2 tablespoons lemon juice
Lemon slices
Dairy sour cream

In a medium saucepan, combine cherries, water, wine, lemon quarters, cinnamon and cloves. Bring to a boil; reduce heat. Cover; simmer 20 minutes, stirring occasionally. Set aside to cool slightly. Discard lemon quarters; pour cherry mixture into a blender or food processor fitted with a metal blade. Process until smooth. Return to saucepan. In a small bowl, dissolve sugar and cornstarch in lemon juice; stir into soup. Stirring constantly, bring to a boil. Stirring constantly, boil 1 minute. Pour into a large bowl; refrigerate until thoroughly chilled.

To serve, ladle into 4 individual bowls or serve in a chilled soup tureen. Garnish with lemon slices and sour cream. Makes 4 servings.

Jellied Raspberry Soup

1 (1-lb.) pkg. frozen whole raspberries
1/4 cup sugar
2 (1/4-oz.) envelopes unflavored gelatin
1/2 cup cold water
4 cups cran-raspberry-juice cocktail
1-1/2 pints vanilla-flavored yogurt (3 cups)

Partially thaw raspberries; reserve 10 or 12 whole raspberries. Place remaining raspberries in a medium bowl; crush slightly. Sprinkle with sugar; toss to coat. Set aside. In a medium saucepan, combine gelatin and water; let stand 3 minutes. Stir over low heat until gelatin dissolves. Pour into a medium decorative glass mold or bowl; stir in juice. Refrigerate until mixture has consistency of unbeaten egg whites, 30 to 45 minutes. Stir in raspberries and any juice that has formed. Spoon yogurt onto raspberry mixture; swirl through, leaving streaks of yogurt. Refrigerate until thoroughly chilled. Decorate with reserved raspberries.

To serve, ladle into individual bowls or serve in a chilled soup tureen. Makes 8 to 10 servings.

Lemon Dessert Soup

3 cups water
1/4 cup uncooked rice
1/2 cup raisins
1-1/2 tablespoons lemon juice
1 tablespoon sugar
1/4 cup whipping cream
Pinch of salt
1 egg yolk, lightly beaten
Ground nutmeg

In a medium saucepan, combine water, rice and raisins. Bring to a simmer; stirring occasionally, simmer until rice is tender. In a small bowl, combine lemon juice, sugar, cream, salt and egg yolk. Using a whisk, slowly beat egg-yolk mixture into hot rice mixture. Pour into a soup tureen. Cool slightly; refrigerate until thoroughly chilled.

To serve, ladel into 4 individual bowls. Garnish each with nutmeg. Makes 4 servings.

Quick Gazpacho

2 slices white bread
1/2 cup cold water
1 red bell pepper, diced
1 green bell pepper, diced
1 small cucumber, peeled, diced
3 medium tomatoes, peeled, seeded, diced
2 garlic cloves, minced
3 tablespoons olive oil
2 to 3 tablespoons red-wine vinegar
Salt and freshly ground black pepper
Ice cubes

Soak bread in water; set aside. In a blender or food processor fitted with a metal blade, combine bell peppers, cucumber and tomatoes. Add garlic, olive oil and vinegar; process until smooth. Add soaked bread. Season with salt and black pepper; process until blended. Refrigerate until thoroughly chilled.
To serve, place ice cubes in soup mugs or individual bowls. Add chilled soup. Makes 4 servings.

Quick Gazpacho

Traditional Gazpacho

3 large ripe tomatoes, peeled, seeded, diced
1 large cucumber, peeled, seeded, diced
1 large green bell pepper, diced
1 large red onion, diced
1 garlic clove, minced
1/4 teaspoon ground cumin
1/4 teaspoon dried leaf basil
1/4 teaspoon dried leaf marjoram
1/4 cup red-wine vinegar
1/4 cup olive oil
3 cups homemade or canned beef stock or tomato juice
Dash hot-pepper sauce
Salt
Chopped fresh parsley
Additional diced vegetables, if desired

In a large bowl, combine tomatoes, cucumber, green pepper and onion. Add garlic. Sprinkle with cumin, basil and marjoram; stir to blend. Stir in vinegar and olive oil. Add stock or tomato juice and hot-pepper sauce. Add salt to taste. Stir well; refrigerate until thoroughly chilled.
To serve, ladle into individual bowls or serve in a chilled soup tureen. Garnish with parsley. Serve with additional diced vegetables, if desired. Makes 4 to 6 servings.

Avocado Soup

2 ripe avocados
2 tablespoons lemon juice
2 cups homemade or canned chicken stock
1/2 pint half and half (1 cup)
2 to 3 tablespoons dry white wine
Salt and freshly ground pepper
Slivered almonds

Peel avocados; cut flesh into cubes. In a blender or food processor fitted with a metal blade, combine avocado cubes, lemon juice and stock. Process until smooth. Pour into a large bowl; stir in half and half and wine. Stir in salt and pepper to taste. Cover; refrigerate until thoroughly chilled.

To serve, ladle into individual bowls or serve in a chilled soup tureen. Garnish with almonds. Makes 4 servings.

Avocado Soup

Cucumber-Yogurt Soup

2 medium cucumbers, peeled, seeded, diced
3 cups homemade or canned chicken stock
2 tablespoons all-purpose flour
1/4 teaspoon ground cloves
Salt and freshly ground pepper
1 pint plain yogurt (2 cups)
Dill sprigs

In a medium saucepan, combine cucumbers and 1 cup stock. Cover; simmer 20 minutes or until cucumbers are soft. Pour into a blender or food processor fitted with a metal blade; process until pureed. Return to saucepan. Combine flour with 2 or 3 tablespoons remaining stock; blend to make a smooth paste. Stir into cucumber puree. Add remaining stock and cloves. Stir in salt and pepper to taste. Simmer 5 minutes, stirring occasionally. Pour into a large bowl; refrigerate until thoroughly chilled.

To serve, stir in yogurt. Ladle into 4 to 6 individual bowls or serve in a chilled soup tureen. Garnish with dill sprigs. Makes 4 to 6 servings.

Vichyssoise

2 large leeks
2 tablespoons butter or margarine
1 lb. potatoes (3 medium)
3 cups homemade or canned chicken stock
1/2 pint half and half (1 cup)
Salt and white pepper
Snipped chives

Wash leeks thoroughly to remove sand. Finely dice leeks. In a medium saucepan, melt butter or margarine over medium heat. Add leeks; sauté until softened. Peel and dice potatoes; add to sautéed leeks. Add stock. Bring to a boil. Reduce heat; simmer 15 minutes or until potatoes are tender. Pour mixture into a blender or food processor fitted with a metal blade; process until smooth. Pour into a large bowl; stir in half and half. Stir in salt and pepper to taste. Cover; refrigerate until thoroughly chilled.

To serve, ladle chilled soup into individual bowls or serve in a chilled soup tureen. Garnish with snipped chives. Makes 4 servings.

Quick Cold Borscht

1 (16-oz.) can diced beets with liquid
1 cup homemade or canned beef stock
1 pint dairy sour cream (2 cups)
3 tablespoons vodka, if desired
Salt and freshly ground black pepper
1/2 cucumber
1 red bell pepper
2 hard-cooked eggs
Snipped chives

Drain beet juice into a large bowl; set beets aside. Stir stock, sour cream and vodka, if desired, into beet juice. Stir in salt and black pepper to taste. Peel and chop cucumber. Dice bell pepper. To beet-juice mixture, add chopped cucumber, diced bell pepper and reserved beets. Refrigerate until thoroughly chilled.

To serve, chop hard-cooked eggs; stir into chilled soup. Ladle into 4 individual bowls or serve in a chilled soup tureen. Garnish with snipped chives. Makes 4 servings.

Quick Cold Borscht

Jellied Consomme with Mushrooms

6 whole cloves
6 black peppercorns
2 bay leaves
12 oz. mushrooms
2 (10-1/2-oz.) cans condensed beef consommé
2 tablespoons lemon juice
Chopped fresh parsley

Tie cloves, peppercorns and bay leaves in a small piece of cheesecloth. Thinly slice mushrooms. In a medium saucepan, combine seasoning bag, sliced mushrooms and condensed consommé. Cover; simmer 10 minutes. Remove seasoning bag. Pour consommé mixture into a medium bowl; stir in lemon juice. Refrigerate until thoroughly chilled.

To serve, ladle into 4 individual bowls or serve in a chilled soup tureen. Garnish with parsley. Makes 4 servings.

Frosty Chicken & Pea Soup

Frosty Chicken & Pea Soup

1 (10-oz.) pkg. frozen green peas
2 green onions
1 cup homemade or canned chicken stock
Salt and freshly ground pepper
1/2 pint half and half (1 cup)
1 cup minced cooked chicken
Watercress sprigs

Cook peas according to package directions. Slice green onions. In a blender or food processor fitted with a metal blade, process cooked peas, stock and sliced green onions. Season with salt and pepper; process until blended. Pour into a large bowl; stir in half and half and chicken. Refrigerate until thoroughly chilled.

To serve, ladle into individual bowls or serve in a chilled soup tureen. Garnish with watercress. Makes 4 servings.

Quick Curried Chicken Soup

2-1/2 cups homemade or canned chicken stock
1/2 to 1 teaspoon curry powder
1/4 teaspoon ground coriander
1/4 teaspoon ground cumin
Pinch of ground allspice
1 (10-3/4-oz.) can condensed cream of chicken soup
1 garlic clove
2 tablespoons finely chopped unpeeled cucumber

In a small bowl, combine 1 tablespoon stock and curry powder. Stir until blended; stir in coriander, cumin and allspice. In a medium saucepan, combine remaining stock and curry mixture. Stir in condensed soup. Skewer garlic with a small wooden pick. Add to stock mixture. Stir over medium heat until mixture comes to a boil. Reduce heat; simmer 3 to 5 minutes, stirring constantly. When hot and smooth, remove from heat. Partially cover pan; set aside to cool. Remove garlic. Pour into a tureen or decorative glass bowl. Refrigerate 2 to 3 hours before serving.

To serve, ladle into 4 individual bowls. Garnish with chopped cucumber. Makes about 4 servings.

Cold Tomato Soup

2 lbs. tomatoes (6 to 8 small)
2 cups tomato juice
1 teaspoon sugar
Salt
Hot-pepper sauce
Cold cooked rice
Chopped fresh basil

Peel and quarter tomatoes. Remove seeds; dice tomatoes. In a blender or food processor fitted with a metal blade, process diced tomatoes until pureed. Pour into a large bowl; add tomato juice and sugar. Season with salt and hot-pepper sauce. Stir until blended. Cover; refrigerate until thoroughly chilled. **To serve,** ladle into 4 individual bowls. Top with cold cooked rice; garnish with basil. Makes 4 servings.

Cold Tomato Soup

Summer Soup

1/4 cup chopped green bell pepper
Water
1/2 cup chopped cucumber
1 cup buttermilk
1 cup tomato juice
Grated peel and juice of 1 lemon
Salt and freshly ground white pepper
Chopped fresh parsley

In a medium saucepan, combine bell pepper and water to cover. Bring to boil. Drain; set aside to cool. Stir in cucumber, buttermilk, tomato juice, lemon peel and lemon juice. Season with salt and white pepper. Pour into a tureen or glass bowl. Refrigerate until thoroughly chilled.
To serve, ladle into individual bowls. Garnish with chopped parsley. Makes 3 to 4 servings.

Cream of Mushroom Soup

1 tablespoon butter
1/4 cup finely chopped onion
2 cups finely chopped mushrooms
1 tablespoon all-purpose flour
2 to 2-1/2 cups homemade or canned chicken stock
1/2 cup whipping cream
Salt and freshly ground white pepper
Chopped chives

Melt butter in a medium saucepan. Add onion; sauté until softened. Add mushrooms. Stirring occasionally, sauté over low heat about 10 minutes. Sprinkle flour over sautéed onion and mushrooms. Cook about 2 minutes, stirring constantly. Slowly stir in stock. Stirring, bring to a boil; reduce heat until mixture barely simmers. Simmer 15 to 20 minutes or until mushrooms are soft. Remove from heat; stir in cream. Season with salt and white pepper. Refrigerate until thoroughly chilled.
To serve, add more stock if mixture is too thick. Serve in individual bowls; garnish each serving with a few chives. Makes about 4 servings.

Chilled Broccoli Soup

Photo on pages 50 and 51.

1 bunch fresh broccoli (about 2 lbs.)
1-1/2 cups homemade or canned chicken stock
1 (10-3/4-oz.) can condensed cream of mushroom soup
1/2 pint dairy sour cream (1 cup)
Salt and freshly ground pepper
4 bacon slices
2 tablespoons chopped fresh parsley
Parsley sprigs

Trim broccoli; break into flowerets. Steam or cook in lightly salted water 10 minutes or until crisp-tender; drain. In a blender or food processor fitted with a metal blade, combine cooked broccoli, stock, condensed soup and sour cream. Process until pureed. Stir in salt and pepper to taste. Spoon into a medium bowl; refrigerate until thoroughly chilled. Cook bacon until crisp; crumble cooked bacon.

To serve, ladle chilled soup into 4 to 6 individual bowls or serve in a chilled soup tureen. Garnish with crumbled bacon, chopped parsley and parsley sprigs. Makes 4 to 6 servings.

Chilled Broccoli Soup

Peanut Soup

1 cup chunk-style peanut butter
1 qt. homemade or canned chicken stock (4 cups)
1/2 pint whipping cream (1 cup)
1/2 teaspoon red (cayenne) pepper
Salt and freshly ground black pepper
2 tablespoons dry sherry
1 cup finely chopped cooked chicken, if desired
Chopped peanuts

Place peanut butter in a medium saucepan. Gradually stir in stock. Bring to a boil. Reduce heat; simmer 5 minutes. Cool slightly; stir in cream and red pepper. Stir in salt and black pepper to taste. Pour into a large bowl; refrigerate until thoroughly chilled.

To serve, stir in sherry and chicken, if desired. Ladle into individual bowls or serve in a chilled soup tureen. Garnish with chopped peanuts. Makes 6 servings.

Chilled Green-Pea Soup

1 large potato
1 medium onion
1 (10-oz.) pkg. frozen green peas
1/2 cup finely shredded Nappa cabbage
2 cups homemade or canned chicken stock
1/2 pint plain yogurt (1 cup)
Salt and ground white pepper
Pinch of sugar

Peel and finely chop potato and onion. Reserve 2 tablespoons peas. In a medium saucepan, combine chopped potato and onion, remaining peas, cabbage and stock. Bring to a boil; reduce heat until mixture barely simmers. Simmer about 10 minutes or until potato is tender. Pour cooked vegetables and stock into a blender or food processor fitted with a metal blade. Process until pureed. Pour into a medium bowl; cool slightly. Reserve about 1/4 cup yogurt. Stir remaining yogurt into pureed mixture. Refrigerate 3 to 4 hours.

To serve, season with salt, white pepper and sugar to taste. Garnish with remaining yogurt and reserved peas. Makes about 4 servings.

Salads

Waldorf Salad

Cucumber-Cheese Salad

2 garlic cloves, if desired
1 large cucumber
16 oz. small-curd cottage cheese (2 cups)
1/2 pint dairy sour cream (1 cup)
Salt and freshly ground pepper
Boston lettuce
Ripe olives

Crush garlic, if used. Peel and finely chop cucumber. In a medium bowl, combine cottage cheese and sour cream; stir until blended. Stir in crushed garlic, if desired, and chopped cucumber; season with salt and pepper. Refrigerate until ready to serve.

To serve, place lettuce on 6 individual salad plates. Spoon cottage-cheese mixture evenly onto plates. Garnish with ripe olives. Makes 6 servings.

Variation

Add 2 tablespoons diced green or red bell pepper, 2 tablespoons chopped fresh herbs or 1 tablespoon toasted caraway seeds.

Waldorf Salad

2 cups sliced unpeeled apples
2 celery stalks, sliced
1/2 cup coarsely chopped walnuts

Creamy Dressing:
1/4 cup whipping cream
1/4 cup mayonnaise
1 teaspoon sugar
1 teaspoon lemon juice
Salt and freshly ground pepper
Curly endive or escarole
Celery leaves

In a large bowl, combine apples, celery and walnuts. Toss to distribute.

To make dressing, in a small bowl, whip cream; stir in mayonnaise. Add sugar and lemon juice. Stir in salt and pepper to taste. Stir dressing into apple mixture.

To serve, line 4 salad plates with endive or escarole. Spoon salad onto lined plates; garnish with celery leaves. Makes 4 servings.

Cucumber-Cheese Salad

On previous pages: Crisp Summer Salad, page 77

Cucumber Salad

4 large cucumbers
1 tablespoon salt
1 large onion
Sour-Cream Dressing:
1-1/2 cups dairy sour cream
3 tablespoons vinegar
1 tablespoon sugar
2 tablespoons finely chopped fresh dill or
   1 teaspoon dried dill weed
Freshly ground pepper
Dill sprigs

Peel cucumbers only if waxed or if skins are tough. Cut cucumbers in half lengthwise; scoop out seeds. Slice as thinly as possible; place in a large bowl. Sprinkle with salt; weight down with a plate or another large bowl. Refrigerate 2 to 3 hours, occasionally draining off liquid that collects. Gently squeeze out remaining liquid. Slice onion into rings. Add sliced onion to drained cucumbers; stir gently.
To make dressing, spoon sour cream into a small bowl. Stir in vinegar, sugar, dill and pepper to taste. Stir until blended; stir into cucumber mixture.
To serve, spoon into a serving dish. Garnish with dill sprigs. Makes 4 to 6 servings.

Asparagus Salad

1 lb. fresh asparagus
1 hard-cooked egg
Lettuce leaves
Italian Dressing:
1 onion
6 tablespoons vegetable oil or olive oil
3 tablespoons vinegar
3 to 4 tablespoons Italian seasoning
Salt and freshly ground pepper

Trim asparagus; cook in lightly salted water until crisp-tender. Drain; refrigerate until chilled. Cut hard-cooked egg in half; separate white from yolk. Finely chop egg white; press egg yolk through a sieve. In a small bowl, combine chopped egg white and sieved egg yolk; toss to distribute. Line 4 salad plates with lettuce leaves. Arrange chilled cooked asparagus on lettuce-lined plates.
To make dressing, mince onion. In a small bowl, beat oil and vinegar until blended. Stir in minced onion and Italian seasoning. Stir in salt and pepper to taste.
To serve, pour dressing over asparagus. Sprinkle prepared hard-cooked egg over top. Makes 4 servings.

Endive-Fruit Salad

Endive-Fruit Salad

2 apples
2 oranges
2 heads Belgian endive
1/4 cup creamy Italian dressing
3 to 4 tablespoons muesli or granola
1 tablespoon chopped fresh parsley

Peel, core and dice apples; peel and dice oranges. Remove 4 outer leaves from each endive head; set aside. Finely chop remaining endive. In a medium bowl, combine chopped endive with diced apples and oranges. Pour dressing over salad; toss to coat. Refrigerate 30 minutes. Stir in muesli or granola.
To serve, arrange reserved endive leaves on 4 individual salad plates. Spoon chilled salad onto leaves; sprinkle with parsley. Makes 4 servings.

Feta-Cheese Rolls

Macaroni-Ham Salad

8 oz. uncooked elbow macaroni
1 cup slivered cooked ham
2 celery stalks, chopped
1 green bell pepper, diced
2 tablespoons chopped pimento

Dressing:
3/4 cup mayonnaise
1 tablespoon prepared mustard
Salt
Hot-pepper sauce

Cook macaroni in slightly salted water until tender; drain. Refrigerate until chilled. In a large bowl, combine cooked macaroni, ham, celery, bell pepper and pimento.

To make dressing, in a small bowl, blend mayonnaise and mustard. Stir in salt and hot-pepper sauce to taste. Spoon over salad; toss gently to coat. Makes 6 servings.

Feta-Cheese Rolls

16 chard or cabbage leaves
1/2 lb. feta cheese, crumbled
1/2 pint dairy sour cream (1 cup)
1 garlic clove, crushed
1 tablespoon chopped green bell pepper
1 teaspoon dried leaf basil
1/2 cup olive oil
1/2 cup white wine
1 tablespoon lemon juice
Salt and freshly ground pepper
Sugar
1 to 1-1/2 lbs. ripe tomatoes (8 to 10 small)
Fresh basil sprigs
French bread

Wash chard or cabbage leaves; blanch in lightly salted water 2 minutes. Pour into a colander; rinse under cold running water. Set aside to cool. In a medium bowl, combine feta cheese, sour cream, garlic, bell pepper and basil. Stir until blended. Spoon 1 to 2 tablespoons cheese mixture onto each blanched leaf. Fold stem-end and sides over filling; roll up toward point of leaf. Arrange in a glass dish. In a small bowl, combine olive oil, wine and lemon juice; beat until blended. Season with salt, pepper and sugar. Pour over filled leaves; refrigerate overnight.

To serve, peel tomatoes; remove seeds. Coarsely chop peeled tomatoes. Using a slotted spoon, remove filled leaves from marinade. Place 2 filled leaves on each of 8 individual plates. Divide chopped tomatoes among plates. Spoon marinade over chopped tomatoes and filled leaves. Garnish with fresh basil leaves; serve with French bread. Makes 8 servings.

Zucchini & Feta Salad

1/2 lb. zucchini
1 small onion
4 small tomatoes
1 green bell pepper
4 to 6 pimento-stuffed green olives
2 hard-cooked eggs

Dill Dressing:
5 tablespoons vegetable oil or olive oil
2 tablespoons vinegar
1/2 teaspoon prepared mustard
About 1 teaspoon sugar
Salt and freshly ground pepper
1 tablespoon finely chopped chives
1 tablespoon finely chopped fresh dill or
    1 teaspoon dried dill weed
1/2 lb. feta cheese

Slice zucchini and onion. Cut each tomato into 4 wedges. Cut bell pepper into strips. Cut each olive in half crosswise. In a large salad bowl, combine sliced zucchini and onion, tomato wedges, bell-pepper strips and olive halves. Cut each hard-cooked egg into 8 wedges.

To make dressing, in a small bowl, beat oil, vinegar and mustard until blended. Season with sugar, salt and pepper. Stir in chives and dill. Pour over vegetables. Garnish with egg wedges. Crumble cheese over top. Serve with freshly baked bread, if desired. Makes 4 servings.

Cheese-Stuffed Tomatoes

4 to 6 medium tomatoes
1 egg yolk
2 teaspoons prepared mustard
2 tablespoons vinegar or lemon juice
1 teaspoon sugar
Pinch of salt
1/2 cup olive oil or vegetable oil
2 tablespoons plain yogurt
2 tablespoons chopped almonds
1 apple
3/4 lb. Emmentaler cheese
1/4 cup slivered almonds

Cut stem ends off tomatoes; scoop out flesh, keeping shells intact. Invert on paper towels to drain. Place egg yolk in a small bowl. Stir in mustard, vinegar or lemon juice, sugar and salt. Beating constantly, add oil very slowly. Beat until thickened. Stir in yogurt and chopped almonds. Peel, core and dice apple. Dice Emmentaler cheese. In a medium bowl, combine diced apple, diced cheese and slivered almonds. Add yogurt mixture; toss to distribute.

To serve, spoon cheese mixture into tomato shells. Place filled tomato shells on individual serving plates. Makes 4 to 6 servings.

Zucchini & Feta Salad

California Salad

Carrot Coins

About 1 lb. carrots
2 to 3 tablespoons lemon juice
1 teaspoon vegetable oil or olive oil
2 tablespoons sugar
1 tablespoon finely chopped fresh dill or
** 1 teaspoon dried dill weed**
Salt and freshly ground pepper

Thinly slice carrots, making about 3 cups. Place carrots in a medium bowl. In a small bowl, beat lemon juice and oil until blended. Add sugar and dill. Stir in salt and pepper to taste. Pour over carrots. Stir to coat. Makes 4 servings.

Variation

Cook carrot slices in lightly salted water until crisp-tender; drain. Add lemon-juice-and-dill mixture. Stir to coat. Spoon into a serving dish.

California Salad

1-1/3 cups water
1/2 teaspoon salt
1/2 cup uncooked long-grain white rice
3 tomatoes
2 ripe avocados
2 hard-cooked eggs
1/4 lb. mushrooms
1/3 lb. cooked ham

Creamy White-Wine Dressing:
3 tablespoons vegetable oil or olive oil
1 tablespoon vinegar
3 tablespoons dry white wine
1 tablespoon half and half
1 teaspoon curry powder
Salt and freshly ground pepper
Basil leaves
Tomato roses, page 216, if desired

In a medium saucepan, combine water and salt; bring to a boil. Add rice. Cover and simmer 20 minutes. Let stand 5 minutes. Stir; refrigerate until chilled. Peel and quarter tomatoes. Remove seeds; cut tomatoes into strips. Dice avocados and hard-cooked eggs. Slice mushrooms; cut ham into julienne strips. In a large bowl, combine cooked rice, tomato strips, diced avocados, diced hard-cooked eggs, sliced mushrooms and julienned ham.
To make dressing, in a small bowl, beat oil, vinegar and wine until blended. Stir in half and half and curry powder until smooth. Stir in salt and pepper to taste. Stir into rice mixture; refrigerate at least 30 minutes.
To serve, garnish salad with basil leaves and tomato roses, if desired. Makes 6 servings.

Pineapple-Tuna Salad

1-1/3 cups water
1/2 teaspoon salt
1/2 cup uncooked long-grain white rice
1 (8-oz.) can chunk pineapple
1 (7-oz.) can solid-pack tuna
1 (10-oz.) pkg. frozen green peas, thawed
1/3 to 1/2 cup vinaigrette dressing
2 tablespoons chopped fresh parsley

In a medium saucepan, combine water and salt; bring to a boil. Add rice; cover and simmer 20 minutes. Let stand 5 minutes. Stir; refrigerate until chilled. While rice chills, drain pineapple and tuna. Flake drained tuna. In a large bowl, combine cooked rice, drained pineapple, flaked tuna and peas.
To serve, pour dressing over salad; toss to distribute. Spoon salad into individual bowls; garnish with parsley. Makes 4 servings.

Three-Bean Salad

Three-Bean Salad

1 (16-oz.) can cannellini beans
1 (15-oz.) can red kidney beans
1 (16-oz.) can cut green beans
1 small red onion
1 garlic clove

Dressing:
5 tablespoons vegetable oil or olive oil
2 tablespoons vinegar
Salt and freshly ground pepper
2 tablespoons finely chopped chives

Pour cannellini, kidney and green beans into a large sieve to drain. Discard juices. Cut onion in half horizontally. Dice 1/2 of onion; cut remaining 1/2 onion in rings. Mince garlic. In a large bowl, combine drained beans, diced onion and minced garlic; set aside. Reserve onion rings for garnish.
To make dressing, in a small bowl, beat oil and vinegar until blended. Stir in salt and pepper to taste. Pour over bean mixture; toss to coat. Garnish with chives and reserved onion rings. Refrigerate until thoroughly chilled before serving. Makes 4 servings.

Green-Bean & Pine-Nut Salad

2 lbs. fresh green beans

Oregano Dressing:
6 tablespoons vegetable oil or olive oil
3 tablespoons tarragon vinegar
1 garlic clove, minced
About 1 tablespoon dried leaf oregano
Salt and freshly ground pepper
1 teaspoon vegetable oil or olive oil
1/4 cup pine nuts

Cook green beans in lightly salted water until crisp-tender; drain. Place cooked beans in a large bowl; set aside.
To make dressing, in a small bowl, beat 6 tablespoons oil and vinegar until blended. Add garlic; stir in oregano, salt and pepper to taste. Pour over beans; toss to coat. Refrigerate several hours. Heat 1 teaspoon oil in a small skillet. Add pine nuts; sauté over low heat until golden brown. Set aside to cool.
To serve, sprinkle browned pine nuts over salad. Makes 6 to 8 servings.

Green-Bean & Pine-Nut Salad

Bean & Salami Salad

Bean & Salami Salad

1 (10-oz.) pkg. frozen whole green beans
1 (10-1/2-oz.) can cannellini beans
1 (10-1/2-oz.) can chick peas or garbanzo beans
1 large onion
2 tomatoes
1/2 lb. Genoa salami

Tarragon Dressing:
6 tablespoons vegetable oil or olive oil
3 tablespoons red-wine vinegar
1 teaspoon prepared mustard
1/2 teaspoon dried leaf tarragon or
    1 tablespoon chopped fresh tarragon
Salt and freshly ground pepper

Cook green beans according to package directions until crisp-tender. Drain; rinse in cold water to stop cooking. Drain cannellini beans and chick peas or garbanzo beans. Slice onion. Cut each tomato into 8 wedges. Cut salami into julienne strips. In a large bowl, combine cooked green beans, drained cannellini beans, drained chick peas or garbanzo beans, onion slices, tomato wedges and salami strips.
To make dressing, in a small bowl, beat oil, vinegar and mustard until blended. Add tarragon. Season with salt and pepper.
To serve, pour dressing over salad; toss to distribute. Makes 4 servings.

Coleslaw

1 large cabbage
1 carrot
1 green bell pepper
2 celery stalks

Coleslaw Dressing:
1/3 cup mayonnaise
1/4 cup dairy sour cream
2 tablespoons vinegar
2 tablespoons sugar
Salt and freshly ground pepper
1 cup slivered almonds
Paprika
4 or 5 green-bell-pepper rings

Shred cabbage; grate carrot. Finely chop bell pepper; slice celery. In a large bowl, combine shredded cabbage, grated carrot, chopped bell pepper and sliced celery.
To make dressing, in a small bowl, combine mayonnaise, sour cream, vinegar and sugar; stir to blend. Stir in salt and pepper to taste.
To serve, stir dressing into cabbage mixture until distributed. Stir in almonds; sprinkle with paprika. Garnish salad with bell-pepper rings. Makes 6 servings.

Pasta Salad

1 bunch fresh broccoli (about 2 lbs.)
1-1/2 to 2 cups uncooked small pasta shells
2 tomatoes
2 green onions

Dressing:
5 tablespoons olive oil
2 tablespoons vinegar
Salt and freshly ground pepper
1 tablespoon chopped fresh parsley

Cut broccoli into flowerets; cook in lightly salted water until crisp-tender. At the same time, cook pasta shells in lightly salted boiling water until tender. Drain cooked broccoli and pasta; refrigerate until chilled. Dice tomatoes; slice green onions. In a large bowl, combine chilled cooked broccoli and pasta, diced tomatoes and sliced green onions.
To make dressing, in a small bowl, beat oil and vinegar until blended. Season with salt and pepper.
To serve, pour dressing over salad. Toss to coat. Garnish with parsley. Makes 6 servings.

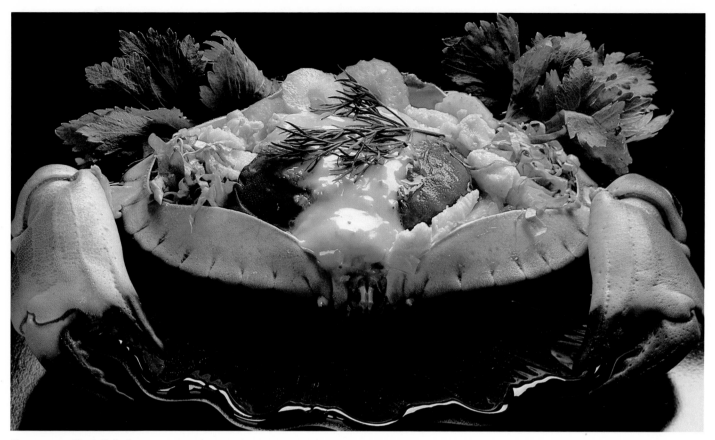

Dungeness-Crab Salad

Dungeness-Crab Salad

4 (1-1/2- to 2-lb.) in-shell Dungeness crabs
6 cups water
1 tablespoon salt
1 onion, cut in half
1 garlic clove
6 black peppercorns
4 parsley sprigs
1 large head lettuce
1 cup chopped celery

Mustard Dressing:
2 cups water
2 eggs
3 tablespoons vinegar
1/4 cup vegetable oil or olive oil
2 tablespoons prepared mustard
2 tablespoons finely chopped chives
Salt and freshly ground pepper
Dill sprigs
Parsley sprigs

Scrub crabs well. In a large pot, combine water, salt, onion, garlic, peppercorns and 4 parsley sprigs. Bring to a boil over medium-high heat. Grasp live crabs, firmly holding back legs. Drop crabs into boiling water, head first. Reduce heat; cover and simmer 12 to 20 minutes. Crabs will turn red when done. Use a slotted spoon or tongs to remove cooked crabs from water; set aside to cool. When cool enough to handle, clean and crack cooked crabs, 1 at a time.

To clean and crack cooked crab, hold base of crab with 1 hand, place thumb of your other hand under shell; pull up. Shell will come off easily. Pull out and discard bile sac. Turn crab on its back. Lift up and pull off *apron,* or rough triangle of shell. Pull out and discard grey feathery gills. Save creamy crab fat, if desired. Use for another purpose. Rinse out top shell and center of crab, removing small white intestine. Scoop out crabmeat; remove any gristle. Place crabmeat in a medium bowl; refrigerate until chilled. Rinse insides of shells; drain. Shred lettuce. Line rinsed shells with shredded lettuce. Mix celery with chilled crabmeat; spoon into shells.

To make dressing, pour 2 cups water into a small saucepan; add eggs. Over medium heat, gradually bring water to a boil; boil 1 minute. Using a slotted spoon, quickly remove eggs from water. Immediately immerse in cold water to stop cooking. Break eggs into a small bowl; beat with a whisk until blended. Add vinegar, oil and mustard; beat until blended. Add chives; stir in salt and pepper to taste.

To serve, spoon dressing over crab salad. Garnish with dill sprigs and parsley sprigs. Makes 4 servings.

Corn & Shrimp Salad

Corn & Shrimp Salad

1 (17-oz.) can whole-kernel corn
2 tomatoes
1 small onion
1/2 lb. cooked, shelled, small shrimp

Oil & Vinegar Dressing:
3 tablespoons vegetable oil or olive oil
1 tablespoon vinegar
Salt and freshly ground pepper
2 tablespoons chopped fresh parsley

Drain corn. Dice tomatoes and onion. In a medium bowl, combine drained corn and diced tomatoes and onion. Add shrimp; toss to distribute.

To make dressing, in a small bowl, beat oil and vinegar until blended. Season with salt and pepper.

To serve, pour dressing over salad; toss to distribute. Garnish with parsley. Makes 4 servings.

Bell-Pepper & Feta Salad

3 green bell peppers
3 tomatoes
2 onions

Dressing:
3 tablespoons vegetable oil or olive oil
1 tablespoon vinegar
Salt and freshly ground pepper
1/2 lb. feta cheese
2 tablespoons finely chopped chives

Cut bell peppers into strips. Cut each tomato into 8 wedges. Slice onions. In a medium bowl, combine bell-pepper strips, tomato wedges and onion slices.

To make dressing, in a small bowl, beat oil and vinegar until blended. Season with salt and pepper.

To serve, pour dressing over salad; toss to distribute. Crumble cheese over salad. Garnish with chives. Makes 4 servings.

Turkey Salad in Tomatoes

4 large firm tomatoes
Salt
2 cups diced cooked turkey or chicken
1/2 cup finely chopped green bell pepper
1/2 cup finely chopped celery
4 green onions, sliced

Dressing:
1/2 cup mayonnaise
1/2 cup bottled French dressing
Freshly ground pepper
Paprika
Chopped fresh parsley

Cut off top 1/4 of each tomato; hollow out centers, discarding seeds and pulp. Sprinkle salt inside tomatoes; invert on paper towels to drain. In a medium bowl, combine turkey or chicken, bell pepper, celery and green onions.

To make dressing, spoon mayonnaise into a small bowl. Stir in French dressing; add pepper to taste. Spoon over poultry mixture; stir gently to coat.

To serve, spoon poultry mixture into drained tomato shells. Sprinkle with paprika; garnish with parsley. Makes 4 servings.

Note: Use leftover turkey or chicken, or poach 4 boneless chicken breasts to make 2 cups diced cooked chicken. For poaching instructions, see Chicken Salad with Sherry Dressing, page 74.

Mussel Salad

Cucumber-Pepper Salad

2 small cucumbers (each about 3 inches long)
1 red bell pepper
2 tablespoons olive oil
1/4 cup red-wine vinegar
1 tablespoon soy sauce
1 tablespoon sugar
1 teaspoon ground ginger
Freshly ground black pepper
Chopped fresh parsley

Peel cucumbers only if waxed. Cut each cucumber in half lengthwise, then crosswise. Remove seeds; cut cucumber pieces lengthwise into 1/4-inch-wide strips. Cut bell pepper into 1/4-inch-wide strips. Heat oil in a medium skillet; add cucumber and bell-pepper strips. Sauté until crisp-tender, about 3 minutes. Remove with a slotted spoon; place in a medium, glass bowl. Pour vinegar and soy sauce over vegetables; season with sugar, ginger and black pepper. Toss gently; refrigerate at least 4 hours.
To serve, spoon onto 4 small individual plates; garnish with parsley. Serve cold. Makes 4 servings.

Mussel Salad

2 (8-3/4-oz.) cans mussels
6 sweet pickles
3 tomatoes
12 pimento-stuffed green olives
12 bottled cocktail onions
Lettuce leaves

Mustard-Chive Dressing:
6 tablespoons mayonnaise
1/4 cup dairy sour cream
1 teaspoon prepared mustard
1 tablespoon finely chopped chives
Salt and freshly ground pepper

Drain mussels. Dice pickles and tomatoes. Cut olives in half. In a medium bowl, combine drained mussels, diced pickles and tomatoes, halved olives and onions. Arrange lettuce leaves on 4 individual salad plates. Spoon salad onto lettuce.
To make dressing, in a small bowl, blend mayonnaise and sour cream. Stir in mustard and chives. Stir in salt and pepper to taste.
To serve, spoon dressing over salad. Makes 4 servings.

Shrimp & Beet Salad

Bismarck-Herring Salad

2 pickled herring fillets
1 dill pickle
2 onions
1 (3-1/2-oz.) can sliced mushrooms

Horseradish Dressing:
1/2 pint dairy sour cream (1 cup)
1 to 2 tablespoons half and half
2 teaspoons prepared horseradish
1 tablespoon finely chopped chives
Dill sprigs

Slice herring fillets and pickle. Cut onions into rings. Drain mushrooms. In a medium bowl, combine sliced herring, pickle, onion rings and drained mushrooms.

To make dressing, in a small bowl, blend sour cream, half and half and horseradish.

To serve, spoon dressing over salad; garnish with chives and dill sprigs. Makes 4 servings.

Shrimp & Beet Salad

1 (16-oz.) can sliced pickled beets, drained
2 bunches watercress, chopped
4 hard-cooked eggs
1/2 lb. cooked, shelled, small shrimp

Creamy Dill Dressing:
1/2 pint dairy sour cream (1 cup)
1/2 cup mayonnaise
3 tablespoons chopped fresh dill
Salt and freshly ground pepper

Arrange beets over bottom of a shallow serving bowl, overlapping slices. Sprinkle watercress over beets, leaving a border of beets uncovered. Cut hard-cooked eggs in half; separate whites from yolks. Chop whites; press yolks through a sieve. Leaving a border of watercress uncovered, sprinkle chopped egg whites in a half circle over watercress. Complete circle with sieved egg yolks. Mound shrimp in center.

To make dressing, in a small bowl, combine sour cream, mayonnaise and dill; stir until blended. Stir in salt and pepper to taste. Pour into a small serving dish; serve with salad. Makes 4 servings.

Bismarck-Herring Salad

Fish & Rice Salad

Fish & Rice Salad

1-1/3 cups water
1/2 teaspoon salt
1/2 cup uncooked long-grain white rice

Steeped Fish:
1/2 lb. white fish fillets
Water
1 lemon slice
1 onion slice
4 parsley sprigs
1/4 teaspoon salt
Pinch of white pepper

Salad:
1/4 celeriac
1 onion
1 apple
1/2 cup diced Gouda cheese (4 oz.)

Curry Dressing:
5 tablespoons vegetable oil or olive oil
2 tablespoons vinegar
About 1 teaspoon curry powder
Salt and freshly ground pepper

In a small saucepan, combine 1-1/3 cups water and salt; bring to a boil. Add rice; cover and simmer 20 minutes. Let stand 5 minutes. Stir; refrigerate until chilled. While rice cooks, steep fish.

To steep fish, rinse fish fillets; set aside. Pour water about 2 inches deep into a fish poacher or large shallow pan. Add lemon, onion, parsley, salt and white pepper. Cover; bring to a full boil. Remove pan from heat. Gently lower rinsed fish fillets into hot liquid. Immediately cover pan. Steep 5 minutes. Lift fish from pan; plunge into iced water to stop cooking. Drain on paper towels. Refrigerate until chilled. Discard steeping mixture.

To prepare salad ingredients, peel and slice celeriac. Thinly slice onion. Peel, core and dice apple. In a large nonmetal bowl, combine sliced celeriac and onion, diced apple and cheese. Flake chilled fish. Add flaked fish and chilled rice to celeriac mixture.

To make dressing, in a small bowl, beat oil and vinegar until blended. Season with curry powder, salt and pepper. Pour over salad; toss to distribute. Refrigerate several hours to let flavors blend. Makes 4 servings.

Chicken Salad with Sherry Dressing

Potato Salad

2 lbs. potatoes (about 6 medium)
2 celery stalks
3 hard-cooked eggs
1/2 small green bell pepper
2 sweet pickles
1 small onion

Mustard-Yogurt Dressing:
1/2 cup mayonnaise
1/2 cup plain yogurt
1 tablespoon prepared mustard
3 tablespoons liquid from sweet pickles
Salt and freshly ground pepper
Lettuce leaves
Paprika
Parsley sprigs

Cook potatoes in lightly salted water until tender. Peel and slice cooked potatoes. Dice celery; chop hard-cooked eggs and bell pepper. Mince pickles and onion. In a large bowl, combine sliced potatoes, diced celery, chopped hard-cooked eggs and bell pepper, and minced pickles and onion.

To make dressing, in a small bowl, combine mayonnaise, yogurt and mustard; stir until blended. Stir in sweet-pickle liquid. Stir in salt and pepper to taste. Spoon dressing over potato mixture; toss to coat.

To serve, line a large salad bowl with lettuce leaves. Spoon potato salad into lettuce-lined bowl; sprinkle with paprika. Garnish with parsley sprigs. Makes 6 servings.

Chicken Salad with Sherry Dressing

2 chicken breasts, skinned, boned
1-1/2 cups water
1/2 cup dry vermouth
1 garlic clove
1 bay leaf
6 black peppercorns
Pinch of salt
1/4 lb. oyster mushrooms or shiitake mushrooms
2 tablespoons butter or margarine
1 tablespoon lemon juice
Salt and freshly ground pepper
1 tomato

Sherry Dressing:
1-1/2 tablespoons olive oil
1-1/2 tablespoons lemon juice
1 tablespoon dry sherry
1-1/2 teaspoons prepared mustard
2 tablespoons whipping cream
3 tablespoons finely chopped chives
Salt and freshly ground pepper
Lettuce leaves
Parsley sprigs

Place chicken breasts between 2 pieces of plastic wrap. Pound with flat side of a meat mallet until flattened.

To poach chicken, in a medium saucepan, combine water, vermouth, garlic, bay leaf, peppercorns and salt. Bring to a boil; reduce heat. Add flattened chicken breasts; simmer 10 to 12 minutes or until barely tender. Lift chicken from pan; plunge into iced water to stop cooking. Drain on paper towels. Refrigerate until cold.

To complete, clean mushrooms; cut in half. Melt butter or margarine in a small skillet. Add mushroom halves; sauté 3 to 4 minutes. Sprinkle with lemon juice. Sprinkle lightly with salt and pepper. Refrigerate until chilled. Quarter tomato; remove core and seeds. Cut seeded tomato into strips.

To make dressing, in a small bowl, beat oil, lemon juice and sherry until blended. Stir in mustard. Add cream; beat until blended. Add 2 tablespoons chives. Stir in salt and pepper to taste.

To serve, line 2 salad plates with lettuce leaves. Place 1 chilled poached chicken breast on each plate. Arrange tomato strips and sautéed mushrooms around chicken. Spoon dressing over top; garnish with parsley sprigs and remaining chives. Makes 2 servings.

Chicken & Mushroom Salad

Mushroom & Beef Salad

1 lb. mushrooms
1/2 lb. cooked roast beef
2 hard-cooked eggs

Russian Dressing:
5 tablespoons vegetable oil or olive oil
2 tablespoons vinegar
1 to 2 tablespoons ketchup
4 to 5 tablespoons half and half
1 teaspoon brandy
About 1 teaspoon sugar
About 1/8 teaspoon paprika
Salt and freshly ground pepper
2 tablespoons chopped fresh parsley

Cut mushrooms in quarters. Slice beef; cut slices in julienne strips. Slice hard-cooked eggs. In a large bowl, combine mushroom pieces, julienned beef and egg slices; set aside.
To make dressing, in a small bowl, beat oil and vinegar until blended. Beat in ketchup, half and half and brandy. Stir in sugar, paprika, salt and pepper to taste.
To serve, pour dressing over salad; toss gently to distribute. Garnish with parsley. Makes 4 servings.

Chicken & Mushroom Salad

2 chicken breasts, skinned, boned
1/4 cup butter or margarine
1/2 lb. mushrooms
4 green onions
1 celery stalk
Salt and freshly ground pepper

Basil Dressing:
1 egg yolk
1 teaspoon prepared mustard
1 tablespoon lemon juice
1 teaspoon sugar
1/2 cup vegetable oil or olive oil
2 tablespoons whipping cream
3 tablespoons chopped fresh basil or
   1 tablespoon dried leaf basil
Salt and freshly ground pepper
Basil or parsley leaves

Place chicken breasts between 2 pieces of plastic wrap. Pound with flat side of a meat mallet until flattened. Melt butter or margarine in a medium skillet. Add flattened chicken; sauté until tender and lightly browned on both sides. Set aside to cool. Slice mushrooms, green onions, celery and cooled cooked chicken; combine in a large bowl. Toss to distribute. Season with salt and pepper to taste.
To make dressing, in a small bowl, beat egg yolk, mustard, lemon juice and sugar until thickened. Beating constantly with a whisk or electric mixer, slowly beat in oil. Beat in cream. Stir in basil; season with salt and pepper to taste. Pour into a small serving bowl.
To serve, garnish salad with basil or parsley; serve with dressing. Makes 4 servings.

Kiwifruit, Citrus & Walnut Salad

Photo on page 224.

3 or 4 kiwifruit
2 oranges
2 pink grapefruit
Lettuce leaves
1/4 cup chopped walnuts
1/3 cup walnut halves
Crème Fraîche, page 162, if desired

Peel and slice kiwifruit, oranges and grapefruit. On 4 individual plates, arrange lettuce leaves. Top with grapefruit slices, orange slices and kiwifruit slices. Sprinkle with chopped walnuts, then walnut halves. Serve with Crème Fraîche, if desired. Makes 4 servings.

Shrimp & Chicken Salad

Fennel & Camembert Salad

1 small fennel bulb
1 small celeriac
1 apple
1/4 lb. ripe Camembert cheese, diced

Piquant Dressing:
2-1/2 tablespoons vegetable oil or olive oil
2-1/2 tablespoons vinegar
1 tablespoon Italian seasoning
1 teaspoon sugar
Salt and freshly ground pepper
Lettuce leaves
2 tablespoons dairy sour cream
1/4 cup chopped walnuts
Lemon slices

Trim and dice fennel; reserve fennel sprigs for garnish. Peel and dice celeriac and apple. In a medium bowl, combine diced fennel, celeriac and apple. Add cheese; toss to distribute.
To make dressing, in a small bowl, beat oil and vinegar until blended. Add Italian seasoning and sugar. Stir in salt and pepper to taste. Pour over fennel mixture; stir to coat. Refrigerate at least 1 hour.
To serve, shred 4 or 5 lettuce leaves. Stir shredded lettuce, sour cream and walnuts into fennel mixture. Adjust seasonings. Line salad plates with lettuce leaves. Spoon salad onto lettuce-lined plates. Garnish with lemon slices and fennel sprigs. Makes 4 servings.

Shrimp & Chicken Salad

1 (15-oz.) can asparagus spears
1/2 lb. boned chicken, cooked
1/4 lb. mushrooms
1 sweet pickle
1/4 lb. cooked, shelled, small shrimp
1 tablespoon slivered almonds
1 orange

Yogurt Dressing:
3 tablespoons mayonnaise
2 tablespoons plain yogurt
1 teaspoon prepared mustard
Salt and freshly ground pepper

Drain asparagus; cut chicken into strips. Slice mushrooms; chop pickle. In a medium bowl, combine drained asparagus, chicken strips, sliced mushrooms and chopped pickle. Stir in shrimp and almonds. Using a citrus scorer, remove peel from orange in thin circular strips, being careful not to include any white pith; set aside. Section orange; add orange sections to chicken mixture.
To make dressing, in a small bowl, blend mayonnaise, yogurt and mustard. Stir in salt and pepper to taste.
To serve, spoon dressing over salad. Garnish salad with reserved orange peel. Makes 4 servings.

Salad Platter

1 small head lettuce
1 red bell pepper
1 green bell pepper
1 medium cucumber
4 tomatoes
1 red onion
1 (12-oz.) can whole-kernel corn, drained
1 (13-oz.) can solid-pack tuna, drained

Pink Sour-Cream Dressing:
1/2 pint dairy sour cream (1 cup)
1/2 cup mayonnaise
2 to 3 tablespoons ketchup
2 to 3 tablespoons half and half
Salt and freshly ground pepper
2 tablespoons chopped fresh parsley

Keeping ingredients separated, prepare the following: Separate lettuce leaves; arrange on a platter. Cut bell peppers into strips. Peel and slice cucumber; slice tomatoes. Cut onion into rings. Arrange bell-pepper strips, cucumber slices, tomato slices and onion rings on lettuce-lined platter. Spoon corn over vegetables. Flake tuna; scatter over corn.
To make dressing, in a small bowl, combine sour cream, mayonnaise, ketchup and half and half. Stir until blended. Stir in salt and pepper to taste.
To serve, spoon dressing over salad. Garnish with parsley. Makes 4 servings.

Kiwifruit Salad

1/2 head Boston lettuce
2 zucchini
2 celery stalks
3 kiwifruit
1/4 lb. cooked ham

Lemon Dressing:
3 tablespoons vegetable oil or olive oil
2 tablespoons lemon juice
1 tablespoon chopped fresh tarragon or
   1 teaspoon dried leaf tarragon
Salt and freshly ground pepper
2 tablespoons pistachios

Shred lettuce; slice zucchini and celery. Peel and slice kiwifruit. Cut ham in thin strips. In a large bowl, combine shredded lettuce and sliced zucchini, celery and kiwifruit. Add ham strips; toss to distribute.

To make dressing, in a small bowl, beat oil and lemon juice until blended. Add tarragon; season with salt and pepper.

To serve, pour dressing over salad; toss to distribute. Garnish salad with pistachios. Makes 4 servings.

Kiwifruit Salad

Crisp Summer Salad

Photo on pages 60 and 61.

1/2 lb. fresh edible pea pods
1/4 lb. mushrooms
4 or 5 radishes
1 cucumber
1 tomato
2 carrots
1 green bell pepper
1 onion
1/4 lb. spinach
1/4 head Romaine lettuce
1 garlic clove

Chive-Parsley Dressing:
6 tablespoons vegetable oil or olive oil
3 tablespoons wine vinegar
2 tablespoons finely chopped chives
2 tablespoons chopped fresh parsley
Salt and freshly ground pepper

Rinse peas pods; drain on paper towels. Slice mushrooms, radishes, cucumber and tomato. Peel and thinly slice carrots. Cut bell pepper and onion into rings. Tear spinach and lettuce into pieces. Cut garlic in half. Rub a large salad bowl with cut surface of garlic. Combine salad ingredients in prepared salad bowl.

To make dressing, in a small bowl, beat oil and vinegar until combined. Stir in chives and parsley. Season with salt and pepper. Pour over salad; toss to distribute. Makes 4 servings.

Marinated-Mushroom Salad

1 onion
2 garlic cloves
1-3/4 lbs. mushrooms
1/4 cup olive oil
1/4 cup lemon juice
3/4 cup water
2 bay leaves
1/4 teaspoon salt
Pinch of freshly ground pepper
Lettuce leaves
Tomato wedges
Chopped fresh parsley

Finely chop onion; crush garlic. Slice mushrooms; set aside. In a medium saucepan, combine chopped onion, crushed garlic, olive oil, lemon juice, water, bay leaves, salt and pepper. Bring to a boil over medium-high heat. Cover; simmer 5 minutes. Add sliced mushrooms. Cover; simmer 8 minutes. Pour into a glass or ceramic bowl; cool to room temperature. Cover; refrigerate several hours or overnight.

To serve, line 6 salad plates with lettuce leaves. Pour off marinade from mushrooms; remove and discard bay leaves. Arrange drained mushrooms on lettuce-lined plates. Garnish with tomato wedges and parsley. Makes 6 servings.

Aspics & Mousses

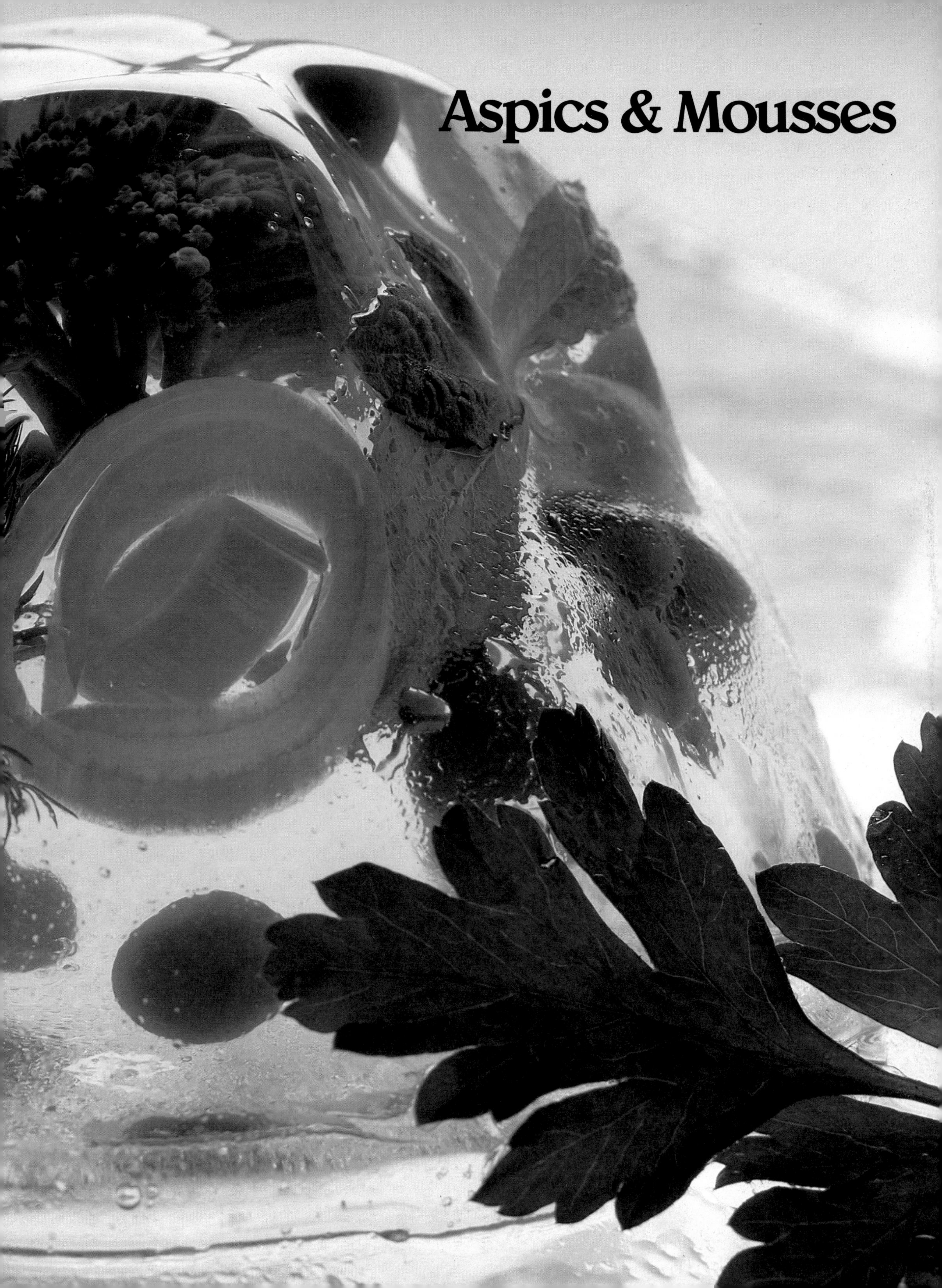

White-Fish Mousse

White-Fish Mousse

3 cups water
1/2 teaspoon salt
6 white peppercorns
4 lemon slices
1 lb. flounder, sole, cod or perch fillets
1-1/2 cups dairy sour cream
1 (1/4-oz.) envelope unflavored gelatin
2 tablespoons lemon juice
Salt and white pepper
Wine Aspic, page 89
8 large shrimp, cooked, peeled
Tomato wedges
Lemon curls, page 215
Dill sprigs

To poach fish, in a pan large enough to hold fish in a single layer, combine water, 1/2 teaspoon salt, peppercorns and lemon slices. Bring to a boil. Add fish; water should completely cover fish. If water does not cover fish, add boiling water to cover. Reduce heat until liquid gently simmers. Cook 6 to 8 minutes or until fish flakes easily. Cooking time will depend on thickness of fish. Remove fish from liquid; drain on paper towels. Strain cooking liquid; reserve 3/4 cup strained cooking liquid.

To make mousse, in a blender or food processor fitted with a metal blade, puree cooked fish until smooth. Add sour cream; process until blended. Spoon pureed fish mixture into a medium bowl; set aside. Pour 3/4 cup reserved cooking liquid into a small saucepan. Sprinkle gelatin over top; let stand 5 minutes. Stir over low heat until gelatin is dissolved. Cool slightly. Stir gelatin mixture and lemon juice into fish mixture. Season with salt and white pepper. Brush 4 (6-ounce) custard cups or small molds with vegetable oil. Drain on paper towels. Spoon fish mixture into oiled cups or molds; refrigerate 3 to 4 hours or until set. Prepare Wine Aspic according to directions; refrigerate until aspic has consistency of unbeaten egg whites.

To complete, run tip of a knife around edge of each cup or mold. Carefully invert onto a wire rack set over a large plate. Remove cup or mold. Arrange 2 shrimp on top of each mousse. Spoon partially set Wine Aspic over each, covering top and side. Refrigerate until set, about 20 minutes. Repeat spooning partially set Wine Aspic over shrimp and mousses 2 or 3 times or until mousses are completely coated. Refrigerate each time aspic is added.

To serve, slide a wide flat spatula under each mousse. Carefully lift onto individual plates. Garnish each with a tomato wedge, lemon curl and dill sprig. Makes 4 servings.

On previous pages: Green-Vegetable Aspic, page 86

Cucumber Mousse

Ham Mousse

1 lb. cooked ham, diced
1-1/4 cups homemade or canned chicken stock
1 (1/4-oz.) envelope unflavored gelatin
2 tablespoons tomato paste
3 tablespoons port or Madeira
1/2 cup minced celery
1 small onion, grated
2 tablespoons chopped fresh parsley
Salt and freshly ground pepper
1/2 cup mayonnaise
1/2 cup whipping cream
Pitted ripe olives
Parsley sprigs

In a blender or food processor fitted with a metal blade, process ham until finely ground; set aside. Pour 1/2 cup stock into a small saucepan. Sprinkle gelatin over top; let stand 5 minutes. Stir over low heat until gelatin is dissolved. Remove from heat; stir in remaining stock, tomato paste and port or Madeira. Pour into a medium bowl; stir in ground ham. Add celery, onion and chopped parsley; season with salt and pepper. Fold in mayonnaise. Refrigerate 20 to 25 minutes or until almost set. In a small bowl, beat cream until stiff peaks form. Fold whipped cream into ham mixture. Rinse a 6-cup decorative mold; drain. Spoon ham mixture into rinsed mold. Refrigerate 3 to 4 hours.
To serve, invert mold onto a platter or serving plate. Wet a dish towel in hot water; wring dry. Place hot wet towel around mold. Leave 5 to 10 seconds; remove mold and cloth. Garnish with olives and parsley sprigs. Makes 8 to 10 servings.

Cucumber Mousse

2 large cucumbers
1/4 cup cold water
1 (1/4-oz.) envelope unflavored gelatin
2 tablespoons cider vinegar
1/2 cup plain yogurt
Salt and white pepper
1/2 pint whipping cream (1 cup)
1 tablespoon chopped fresh dill
1 tablespoon chopped fresh parsley
Dill sprigs
Radish sprouts or watercress
Pumpernickel or dark rye bread

Peel and grate cucumbers. Place grated cucumbers in a sieve over a medium bowl. Let drain 30 minutes. Pour water into a small saucepan. Sprinkle gelatin over top; let stand 5 minutes. Stir over low heat until gelatin is dissolved. Remove from heat; stir in vinegar and yogurt. Pour yogurt mixture into a medium bowl. Spoon drained cucumbers onto a clean dish towel. Wring out as much moisture as possible. Stir drained cucumbers into yogurt mixture. Season with salt and white pepper. Refrigerate until mixture mounds when dropped from a spoon. In a medium bowl, beat cream until stiff peaks form. Fold whipped cream, chopped dill and parsley into cucumber mixture. Pour into a 4-cup decorative mold; smooth top. Refrigerate 3 to 4 hours or until set.
To serve, invert mold onto a platter or serving plate. Wet a dish towel in hot water; wring dry. Place hot wet towel around mold. Leave 5 to 10 seconds; remove mold and cloth. Garnish with dill sprigs and radish sprouts or watercress. Serve with pumpernickel or dark rye bread. Makes 10 to 12 servings.

Beef Stock for Aspic

1 unpeeled onion
3 or 4 whole cloves
2 lbs. beef soup bones
1 bay leaf
3 parsley sprigs
1 teaspoon coarse salt
6 to 8 black peppercorns
6 cups cold water

Stud unpeeled onion with whole cloves. In a large saucepan or stockpot, combine clove-studded onion, bones, bay leaf, parsley, salt, peppercorns and water. Bring to a boil. Skim foam from surface until surface is clear. Reduce heat; cover and simmer 2-1/2 to 3 hours, adding more water as necessary. Cool slightly. Strain stock into a 5- or 6-cup container with a tight-fitting lid. Refrigerate or freeze until fat solidifies on top of stock; remove fat. Cover container; refrigerate 2 to 3 days or freeze up to 4 months. Makes about 4-1/2 cups.

Fresh-Salmon Mousse with Salmon Steaks

Water
2 bay leaves
1/4 cup tarragon vinegar
2 thick lemon slices
1/4 teaspoon salt
About 1 lb. fresh salmon
4 small salmon steaks
2 tablespoons lemon juice
1 (1/4-oz.) envelope unflavored gelatin
Salt and white pepper
3/4 cup whipping cream
2 tablespoons chopped fresh dill
Tomato roses, page 216
Dill sprigs

To cook salmon, in a large saucepan or fish poacher, combine 4 cups water, bay leaves, vinegar, lemon and salt. Bring to a boil; reduce heat until water simmers. Add large salmon piece and salmon steaks; simmer 5 to 10 minutes or until fish flakes easily. Cooking time will depend on thickness of salmon. Undercook salmon slightly; it will continue to cook as it cools. Cool salmon in cooking liquid. Using a slotted spoon, remove salmon from cooking liquid. Refrigerate cooked salmon steaks until ready to serve.

To make mousses, remove skin and bones from large piece of cooked salmon. In a blender or food processor fitted with a metal blade, puree boned salmon. In a medium bowl, combine salmon puree and lemon juice; set aside. Pour 1/4 cup water into a small saucepan. Sprinkle gelatin over top; let stand 5 minutes. Stir over low heat until gelatin is dissolved. Set aside to cool. Stir cooled gelatin mixture into salmon puree. Season with salt and white pepper. Brush 4 (6-ounce) custard cups or molds with vegetable oil; drain on paper towels. In a medium bowl, beat cream until stiff peaks form. Fold whipped cream and chopped dill into salmon puree. Spoon into oiled each cups or molds; smooth tops. Refrigerate 3 to 4 hours or until firm.

To serve, run tip of a knife around inside edge of each cup or mold. Carefully invert mousses onto a platter or serving plate. Remove cups or molds. Add reserved salmon steaks. Garnish with tomato roses and dill sprigs. Makes 4 servings.

Fresh-Salmon Mousse with Salmon Steaks

Gorgonzola Mousse

1/2 lb. Gorgonzola cheese, crumbled
1/4 cup dry sherry
1/2 pint dairy sour cream (1 cup)
White pepper
Hot-pepper sauce
1/4 cup water
1 (1/4-oz.) envelope unflavored gelatin
1/2 cup whipping cream
Lime slices

In a blender or food processor fitted with a metal blade, process cheese and sherry until almost smooth. Add sour cream; process until blended. Spoon into a medium bowl; season with white pepper and hot-pepper sauce. Pour water into a small saucepan. Sprinkle gelatin over top; let stand 5 minutes. Stir over low heat until gelatin is dissolved. Cool slightly. Stir 1/2 cup cheese mixture into gelatin mixture until well blended. Stir gelatin mixture into remaining cheese mixture; refrigerate 15 minutes. Brush inside of a 3-cup decorative mold with vegetable oil; drain on paper towels. In a small bowl, beat cream until stiff peaks form. Fold whipped cream into cheese mixture until no streaks of whipped cream remain. Spoon cheese mixture into oiled mold; smooth top. Refrigerate 3 to 4 hours or until set.

To serve, invert mold onto a platter or serving plate. Wet a dish towel in hot water; wring dry. Place hot wet towel around mold. Leave 5 to 10 seconds; remove mold and cloth. Garnish with lime slices. Makes 10 to 12 servings.

Chicken & Asparagus Mold

Chicken & Asparagus Mold

1 (3-oz.) pkg. lemon-flavored gelatin
1 (1/4-oz.) envelope unflavored gelatin
2 cups boiling water
1-1/2 cups orange juice
1 tablespoon chopped fresh parsley
Salt
1 (8-3/4-oz.) can white asparagus spears, drained
2 hard-cooked eggs, sliced
1-3/4 cups cubed cooked chicken
Orange slices, halved
Parsley

To make aspic, in a medium bowl, blend lemon-flavored gelatin and unflavored gelatin. Add boiling water; stir until gelatins are completely dissolved. Stir in orange juice. Cool to room temperature. Stir in chopped parsley; season with salt. Rinse a 6-cup decorative mold with cold water; drain. Pour about 1/2 cup aspic into bottom of rinsed mold. Refrigerate until set. Let remaining aspic stand at room temperature.

To complete, cut asparagus spears in half crosswise. Arrange 1/2 of asparagus spears and 1/2 of egg slices alternately around edge of mold. Place 1/2 of chicken in center of mold. Pour in enough reserved aspic to cover. Refrigerate until set. Repeat with remaining cut asparagus spears, egg slices and chicken. Pour remaining aspic over chicken; refrigerate 3 to 4 hours or until set.

To serve, invert mold onto a platter or serving plate. Wet a dish towel in hot water; wring dry. Place hot wet towel around mold. Leave 5 to 10 seconds; remove mold and cloth. Garnish by arranging halved orange slices around bottom of aspic. Top aspic with parsley sprigs. Makes 8 to 10 servings.

Avocado Mousse

1/2 cup homemade or canned chicken stock
1 (1/4-oz.) envelope unflavored gelatin
2 large ripe avocados
2 tablespoons lemon juice
Salt and white pepper
1/2 cup mayonnaise
1 teaspoon Worcestershire sauce
Hot-pepper sauce
3/4 cup whipping cream
Chopped red and green bell pepper

Pour stock into a small saucepan. Sprinkle gelatin over top; let stand 5 minutes. Stir over low heat until gelatin is dissolved. Set aside to cool. In a medium bowl, mash avocados with a fork; stir in lemon juice. Season with salt and white pepper. Stir in cooled gelatin mixture. Fold in mayonnaise, Worcestershire sauce and hot-pepper sauce. Refrigerate until thickened and almost set. Brush a 4-cup ring mold or decorative mold with vegetable oil; drain on paper towels. In a medium bowl, beat cream until stiff peaks form. Fold whipped cream into avocado mixture until no streaks of whipped cream remain. Spoon avocado mixture into oiled mold; smooth top. Refrigerate 2 to 3 hours or until set.

To serve, run tip of a knife around inside edge of mold. Invert mousse onto a platter or serving plate; remove mold. Garnish with bell peppers. Makes 8 to 10 servings.

Firm Aspic

1-3/4 cups homemade or canned chicken, beef or
  vegetable stock
2 (1/4-oz.) envelopes unflavored gelatin
1/4 cup Madeira, sherry, dry red wine or dry white wine

To make aspic, clarify stock, page 89, if desired.
Pour 1/2 cup stock into a small saucepan. Sprinkle
gelatin over top; let stand 5 minutes. Stir over low
heat until gelatin is dissolved. Stir in remaining
1-1/4 cups stock; cool slightly. Stir in wine until
blended. Pour into an 11" x 7" glass baking dish.
Refrigerate 2 hours or until very firm. Cover; store
in refrigerator until ready to use. Aspic can be
cubed, diced or finely chopped, or cut in diamond
shapes. Use firm pieces of aspic as a garnish for
many cold dishes.
To remove aspic in a solid piece, lightly brush dish
with a thin coating of vegetable oil; drain on paper
towels, or wipe excess oil from dish with a paper
towel before adding aspic. Makes 2 cups.

Smoked Trout in Aspic

Summer Aspic

1 (3-oz.) pkg. lemon-flavored gelatin
1 (1/4-oz.) envelope unflavored gelatin
1-1/2 cups boiling water
1/2 cup cold water
1 green or red bell pepper
1 cup diced unpeeled zucchini
1 cup coarsely chopped celery
1/2 cup coarsely chopped radishes
1/2 cup bottled Italian dressing

To make aspic, in a large bowl, blend lemon-
flavored gelatin and unflavored gelatin. Add boiling
water; stir until gelatins are completely dissolved.
Stir in cold water. Refrigerate until aspic has
consistency of unbeaten egg whites.
To complete, dice bell pepper. In a large bowl,
combine zucchini, celery, radishes and diced bell
pepper. Add Italian dressing; toss lightly to
distribute. Fold vegetable mixture into partially set
aspic. Brush a 6-cup decorative mold or ring mold
with vegetable oil; drain on paper towels. Pour aspic
into oiled mold; smooth top. Refrigerate 3 to 4
hours or until set.
To serve, run tip of a knife around edge of mold.
Invert onto a serving plate; remove mold. Makes 8
to 10 servings.

Smoked Trout in Aspic

1-1/2 cups homemade or canned chicken stock
1 small onion
4 black peppercorns
Pinch of saffron
1/4 cup cold water
1 (1/4-oz.) envelope plus
  1 teaspoon unflavored gelatin powder
1 cup dry white wine
1 tablespoon white vinegar
2 to 3 drops hot-pepper sauce
Salt and white pepper
2 hard-cooked eggs
2 tomatoes
6 smoked-trout fillets (about 1-1/2 lbs.)
1 (8-3/4-oz.) can white asparagus spears, drained
Dill sprigs

Horseradish Sauce:
1/2 pint dairy sour cream (1 cup)
2 to 3 teaspoons prepared horseradish, well drained
About 1 teaspoon lemon juice
Salt and white pepper

Bloody Mary Aspic

1/2 cup cold water
2 (1/4-oz.) envelopes unflavored gelatin
2-3/4 cups tomato juice
2 tablespoons lemon juice
4 to 5 tablespoons vodka
1 teaspoon Worcestershire sauce
Hot-pepper sauce
Celery salt
Pepper
2 medium tomatoes
1 small onion
2 tablespoons chopped chives
1 hard-cooked egg, sliced
Radish sprouts, alfalfa sprouts or watercress

To make aspic, pour water into a medium saucepan. Sprinkle gelatin over top; let stand 5 minutes. Stir over low heat until gelatin is dissolved. Remove from heat; stir in tomato juice, lemon juice, vodka and Worcestershire sauce. Season with hot-pepper sauce, celery salt and pepper. Pour into a medium bowl; refrigerate until mixture has consistency of unbeaten egg whites, about 45 minutes.

To complete, peel tomatoes. Remove seeds; chop tomatoes. Finely chop onion. Fold chopped tomatoes, chopped onion and chives into partially set aspic. Pour into a 4-cup ring mold; refrigerate 3 to 4 hours or until set.

To serve, invert mold onto a platter or serving plate. Wet a dish towel in hot water; wring dry. Place hot wet towel around mold. Leave 5 to 10 seconds; remove mold and cloth. Garnish with slices of hard-cooked egg and radish sprouts, alfalfa sprouts or watercress. Makes 8 to 10 servings.

To make aspic, clarify stock, page 89, if desired. In a medium saucepan, combine stock, onion, peppercorns and saffron; bring to a boil. Boil rapidly 5 minutes. Line a sieve with a double layer of cheesecloth. Pour stock mixture through lined sieve into a medium bowl. Discard onion, peppercorns and saffron. Pour water into a small saucepan. Sprinkle gelatin over top; let stand 5 minutes. Stir over low heat until gelatin is dissolved. Remove from heat. Stir in strained stock, wine, vinegar and hot-pepper sauce until blended. Season with salt and white pepper. Refrigerate until aspic has consistency of unbeaten egg whites.

To complete, slice hard-cooked eggs and tomatoes. Place 1 trout fillet on each of 6 salad plates. Place egg slices, tomato slices and asparagus spears on each dish, arranging vegetables decoratively around trout fillets. Garnish with dill sprigs. Spoon 5 to 6 tablespoons partially set aspic over vegetables and trout. Refrigerate 2 to 3 hours or until aspic is set.

To prepare sauce, in a small bowl, combine sour cream and horseradish; stir until blended. Season with lemon juice, salt, and white pepper. Serve with trout in aspic. Makes 6 servings.

Bloody Mary Aspic

Asparagus Mousse with Caviar

Asparagus Mousse with Caviar

1-1/4 lbs. fresh asparagus
Water
1 teaspoon butter
1/2 teaspoon salt
1/2 teaspoon sugar
1 (1/4-oz.) envelope unflavored gelatin
1/2 cup dairy sour cream
1 egg white, lightly beaten
White pepper
1 small tomato
6 tablespoons black lumpfish caviar
1/2 cup whipping cream
1 teaspoon browning sauce

Snap off woody ends of asparagus stalks; discard ends. Cut tips off asparagus 2 to 3 inches from end; set aside. Peel stalks. In a medium saucepan, combine peeled asparagus stalks, 2-1/2 cups water, butter, salt and sugar. Bring to a gentle boil. Simmer 20 to 25 minutes or until asparagus stalks are very soft. In a blender or food processor fitted with a metal blade, puree cooked asparagus stalks and cooking liquid. Pour asparagus puree into a medium bowl; set aside. Brush 6 (4-ounce) ring molds with vegetable oil; drain on paper towels. Pour 1/4 cup water into a small saucepan. Sprinkle gelatin over top; let stand 5 minutes. Stir over low heat until gelatin is dissolved. Stir into asparagus puree until blended. Cool to room temperature. Add sour cream and egg white to puree mixture; beat vigorously with a whisk until blended and smooth. Season with white pepper. Place oiled molds on a small baking sheet. Pour asparagus mixture into oiled molds; refrigerate until set. In a small saucepan, cook reserved asparagus tips in lightly salted boiling water until crisp-tender. Drain; refrigerate until chilled. Peel tomato; remove seeds. Press seeded tomato pulp through a sieve.

To serve, run tip of a knife around edge of each mold. Unmold onto individual plates. Spoon 1 tablespoon caviar into center of each mousse; top caviar with about 1 teaspoon sieved tomato. In a small bowl, beat whipping cream until slightly thickened. Add browning sauce; swirl lightly through whipped cream. Spoon around mousses. Garnish with cooked asparagus tips. Makes 6 servings.

Green-Vegetable Aspic

Photo on pages 78 and 79.

1 qt. homemade or canned chicken stock (4 cups)
2 (1/4-oz.) envelopes unflavored gelatin
Green food coloring
4 broccoli flowerets
2 or 3 cauliflowerets
1 tablespoon frozen green peas
1 leek, white part only, sliced
2 or 3 fresh basil, thyme or dill sprigs
Parsley sprigs
Cold cooked meat

To make aspic, clarify stock, page 89, if desired. Pour 1/2 cup stock into a medium saucepan. Sprinkle gelatin over top; let stand 5 minutes. Stir over low heat until gelatin dissolves. Stir in remaining 3-1/2 cups stock. Pour into a large bowl. Stir in 1 or 2 drops green food coloring until blended. Cool to room temperature. Rinse a 5-cup decorative mold with water; drain. Pour a thin layer of aspic in bottom; refrigerate until set.

To complete, cook broccoli, cauliflower, peas and leek separately in lightly salted water until crisp-tender. Drain well; plunge into iced water to cool. Drain well. Arrange cooked vegetables decoratively over set aspic. Place basil, thyme or dill sprigs around inside edge of mold. Slowly pour remaining aspic into mold without disturbing vegetables. Refrigerate 3 to 4 hours or until set.

To serve, invert mold onto a platter or serving plate. Wet a dish towel in hot water; wring dry. Place hot wet towel around mold. Leave 5 to 10 seconds; remove mold and cloth. Garnish with parsley sprigs. Serve with cold meat. Makes 6 to 10 servings.

Herbed Ham in Aspic

Herbed Ham in Aspic

3-1/2 cups homemade or canned chicken stock
2 (1/4-oz.) envelopes unflavored gelatin
2 tablespoons brandy
1/4 cup port or Madeira
Salt and freshly ground pepper
1/2 cup chopped fresh parsley
2 tablespoons chopped fresh tarragon or chives
3-1/2 cups cubed cooked ham
Parsley sprigs, tarragon sprigs or chopped chives
Rémoulade Sauce, page 158

To make aspic, clarify stock, page 89, if desired. Pour 1/2 cup stock into a medium saucepan. Sprinkle gelatin over top; let stand 5 minutes. Stir over low heat until gelatin is dissolved. Stir in remaining 3 cups stock; cool slightly. Stir in brandy and port or Madeira. Season with salt and pepper. Stir in chopped parsley and tarragon or chives. Rinse a 9'' x 5'' loaf pan or 1-1/2-quart terrine with water. Pour 3/4 cup aspic into rinsed loaf pan or terrine. Refrigerate 20 minutes or until set enough to hold ham in place. Scatter 1/3 of ham over set aspic. Pour in enough remaining aspic to barely cover ham; refrigerate until set. Repeat layers of ham and aspic ending with a layer of aspic. Refrigerate 3 to 4 hours or until firm.

To serve, invert mold onto a platter or serving plate. Wet a dish towel in hot water; wring dry. Place hot wet towel around mold. Leave 5 to 10 seconds; remove mold and cloth. Or, serve from mold. Garnish with parsley, tarragon or chives. Serve with Rémoulade Sauce. Makes 8 to 10 servings.

Stuffed Greek Aspic

Stuffed Greek Aspic

2-1/2 cups homemade or canned chicken stock
2 (1/4-oz.) envelopes unflavored gelatin
1 cup dry white wine
1/2 cup tarragon vinegar
1 teaspoon Worcestershire sauce
8 slices boiled ham
8 canned pickled vine leaves, drained,
    stem ends removed
10 oz. goat cheese or Neufchâtel cheese,
    room temperature
3 tablespoons butter or margarine, room temperature
3 tablespoons whipping cream
1 teaspoon dried leaf basil
1 (10-oz.) pkg. frozen tiny green peas, thawed, drained
1 (12-oz.) can whole-kernel corn with sweet peppers,
    drained

Yogurt Sauce:
3/4 cup plain yogurt
3/4 cup dairy sour cream
1 teaspoon Dijon-style mustard
3 tablespoons chopped fresh parsley, chives or tarragon
Salt and white pepper
2 or 3 lemon slices, cut in quarters
Parsley sprigs

To make aspic, clarify stock, opposite, if desired. Pour 1/2 cup stock into a medium saucepan. Sprinkle gelatin over top; let stand 5 minutes. Stir over low heat until gelatin is dissolved. Stir in remaining 2 cups stock, wine, vinegar and Worcestershire sauce; cool slightly. Rinse an 11'' x 4'' loaf pan with water; drain. Pour 3/4 cup cooled aspic into rinsed pan; refrigerate until set. Refrigerate remaining aspic until it has consistency of unbeaten egg whites. Place 3 or 4 ham slices, slightly overlapping, over set aspic in pan. Place a layer of vine leaves over ham. Arrange remaining ham slices over vine leaves and up sides of pan. Cover with remaining vine leaves.

To complete, in a small bowl, beat cheese, butter or margarine, cream and basil until blended. Spoon cheese mixture down center of pan over vine leaves. Shape into a roll by folding vine leaves from sides of pan over cheese roll. Then fold ham from sides of pan over vine leaves. Fold peas and corn into reserved partially set aspic. Spoon into pan around sides and over top of cheese roll, covering roll completely. Refrigerate 3 to 4 hours or until set.

To make sauce, in a small bowl, combine yogurt, sour cream, mustard and herbs. Season with salt and white pepper; stir until blended. Pour into a small serving bowl.

To serve, invert mold onto a platter or serving plate. Wet a dish towel in hot water; wring dry. Place hot wet towel around mold. Leave 5 to 10 seconds; remove mold and cloth. Garnish top of aspic with lemon slices and parsley sprigs. Serve with Yogurt Sauce. Makes 10 to 12 servings.

Chicken in Sherry Aspic

Sherry Aspic:
3-1/4 cups homemade or canned chicken stock
2 (1/4-oz.) envelopes unflavored gelatin
1/2 cup dry sherry
3 tablespoons lemon juice
1 teaspoon Worcestershire sauce
Salt and white pepper

Filling:
1 (10-oz.) pkg. frozen crinkle-cut carrots,
   partially thawed
Parsley sprigs
2-1/2 cups diced cooked chicken
2 celery stalks, sliced
1 (2-1/2-oz.) jar whole mushrooms, drained, halved
Parsley sprigs
Carrot sticks
Celery slices

To make aspic, clarify stock, below, if desired. Pour 1/2 cup stock into a medium saucepan. Sprinkle gelatin over top; let stand 5 minutes. Stir over low heat until gelatin is dissolved. Remove from heat. Stir in remaining stock, sherry, lemon juice and Worcestershire sauce. Season with salt and white pepper.
To complete, layer filling ingredients in a 2-quart mold, 1 layer at a time, using enough aspic to cover each layer. Refrigerate between layering until aspic sets enough to hold layers in place. *Layer in order:* carrots with parsley sprigs between carrot slices; chicken; carrots and celery; chicken and mushrooms. Continue layering carrots and celery, then chicken and mushrooms, with aspic between layers, until all ingredients are used. Begin and end with a layer of aspic. Refrigerate 3 to 4 hours or until set.
To serve, invert mold onto a platter or serving plate. Wet a dish towel in hot water; wring dry. Place hot wet towel around mold. Leave 5 to 10 seconds; remove mold and cloth. Garnish with parsley sprigs, carrot sticks and sliced celery. Makes 8 to 10 servings.

Chicken in Sherry Aspic

Wine Aspic

1-1/2 cups homemade or canned chicken, beef or
   vegetable stock
1 (1/4-oz.) envelope unflavored gelatin
1/3 cup dry sherry, dry white wine or Madeira

To make aspic, clarify stock, below, if desired. Pour 1/2 cup stock into a medium saucepan. Sprinkle gelatin over top; let stand 5 minutes. Stir over low heat until gelatin is dissolved. Stir in remaining 1 cup stock. Cool to room temperature; stir in wine. Refrigerate 20 to 25 minutes or until mixture has consistency of unbeaten egg whites. Spoon over cold foods; refrigerate until set. Makes about 2 cups.

Note: This aspic may be poured over terrines, mousses, poultry, fish, cold meat or other cold foods that require a light covering of aspic.

To Clarify Stock

Pour 4 to 6 cups stock into a large saucepan or stockpot. Add 3 egg whites. Stirring constantly, bring to a boil. Reduce heat; simmer 40 minutes without stirring or disturbing crust that forms on top. Remove from heat; let stand 15 minutes. Line a large sieve with a double thickness of cheesecloth or paper towels. Place lined sieve over a large bowl. Pour stock mixture into lined sieve without disturbing surface crust. Let stand 1 hour before using. If any fat appears on top of stock, blot off with paper towels.

Pureed-Vegetable Terrine

Celery Puree:
6 large celery stalks
1 cup water
1/4 teaspoon salt
2 tablespoons cold water
2 teaspoons unflavored gelatin powder
2 tablespoons dairy sour cream
2 egg whites
Salt and white pepper

Broccoli Puree:
About 1 lb. broccoli
2 cups water
1/4 teaspoon salt
2 tablespoons cold water
2 teaspoons unflavored gelatin powder
2 tablespoons dairy sour cream
2 egg whites
1/4 teaspoon ground nutmeg

Carrot Puree:
1 lb. carrots
1-1/2 cups water
1/2 teaspoon sugar
1/4 teaspoon salt
2 tablespoons cold water
2 teaspoons unflavored gelatin powder
2 tablespoons dairy sour cream
1/4 teaspoon ground ginger
2 egg whites
Salt and white pepper

To make celery puree, trim celery, removing large ribs from back of stalks. Thinly slice trimmed celery. In a medium saucepan, bring 1 cup water and salt to a boil. Add sliced celery; cook until tender, about 25 minutes. In a blender or food processor fitted with a metal blade, puree cooked celery and cooking liquid. Pour puree into a medium bowl; set aside. Pour 2 tablespoons water into a small saucepan. Sprinkle gelatin over top; let stand 5 minutes. Stir over low heat until gelatin is dissolved. Stir into celery puree. Stir in sour cream. In a small bowl, beat egg whites until foamy. Add to celery puree; beat vigorously with a whisk until blended and smooth. Season with salt and white pepper; set aside.

To make broccoli puree, trim broccoli stalks, removing leaves; peel stalks. Remove 6 to 8 broccoli flowerets; set aside. Coarsely chop remaining broccoli. In a medium saucepan, combine 2 cups water and salt; bring to a boil. Add chopped broccoli; cook until tender, about 20 minutes. In a blender or food processor fitted with a metal blade, puree cooked broccoli and cooking liquid. Pour puree into a medium bowl; set aside. Pour 2 tablespoons water into a small saucepan. Sprinkle gelatin over top; let stand 5 minutes. Stir over low heat until gelatin is dissolved. Stir into broccoli puree. Stir in sour cream. In a small bowl, beat egg whites until foamy. Add to broccoli puree; beat vigorously with a whisk until blended and smooth. Stir in nutmeg; set aside. Cook reserved broccoli flowerets in lightly salted water 5 minutes. Drain well; set aside.

To make carrot puree, peel and thinly slice carrots. In a medium saucepan, bring 1-1/2 cups water, sugar and salt to a boil. Add sliced carrots; cook until tender, about 25 minutes. In a blender or food processor fitted with a metal blade, puree carrots and cooking liquid. Pour puree into a medium bowl; set aside. Pour 2 tablespoons water into a small saucepan. Sprinkle gelatin over top; let stand 5 minutes. Stir over low heat until gelatin is dissolved. Stir into carrot puree. Stir in sour cream and ginger. In a small bowl, beat egg whites until foamy. Add to carrot puree; beat vigorously with a whisk until blended and smooth. Season with salt and white pepper; set aside.

To complete, brush a 2-quart soufflé dish or 9'' x 5'' loaf pan with vegetable oil; drain on paper towels. Pour celery puree into bottom of oiled dish or pan; smooth top. Refrigerate 20 to 30 minutes or until almost set. Pour 1/2 of broccoli puree evenly over partially set celery puree. Gently press cooked flowerets into broccoli puree, stem-ends up. Carefully pour remaining broccoli puree around and over protruding broccoli flowerets; smooth top. Refrigerate 20 to 30 minutes or until almost set. Pour carrot puree over broccoli puree; smooth top. Preheat oven to 375F (190C). Cover dish or pan with foil. Place dish in a roasting pan; pour in enough boiling water to come 3/4 up sides of dish or pan. Bake 1 hour. Remove foil cover; cool completely on a wire rack. Cover cooled terrine with foil; refrigerate until firm, 4 to 5 hours.

To serve, invert mold onto a platter or serving plate. Wet a dish towel in hot water; wring dry. Place hot wet towel around mold. Leave 5 to 10 seconds; remove mold and cloth. Cut terrine into slices. Makes 12 to 14 servings.

Pureed-Vegetable Terrine

Festive Aspic Loaf

Festive Aspic Loaf

3-1/2 cups homemade or canned chicken or beef stock
2 (1/4-oz.) envelopes unflavored gelatin
1/2 cup tarragon vinegar
6 hard-cooked eggs
1/2 lb. cooked ham
4 medium, kosher dill pickles, sweet pickles or
    Polish pickles
4 medium tomatoes
1/3 cup chopped fresh parsley

To make aspic, clarify stock, page 89, if desired. Pour 1/2 cup stock into a medium saucepan. Sprinkle gelatin over top; let stand 5 minutes. Stir over low heat until gelatin is dissolved. Remove from heat; stir in remaining 3 cups stock and vinegar. Rinse a 9'' x 5'' loaf pan with water; drain. Pour about 2/3 cup aspic into rinsed pan; refrigerate until softly set. Refrigerate remaining aspic until it has consistency of unbeaten egg whites. Cut 2 eggs in thick slices; coarsely chop remaining 4 eggs. Dice ham, pickles and tomatoes.

To complete, arrange egg slices over softly set aspic in loaf pan. Scatter 1/2 of diced ham over egg slices. Pour in enough partially set aspic to cover. Refrigerate until set enough to hold ham in place. Scatter 1/2 of diced pickles over ham layer. Add enough aspic to cover; refrigerate until set enough to hold pickles in place. Add 1/2 of chopped tomatoes and 1/2 of parsley; add enough aspic to cover. Refrigerate until set enough to hold tomatoes and parsley in place. Add chopped eggs; add enough aspic to cover. Refrigerate until set enough to hold eggs in place. Repeat with remaining tomatoes, parsley, pickles and ham, adding aspic between each layer and ending with aspic. Refrigerate 3 to 4 hours or until firm.

To serve, invert mold onto a platter or serving plate. Wet a dish towel in hot water; wring dry. Place hot wet towel around mold. Leave 5 to 10 seconds; remove mold and cloth. Makes 8 to 10 servings.

Note: To shorten setting time, keep all ingredients refrigerated until needed.

Gazpacho Aspic

1/4 cup cold water
2 tablespoons lemon juice
1 (1/4-oz.) envelope plus
    1 teaspoon unflavored gelatin powder
2-1/2 cups vegetable-juice cocktail
2 to 3 drops hot-pepper sauce
Salt and white pepper
1 medium cucumber
1 medium tomato
1 green bell pepper
1 small onion
1 to 2 tablespoons chopped fresh parsley

To make aspic, pour water and lemon juice into a medium saucepan. Sprinkle gelatin over top; let stand 5 minutes. Stir over low heat until gelatin is dissolved. Remove from heat; stir in vegetable-juice cocktail and hot-pepper sauce until blended. Season with salt and white pepper. Pour into a medium bowl; refrigerate until mixture has consistency of unbeaten egg whites.

To complete, peel cucumber; cut in half and remove seeds. Dice seeded cucumber, tomato, bell pepper and onion. Fold parsley and diced cucumber, tomato, green pepper and onion into partially set aspic. Brush a 4-cup ring mold with vegetable oil. Drain on paper towels. Pour aspic into oiled mold; refrigerate 3 to 4 hours or until set.

To serve, run tip of a knife around edge of mold. Invert mold onto a serving platter or plate; remove mold. Makes 6 to 8 servings.

Fish & Shellfish

Foil-Baked Salmon Steaks

Egg Salad in Salmon Rolls

1 or 2 celery stalks
6 hard-cooked eggs
1/4 cup mayonnaise
2 teaspoons Dijon-style mustard
1/4 teaspoon Worcestershire sauce
2 tablespoons snipped chives
Salt and freshly ground pepper
8 slices smoked salmon
Lettuce leaves
1 (16-oz.) can asparagus spears, drained
2 or 3 pimento-stuffed olives, sliced
Radish sprouts, alfalfa sprouts or chopped parsley
Buttered toast triangles

Finely chop celery; place in a medium bowl. Press hard-cooked eggs through a sieve into bowl. Add mayonnaise, mustard, Worcestershire sauce and chives. Season with salt and pepper; stir well. Spread egg salad evenly on salmon slices. Roll salmon around egg salad.
To serve, line a platter or serving dish with lettuce leaves. Place salmon rolls on lettuce-lined platter or dish. Place 2 asparagus spears on top of each salmon roll; top each with an olive slice. Garnish with radish sprouts, alfalfa sprouts or parsley. Serve with buttered toast triangles. Makes 8 servings.

Foil-Baked Salmon Steaks

4 salmon steaks, about 1 inch thick
4 teaspoons lemon juice
Salt and freshly ground pepper
Boston lettuce
Tomato wedges
Parsley sprigs
Tartar Sauce, page 158

Preheat oven to 425F (220C). Cut 4 pieces of foil large enough to wrap around each salmon steak. Generously brush foil with vegetable oil. Sprinkle salmon steaks with lemon juice, salt and pepper. Wrap tightly in foil; place on an ungreased baking sheet. Bake 10 to 15 minutes or until fish flakes easily. Remove from foil; refrigerate until chilled.
To serve, arrange lettuce on a platter or serving dish. Place chilled cooked salmon steaks on lettuce-lined platter or dish. Garnish with tomato wedges and parsley sprigs. Serve with Tartar Sauce. Makes 4 servings.

Egg Salad in Salmon Rolls

On previous pages: Gravlax with Dill Sauce, opposite

Gravlax with Dill Sauce

Photo on pages 92 and 93.

3 to 4 lbs. center-cut salmon fillets, with skin
1/3 cup sugar
1/4 cup coarse salt
1 bunch fresh dill, separated into short sprigs
1 tablespoon white peppercorns, crushed
1 teaspoon brandy, if desired

Dill Sauce:
3 tablespoons Dijon-style mustard
1 tablespoon sugar
1 tablespoon red-wine vinegar
Salt and white pepper
3 tablespoons olive oil or vegetable oil

Gravlax with Dill Sauce

Find any bones in salmon by running your fingers over cut surface of salmon; if necessary, use tweezers to remove bones. In a small bowl, combine sugar and salt. Sprinkle a little of sugar mixture in bottom of a glass or ceramic baking dish. Rub boneless salmon with remaining sugar mixture. Reserve 2 to 3 tablespoons dill for Dill Sauce. Sprinkle 1/2 of remaining dill over sugar mixture in baking dish. Place 1 salmon fillet, skin-side down, in baking dish. Sprinkle with peppercorns and brandy, if desired. Cover with remaining dill. Place remaining salmon fillet, skin-side up, over dill; cover with foil. If a compact texture is desired, top with a small chopping board or a slightly smaller baking dish. Place several cans of food on board or in top dish for weight. Refrigerate about 5 hours; drain. Cover again with foil; refrigerate 2 to 3 days, draining occasionally.
To make sauce, in a small bowl, combine mustard, sugar, vinegar, salt and white pepper. Gradually add oil, beating constantly. Chop reserved dill; add to sauce. Refrigerate until ready to serve.
To serve, remove skin from marinated salmon; cut in thin slices. Serve with Dill Sauce. Makes 12 to 16 servings.

Variation

Add strips of carrot, diced celeriac, chopped green onions, juniper berries, red-onion rings, bay leaves, sage or parsley to marinade. Wipe marinade ingredients from salmon fillets before cutting and serving.

Cold Salmon Loaf

1 (8-oz.) pkg. cream cheese, room temperature
1 (16-oz.) can red salmon
1/2 cup finely chopped celery
1 tablespoon lemon juice
2 teaspoons prepared horseradish
Salt and freshly ground pepper
Walnut halves
Pimento strips

In a medium bowl, stir cream cheese until smooth. Drain salmon; remove bones, if desired. Flake salmon; add to stirred cream cheese. Mash with a fork until nearly smooth. Stir in celery, lemon juice and horseradish. Season with salt and pepper.
To serve, shape into a loaf. Place salmon loaf on a serving plate. Garnish with walnut halves and pimento strips. Refrigerate until thoroughly chilled. Makes 6 servings.

Mixed Seafood Platter

Mixed Seafood Platter

24 mussels
2 cups dry white wine
1 onion, cut in half
4 parsley sprigs
1/2 lb. squid
1/2 lb. medium shrimp (10 to 12 shrimp)
1 (3-3/4 oz.) can sardines, drained
1 cup sliced pimento-stuffed olives
About 1/3 cup bottled Italian dressing
Lamb's lettuce or other small-leaf lettuce
3 to 4 tablespoons dairy sour cream
1 tablespoon black lumpfish caviar, if desired
Dill sprigs
French bread
Butter

To clean and cook mussels, scrub mussels under cold running water; pull off beards. Discard any mussels that remain open. Place cleaned mussels in a large kettle; add wine, onion and parsley. Bring to a simmer. Cover; cook 3 to 5 minutes or until mussels open. After 2 minutes turn mussels with a large spoon. Using a slotted spoon, place cooked mussels in a large bowl; set aside to cool. Discard any mussels that do not open. Strain cooking liquid into a medium saucepan. Reserve cooking liquid.

When mussels are cool enough to handle, remove from shells. Refrigerate.

To clean and cook squid, gently pull tentacles, viscera and ink sac from body. Pull out and discard transparent sword-shaped pen from body. Cut off tentacles just above eyes; discard eyes, viscera and ink sac. Squeeze small hard, round beak, that looks like a garbanzo bean, from base of tentacles. Discard beak. Rinse body cavity. Trim wings, if desired. Pull off and discard transparent, speckled membrane covering large squid. Membrane of small squid is tender and edible. Cut squid body into rings. If tentacles are long, cut in half. Bring mussel cooking liquid to a boil. Reduce heat; add squid rings and tentacles. Cook in simmering water 1 to 3 minutes. Drain; rinse under cold running water to stop cooking. Place in large bowl with shucked mussels. Return bowl to refrigerator.

To cook shrimp, place shrimp in a large saucepan; cover with water. Place cover on saucepan at a slight angle. Bring to a boil over high heat. Boil until steam begins to escape from saucepan. Remove from heat; drain off water immediately, holding cover in place to prevent steam from escaping. Cover pan tightly; set covered pan aside. Let shrimp finish cooking in steam, about 12 minutes. When cool enough to handle, shell and devein cooked shrimp. Arrange deveined shrimp on a plate in a single layer; refrigerate until chilled.

To complete, add chilled shrimp to bowl with chilled mussels and squid. Add sardines and olives. Pour Italian dressing over top; toss to coat evenly. Refrigerate until thoroughly chilled.

To serve, arrange lettuce on a large platter. Spoon shellfish mixture onto lettuce. Spoon sour cream in center; top with caviar, if desired. Garnish with dill sprigs. Serve with French bread and butter. Makes 4 servings.

Crayfish & Trout Platter

Crayfish & Trout Platter

Photo on pages 98 and 99.

16 large live crayfish
4 qts. water
1 tablespoon salt
4 teaspoons Crab-Boil Mix, page 104
1/2 cup dry white wine
10 black peppercorns
1 parsley sprig
1 bay leaf
1 garlic clove
2 trout fillets
1/2 cup whipping cream
Salt and freshly ground pepper
1 ripe avocado
1/2 lb. mushrooms
Watercress
Dill sprigs

Rinse crayfish under cold running water to remove any sand or mud. If not cooking immediately, place rinsed crayfish in a large bowl of salted cold water. Refrigerate up to 1 hour or until ready to cook.

To cook crayfish, in a 6 to 8-quart kettle, combine 4 quarts water, 1 tablespoon salt and Crab-Boil Mix. Bring to a boil; boil gently 5 to 10 minutes to let flavors blend. Using tongs, carefully lower crayfish into boiling liquid, head first. When liquid returns to a boil, cook about 8 minutes. Crayfish will turn bright red when cooked. Test 1 cooked crayfish for doneness by breaking tail from body with a twisting motion. If tail comes off easily, crayfish is done. Use a slotted spoon to remove cooked crayfish from cooking liquid. Set aside to cool; discard cooking liquid.

To cook trout fillets, in a fish poacher or skillet large enough to hold trout fillets in a single layer, combine wine, 1/2 cup water, peppercorns, parsley, bay leaf, garlic and 1 teaspoon salt. Bring to a boil; add trout fillets. Reduce heat so liquid barely simmers. Cover; cook about 5 minutes. Using a slotted spoon, remove cooked trout fillets from

poaching liquid; set aside to cool. Strain poaching liquid, reserving 1/2 cup in a small saucepan. Bring reserved poaching liquid to a simmer; slowly stir in cream. Bring back to a simmer, stirring constantly; do not boil. Season with salt and pepper; set aside to cool.

To serve, peel and slice avocado. Slice mushrooms. On a large platter, arrange cooked crayfish, cooked trout, avocado slices and mushroom slices. Garnish with watercress and dill. Serve with sauce. Makes 4 servings.

Kitchen Herbs

Fresh or dried herbs are welcome additions to dressings and marinades. Years ago, nearly every kitchen had its herb garden. Today, this is still possible. For information on growing your own herbs, see *Herbs: How to Select, Grow and Enjoy,* by Norma Jean Lathrop. Also see *How to Cook With Herbs, Spices & Flavorings,* by Doris Townsend. Both are published by HPBooks, Inc.

Use fresh herbs when possible for maximum flavor in cold cuisine. The flavor is superior to dried herbs. When fresh herbs are not available, substitute dried ones, *using 1/2 to 1 teaspoon dried herb for 1 tablespoon fresh herb.* When using any herb, add some, then taste, and add more, if desired.

Danish Herring Salad

4 salted herring fillets
2 medium potatoes
2 medium, tart apples
1 dill pickle
1 small onion
1 (8-oz.) can pickled beets

Creamy Sauce:
2 tablespoons butter or margarine
2 tablespoons all-purpose flour
1-1/4 cups half and half
1 teaspoon prepared mustard
1/4 teaspoon sugar
Freshly ground pepper
Parsley sprigs

Soak herring in cold water overnight. Cook potatoes until tender. When cool enough to handle, peel and dice cooked potatoes. Peel and dice apples. Dice pickle and onion. Drain beets, reserving 2 tablespoons juice for dressing. Finely dice 2 or 3 beets; set aside. Use remaining beets and juice for another purpose.

To make sauce, melt butter or margarine in a small saucepan. Stir in flour; cook 1 minute. Slowly stir in half and half. Stirring constantly, cook over medium heat until thickened. Add 2 tablespoons reserved pickled-beet juice. Add mustard, sugar and pepper. Stir well; cook 1 minute. Set aside to cool.

To complete, drain soaked herring; cut into small pieces. In a medium bowl, combine herring pieces and diced beets, potatoes, apples, pickle and onion. Stir in Creamy Sauce. Refrigerate until thoroughly chilled.

To serve, garnish with parsley sprigs. Makes 6 servings.

Pickled Herring in Cream Sauce

Pickled Herring in Cream Sauce

8 salted herring fillets
2 onions
1-1/2 cups white-wine vinegar
1/2 cup boiling water
1/2 cup dairy sour cream
2 teaspoons sugar
2 teaspoons pickling spices
2 bay leaves
Parsley sprigs
Boiled potatoes, if desired

Soak herring in cold water overnight. Drain. Slice onions. Arrange 1/2 of onion slices in a 9-inch-square glass baking dish. Add soaked herring fillets. Top with remaining onion slices. In a medium bowl, combine vinegar, 1/2 cup boiling water, sour cream, sugar and pickling spices; stir to blend. Pour over soaked herring; add bay leaves. Cover; refrigerate 48 hours.

To serve, remove and discard bay leaves. Place marinated herring on a platter. Garnish with parsley sprigs. Serve with boiled potatoes, if desired. Makes 4 servings.

On previous pages: Crayfish & Trout Platter, page 97

Shrimp with Pernod Cream

Shrimp with Pernod Cream

1 lb. jumbo shrimp (16 to 25 shrimp)

Pernod Cream:
1/2 pint dairy sour cream (1 cup)
3 to 4 teaspoons Pernod
1/4 teaspoon ground ginger
Salt and freshly ground pepper
Chopped pistachios

To cook shrimp, place shrimp in a large saucepan; cover with water. Place cover on saucepan at a slight angle. Bring to a boil over high heat. Boil until steam begins to escape from saucepan. Remove from heat; drain off water immediately, holding cover in place to prevent steam from escaping. Cover pan tightly; set covered pan aside. Let shrimp finish cooking in steam, about 12 minutes. When cool enough to handle, shell and devein cooked shrimp. Refrigerate until chilled.
To make cream, spoon sour cream into a small bowl. Stir in Pernod and ginger; season with salt and pepper.
To serve, place bowl with Pernod Cream on a platter or serving plate. Garnish Pernod Cream with pistachios. Arrange cooked shrimp around bowl. Makes 4 servings.

Shrimp in Tomato Marinade

2 lbs. medium shrimp (40 to 48 shrimp)

Tomato Marinade:
1 onion
1 garlic clove
2 tablespoons butter or margarine
1 (16-oz.) can tomato sauce
1/3 cup dry white wine
1 teaspoon Worcestershire sauce
1/2 teaspoon Italian seasoning
Hot-pepper sauce
Dill sprigs
French bread

To cook shrimp, place shrimp in a large saucepan; cover with water. Place cover on saucepan at a slight angle. Bring to a boil over high heat. Boil until steam begins to escape from saucepan. Remove from heat; drain off water immediately, holding cover in place to prevent steam from escaping. Cover pan tightly; set covered pan aside. Let shrimp finish cooking in steam, about 12 minutes. When cool enough to handle, shell and devein cooked shrimp. Refrigerate until chilled.
To make marinade, finely chop onion and garlic. Melt butter or margarine in a medium saucepan. Add chopped onion and garlic; sauté until onion is transparent. Stir in tomato sauce, wine, Worcestershire sauce, Italian seasoning and hot-pepper sauce. Set aside to cool. Pour cooled marinade over cooked shrimp; refrigerate 2 to 3 hours.
To serve, spoon marinated shrimp and marinade into a serving dish. Garnish with dill sprigs. Serve with French bread. Makes about 8 servings.

Shrimp in Tomato Marinade

Royal Lobster

Royal Lobster

Salt, if desired
1 (2-1/2- to 3-lb.) lobster
Mayonnaise
Salt and freshly ground pepper
6 artichoke bottoms
1 (14-1/2-oz.) can white or green asparagus tips,
   drained
Pimento strips or red bell-pepper rings, cut in half
1 hard-cooked egg, sliced
Radish sprouts or alfalfa sprouts
Butter, melted

Pour water 8 to 10 inches deep in a large kettle. Add 1 teaspoon salt for each quart of water used, if desired. Cover kettle; bring water to a boil. Use tongs to grasp lobster firmly behind head. Plunge head-first into boiling water. Partially cover kettle; bring water back to a simmer. Begin timing; cook 13 to 15 minutes. Use tongs to remove cooked lobster from kettle. Plunge into cold water to cool and prevent overcooking; drain on paper towels. Refrigerate until chilled. *Do not bend lobster to crack shell.*

To remove meat without breaking lobster shell, turn lobster on back to expose stomach. Cut through soft membrane on both sides of tail and stomach undershell with kitchen shears; remove bottom shell from tail and body. Carefully pull out meat in 1 piece; slice meat.

To complete, collect bits of lobster meat that have fallen off sliced lobster and any meat left in body. Chop into small pieces to make 1/2 cup; place in a small bowl. If necessary, chop 1 or 2 lobster slices; add to meat in bowl. Stir in enough mayonnaise to moisten; season with salt and pepper. Spoon mixture onto artichoke bottoms. Arrange asparagus tips over chopped-lobster mixture; place a pimento strip or bell-pepper slice across top of each to create *basket handles.*

To serve, place unbroken lobster shell on a serving tray. If desired, arrange sliced lobster meat and egg slices alternately along back of lobster, as shown. Use wooden skewers to hold in place. Garnish with radish sprouts or alfalfa sprouts; serve with butter. Place filled artichoke bottoms on tray. Makes 2 servings.

Lobster Tails with Garlic Sauce

8 (4- to 5-oz.) lobster tails
White vinegar
Dill sprigs

Garlic Sauce:
2 egg yolks
1 teaspoon prepared mustard
4 garlic cloves, crushed
Salt and white pepper
1 cup olive oil
Chopped nuts

If lobster tails are uncooked, pour enough water into a large kettle to cover lobster tails. Add 1 tablespoon vinegar for each quart of water used. Cover kettle; bring water to a boil. Use tongs to lower lobster tails into boiling water. Bring water back to a boil; cook about 6 minutes. Use tongs to remove cooked tails from boiling water. Plunge into cold water to cool and prevent overcooking; drain on paper towels. When cool enough to handle, remove meat from shells, keeping meat in 1 piece.
To remove lobster meat from shells, use kitchen shears to cut through soft membrane on both sides of undershell of cooked lobster tails. Pull shell away from meat. Refrigerate lobster meat until chilled.
To make sauce, in a blender or food processor fitted with a metal blade, combine egg yolks, mustard, garlic, salt and white pepper. Process a few seconds. With motor running, pour oil into container in a slow, steady stream. Continue processing until mixture thickens.
To serve, spoon Garlic Sauce into a serving bowl; garnish with nuts. Place bowl in center of a platter or serving plate. Or, spoon Garlic Sauce onto center of platter or plate; garnish with nuts. Arrange shelled cooked lobster meat around sauce. Garnish with dill sprigs. Makes 4 servings.

Lobster Tails with Garlic Sauce

Shrimp & Potato Salad

Photo on pages 106 and 107.

1 lb. new potatoes (3 medium potatoes)
2 hard-cooked eggs
1 lb. medium shrimp (20 to 24 shrimp)
Chopped fresh dill

Velvet Salad Dressing:
1/2 cup mayonnaise
1/2 cup dairy sour cream
2 tablespoons ketchup
1 teaspoon white-wine vinegar
1 teaspoon sugar
Salt and freshly ground pepper

Cook potatoes until tender; peel and slice cooked potatoes. Coarsely chop hard-cooked eggs. Refrigerate separately until chilled.
To cook shrimp, place shrimp in a large saucepan; cover with water. Place cover on saucepan at a slight angle. Bring to a boil over high heat. Boil until steam begins to escape from saucepan. Remove from heat; drain off water immediately, holding cover in place to prevent steam from escaping. Cover pan tightly; set covered pan aside. Let shrimp finish cooking in steam, about 12 minutes. When cool enough to handle, shell and devein cooked shrimp; refrigerate until chilled.
To make salad dressing, in a small bowl, combine mayonnaise and sour cream; stir until blended. Stir in ketchup, vinegar and sugar. Season with salt and pepper. Refrigerate until ready to serve.
To serve, in a medium serving bowl, combine deveined shrimp, sliced potatoes and chopped eggs; toss lightly. Garnish with chopped dill. Serve with Velvet Salad Dressing. Makes 6 to 8 servings.

Boiled Crayfish with Mustard Sauce

Boiled Crayfish with Mustard Sauce

24 large live crayfish
6 qts. water
1/4 cup salt
4 teaspoons Crab-Boil Mix, opposite

Mustard Sauce:
3/4 cup mayonnaise
2 tablespoons hot spicy prepared mustard
Hot-pepper sauce
Lemon wedges
Dill sprigs

Rinse crayfish under cold running water to remove any sand or mud. If not cooking immediately, place rinsed crayfish in a large bowl of salted cold water. Refrigerate up to 1 hour or until ready to cook.

To cook crayfish, in a large kettle, combine water, salt and Crab-Boil Mix. Bring to a boil; boil gently 5 to 10 minutes to let flavors blend. Using tongs, carefully lower crayfish into boiling liquid, head first. When liquid returns to a boil, cook about 8 minutes. Crayfish will turn bright red when cooked. Test 1 cooked crayfish for doneness by breaking tail from body with a twisting motion. If tail comes off easily, crayfish is done. Use a slotted spoon to remove cooked crayfish from cooking liquid. Set aside to cool; discard cooking liquid.

To make sauce, spoon mayonnaise into a small bowl. Stir in mustard; season with hot-pepper sauce.
To serve, place 6 cooled cooked crayfish on each of 4 plates. Garnish with lemon wedges and dill sprigs. Serve with Mustard Sauce. Makes 4 servings.

Crab-Boil Mix

6 black peppercorns
8 whole cloves
8 whole allspice
1-1/2 teaspoons dried leaf thyme
1 teaspoon dry mustard
1 teaspoon celery seeds
1 to 2 teaspoons red (cayenne) pepper

In a small bowl, combine all ingredients, adding red pepper to taste. Makes about 8 teaspoons.

Note: When a spicy flavor is desired for poached fish, use this flavorful combination. Add about 1/2 teaspoon for each quart of liquid. Simmer 5 to 10 minutes to let flavors blend before adding fish.

Oysters on-the-Half-Shell

About 24 live oysters

Cocktail Sauce:
3 tablespoons ketchup
1 tablespoon prepared horseradish
1/4 cup lemon juice
Salt
Hot-pepper sauce
Crushed ice
Lemon wedges
Pumpernickel or other dark bread
Butter

Oysters on-the-Half-Shell

Discard any oysters that are not tightly closed or that do not close when tapped with your fingers.

To shuck oysters, scrub shells thoroughly under cold running water. Open 1 oyster at a time. Place a folded towel or potholder on a flat surface. Place oyster, deep-shell-side down, on towel or potholder. Cover with part of towel or potholder to protect your hand. Push tip of an oyster knife or punch-type can opener between shell halves, close to hinge. Pry upward. This will open shell halves enough to slide knife blade inside. Slide knife blade around top shell to sever muscle holding shells together. Be careful not to puncture oyster. Discard top shell.

To make sauce, in a small bowl, combine ketchup, horseradish and lemon juice. Season with salt and hot-pepper sauce. Stir to blend.

To serve, make a layer of crushed ice on a deep platter. Arrange oysters, on deep shells, on crushed ice. Serve cold with Cocktail Sauce, lemon wedges, bread and butter. Makes 4 servings.

Care of Oysters

Refrigerate live oysters with their deep-cup shell down so juice, called *liquor,* doesn't leak out. Cover with a damp towel. Do not cover with fresh water; fresh water will kill any shellfish. Discard any oysters that are open, bad-smelling or dried out when opened. Shucked oysters should be plump, have a natural creamy color, fresh aroma and clear liquor surrounding them.

Oysters Vermouth

1 pint shucked oysters, with liquor
1/4 cup dry vermouth or dry white wine
1 small onion
1/2 lemon
6 black peppercorns
1/4 teaspoon mustard seeds
1 bay leaf
Salt
Cocktail bread

To cook oysters, place oysters and oyster liquor in a medium saucepan. Cook over medium heat until edges of oysters start to curl and become firm. Use a slotted spoon to remove oysters from liquor; place in a glass or ceramic bowl. Continue cooking liquor over high heat until reduced to 1/2 cup. Remove from heat; stir in vermouth or wine. Set aside to cool. Thinly slice onion and lemon. Add sliced onion, sliced lemon, peppercorns, mustard seeds and bay leaf to oysters. Season with salt; stir well. Pour cooled reduced liquor over oyster mixture; refrigerate 3 to 4 hours.

To serve, remove and discard bay leaf. Serve with cocktail bread. Makes 6 servings.

Special-Occasion Breakfast

Double recipe Vichyssoise, page 55
Shrimp & Potato Salad, page 103

Seafood & Radish Board:
8 herring fillets
8 large onion rings
Dill sprigs
2 bunches radishes
1 large kipper

Cheese Bowl:
1/2 lb. Swiss cheese
1/2 lb. Roquefort cheese
Other cheeses as desired
2 or more tomato wedges

Caviar Treat:
1 (3-1/2-oz.) jar golden lumpfish caviar or
    salmon caviar
1 small onion
Chopped fresh dill

Salmon Plate:
Lettuce
3/4 lb. smoked salmon
2 or 3 lemon slices

Sausage Plate:
1/4 lb. thinly sliced Genoa salami
1/4 lb. thinly sliced pepperoni
1 (1/2-lb.) piece liverwurst, sliced, if desired
French Bread, page 124, sliced
Whipped butter
White wine

Prepare Vichyssoise, doubling recipe. Prepare Shrimp & Potato Salad.

To make seafood and radish board, roll herring fillets; slide an onion ring around each roll; garnish each with a dill sprig. Arrange in 2 rows on a serving board. Wash and trim radishes. Arrange trimmed radishes and kipper on board.

To make cheese bowl, cut cheeses into cubes. Arrange cheese cubes and tomato wedges in a shallow serving bowl.

To make caviar treat, spoon caviar into a small bowl. Mince onion; arrange around caviar. Garnish with chopped dill.

To make salmon plate, arrange lettuce on a serving plate; add smoked salmon, curling slightly to add interest. Garnish with lemon slices.

To make sausage plate, arrange salami, pepperoni and liverwurst on a serving dish.

To serve, arrange dishes on a serving table in an attractive arrangement. Serve with sliced bread, butter and wine. Makes 6 to 8 servings.

Special-Occasion Breakfast, clockwise from top left: Vichyssoise, page 55; Shrimp & Potato Salad, page 103; Whipped butter, Caviar Treat, Cheese Bowl; French Bread, page 124; Seafood & Radish Board. In center: Sausage Plate, Salmon Plate.

Boiled Lobster

4 (1-lb.) live lobsters
Butter, melted
Lemon wedges

To cook lobsters, pour water 6 to 8 inches deep in a large kettle. Add 1 teaspoon salt for each quart of water used, if desired. Cover kettle; bring water to a boil. Use tongs to grasp a lobster firmly behind head. Plunge head-first into boiling water. Partially cover kettle; bring water back to a simmer. Begin timing; cook 1-pound lobsters 8 to 10 minutes. Add 2 to 3 minutes for each additional pound. Use tongs to remove cooked lobster from kettle. Plunge into cold water to cool and prevent overcooking; drain on paper towels. Repeat with remaining lobsters. Set aside to cool. Refrigerate until chilled.
To serve, provide small forks and pincers to crack shells. Serve with butter and lemon wedges. Makes 4 servings.

Cold Fish Salad

3 cups water
1/2 onion, diced
1/2 cup dry white wine
1/2 carrot, thinly sliced
1/2 celery stalk, thinly sliced
1 bay leaf
1/2 teaspoon salt
1 lb. white fish fillets
1/2 cup chopped pimento-stuffed olives
1/2 cup chopped celery
3/4 cup mayonnaise
2 tablespoons lemon juice
2 tablespoons prepared mustard
Salt and freshly ground pepper
Lettuce
Parsley sprigs

To cook fish fillets, in a large saucepan, combine water, onion, wine, carrot, 1/2 celery stalk, bay leaf and 1/2 teaspoon salt. Bring to a boil. Reduce heat; simmer 10 minutes. Add fish fillets; bring liquid back to a simmer. Simmer gently 5 to 8 minutes or until fish flakes easily. Immediately plunge cooked fish fillets into cold water to stop cooking. Discard cooking liquid.
To complete, flake cooled cooked fish fillets into a medium bowl. Add olives and chopped celery; stir gently. In a small bowl, combine mayonnaise, lemon juice and mustard. Season with salt and pepper. Stir into fish mixture.
To serve, line a serving bowl with lettuce leaves. Spoon fish mixture into lettuce-lined bowl. Garnish with parsley sprigs. Makes 4 to 6 servings.

Meat & Poultry

Corned-Beef Platter

Steak Tartare

Photo on pages 108 and 109.

2 lbs. lean beef-top round or beef-loin tenderloin
1 onion
1 (2-oz.) can anchovy fillets
1/2 cup drained capers
4 egg yolks
Chopped sweet pickle, if desired
Snipped chives, if desired
Salt and freshly ground pepper
Onion rings, if desired
Marjoram leaves, if desired
Cocktail bread
Assorted crackers

In a food processor fitted with a metal blade, process beef until finely ground. Finely chop onion; drain and finely chop anchovies. In a large bowl, combine ground meat, chopped onion, chopped anchovies, capers and egg yolks. Add pickles and chives, if desired. Toss lightly with 2 forks until thoroughly blended. Season with salt and pepper. Spoon into a mound on a platter or serving plate. Cover with plastic wrap or foil; refrigerate up to 1 hour.

To serve, garnish with onion rings and marjoram leaves, if desired. Serve with cocktail bread and assorted crackers. Makes 16 to 20 servings.

Corned-Beef Platter

1 lb. fresh green beans
3 or 4 tomatoes
1 small onion
1 garlic clove
2 tablespoons lemon juice or tarragon vinegar
1 teaspoon sugar
Salt and freshly ground pepper
1/4 cup vegetable oil or olive oil
8 slices corned beef
Hard rolls

Trim beans; cut or snap in half crosswise. Cook in lightly salted water until crisp-tender, about 15 minutes. Drain; place in a medium glass bowl. Cut tomatoes into wedges; cut wedges in half crosswise. Add tomato pieces to cooked green beans. Finely dice onion; crush garlic. In a medium bowl, combine diced onion, crushed garlic, lemon juice or vinegar and sugar. Season with salt and pepper. Gradually beat in oil until blended. Pour over bean mixture; stir to coat. Refrigerate until chilled.

To serve, spoon marinated beans and tomatoes into a serving dish. Roll up corned-beef slices; arrange over vegetables. Serve with rolls. Makes 4 servings.

On previous pages: Steak Tartare, above

Roast Beef with Herbs de Provence

1 (4-lb.) boneless beef rib-eye roast or
   beef round-tip roast
1 garlic clove
Salt and freshly ground pepper
2 to 3 tablespoons Dijon-style mustard
Herbs de Provence
Rémoulade Sauce, page 158

Roast Beef with Herbs de Provence

Preheat oven to 350F (175C). Cut garlic in half
lengthwise. Rub surface of beef with cut surface of
garlic. Sprinkle beef with salt and pepper. Spread
mustard over top and sides of seasoned beef; coat
generously with Herbs de Provence. Place coated
beef on a rack in a roasting pan. Bake 20 to 30 minutes per pound or until a thermometer inserted in
thickest part registers 140F (60C) for rare, 160F
(70C) for medium and 170F (75C) for well done.
Remove from oven; cool to room temperature.
Cover with foil; refrigerate until ready to serve.

To serve, thinly slice cooked beef. Serve with Rémoulade Sauce. Makes 12 servings.

Summer Meat Loaf

1 lb. lean ground beef
1/2 lb. ground veal
1/2 lb. lean ground pork
2 eggs
1/4 cup seasoned dry bread crumbs
2 tablespoons Italian seasoning
Salt and freshly ground pepper
2 hard-cooked eggs, if desired
Sliced pickles
Parsley sprigs
Ketchup

Preheat oven to 350F (175C). Place beef, veal and
pork in a large bowl; use a fork to break into small
pieces. In a small bowl, lightly beat eggs. Stir in
bread crumbs, Italian seasoning, salt and pepper.
Pour over meat; use a fork or your hands to blend
egg mixture into meat until thoroughly combined.
Turn mixture out onto a large piece of waxed paper;
shape meat mixture into a loaf. If desired, press
hard-cooked eggs into center of loaf, about 3 inches
apart. Cover top of eggs with meat so eggs are
completely enclosed inside loaf. Place loaf on a rack
in a roasting pan to let fat drain during cooking.
Bake 1-1/2 hours. Remove from oven; let cool to
room temperature. Cover with foil; refrigerate until
ready to serve.

To serve, thinly slice meat loaf; arrange on a platter
or serving plate. Garnish with sliced pickles and
parsley sprigs. Serve with ketchup. Makes 6
servings.

Tongue with Horseradish Cream

1 (4- to 5-lb.) beef tongue
6 black peppercorns
3 or 4 parsley sprigs
2 bay leaves
1 onion, halved
Horseradish Cream, page 158
Hot mustard

Rinse tongue; place in a large saucepan. Cover with
water. Add peppercorns, parsley, bay leaves and
onion. Bring to a boil. Skim foam from surface of
water until surface is clear. Reduce heat until water
barely simmers. Cover saucepan; simmer 2 to 2-1/2
hours or until tender. Remove from saucepan; set
aside to cool. When cool enough to handle, cut off
outer skin and root. Cover cooked tongue with foil;
refrigerate until ready to serve.

To serve, slice cooked tongue; arrange on a platter
or serving plate. Serve with Horseradish Cream and
hot mustard. Makes 8 servings.

Fillet of Beef with Walnut Cream

Fillet of Beef with Walnut Cream

1 (4- to 6-lb.) beef-loin tenderloin roast
Salt and freshly ground pepper
1/4 cup butter or margarine, room temperature
1 cup finely chopped walnuts

Walnut Cream:
1/2 pint dairy sour cream (1 cup)
1 garlic clove, crushed
1/2 cup finely chopped walnuts
Salt and freshly ground pepper

Preheat oven to 500F (260C). Fold narrow end of roast under; tie with kitchen string. Sprinkle salt and pepper over entire roast. Rub butter or margarine over entire surface of roast; firmly press nuts into butter or margarine on top and sides of roast. Place coated roast on a rack in a roasting pan; place in preheated oven. Immediately reduce oven temperature to 400F (205C); bake 30 minutes or until a thermometer inserted in thickest part registers 140F (60C) for rare, 160F (70C) for medium and 170F (75C) for well done. Remove cooked roast from oven; let cool to room temperature. Cover with foil; refrigerate until ready to serve.

To make cream, spoon sour cream into a small bowl. Stir in garlic and walnuts. Season with salt and pepper.

To serve, remove string from chilled roast; slice. Serve with Walnut Cream. Makes 12 to 16 servings.

Vitello Tonnato

2 to 3 tablespoons vegetable oil or olive oil
1 (3-lb.) boneless veal roast, tied
5 cups homemade or canned chicken stock
1 cup dry vermouth or dry white wine
1 onion
1 carrot
1 celery stalk
6 black peppercorns
4 parsley sprigs
2 garlic cloves
1 bay leaf
1 teaspoon dried leaf thyme

Tuna Sauce:
1 (7-oz.) can tuna, drained
1 (2-oz.) can anchovy fillets, drained
1 cup mayonnaise
2 tablespoons drained capers

Heat oil in a large skillet. Add veal; brown on all sides. Pour stock and vermouth or wine into a large saucepan. Add browned veal; bring liquid to a boil. Skim foam from surface of liquid until surface is clear. Coarsely chop onion, carrot and celery; add to saucepan. Add peppercorns, parsley, garlic, bay leaf and thyme. Reduce heat until liquid barely simmers. Cover saucepan; simmer about 1-1/2 hours or until meat is tender. Cool meat in cooking liquid. When cool, remove from liquid. Cover with foil; refrigerate until chilled. Strain cooking liquid; reserve cooking liquid to use in sauce.

To make sauce, in a blender or food processor fitted with a metal blade, combine tuna and 6 anchovy fillets; process until pureed. Reserve remaining anchovies for garnish. Spoon pureed mixture into a medium bowl; stir in mayonnaise. Gradually beat in about 1 cup reserved cooking liquid. Sauce should be thick enough to coat back of a spoon. Stir in capers.

To serve, remove string from chilled cooked veal. Thinly slice chilled veal; arrange on a platter or serving plate. Spoon some of Tuna Sauce over top. Garnish with reserved anchovy fillets. Serve remaining Tuna Sauce separately. Makes 8 to 10 servings.

Westphalian-Ham Platter

8 sweet pickles
4 red radishes
1 (5-inch) white radish
2 tomatoes
1 cucumber
Pimento-stuffed olives
1 lb. sliced Westphalian ham or prosciutto
Parsley sprigs
Pumpernickel or other dark bread
Whipped butter or Mustard Butter, page 167

Slice pickles lengthwise almost all the way from blossom end to stem end. Spread apart to make *pickle fans*. Cut red radishes in decorative patterns and white radish in a spiral, page 217. Cut tomatoes into wedges. Slice cucumber with a waffle-edged cutter; slice olives.

To serve, fold or roll meat slices; arrange decoratively on a platter. Place an olive slice on each cucumber slice; arrange over folded meat slices. Arrange cut red radishes, pickle fans and tomato wedges on platter. Open white radish spiral; place in center of platter. Garnish with parsley sprigs. Serve with bread and whipped butter or Mustard Butter. Makes 4 servings.

Westphalian-Ham Platter

Canadian-Bacon Platter

Canadian-Bacon Platter

3 lbs. unsliced Canadian-style bacon
Pineapple juice
Lemon slices
Fresh herbs
Potato Salad, page 74

Preheat oven to 350F (175C). Remove casing from meat, if necessary. Place meat on a rack in a roasting pan. Bake 35 to 40 minutes per pound or until a thermometer inserted in center registers 160F (70C). Baste with pineapple juice every 15 minutes. Remove from oven; cool to room temperature. Cover with foil; refrigerate until ready to serve.

To serve, cut cooked meat in thick slices; arrange on a serving plate. Garnish with lemon slices and fresh herbs. Serve with Potato Salad. Makes 8 to 12 servings.

Pork Roast with Avocado Cream

Pork Roast with Avocado Cream

4 teaspoons Italian seasoning
2 teaspoons ground ginger
Salt
Pinch of freshly ground pepper
1 (2- to 2-1/2-lb.) boneless pork-loin center-loin roast
2 fennel bulbs
4 carrots
2 leeks
4 celery stalks
Cherry tomatoes

Marinade:
1/4 cup white-wine vinegar
1/4 cup vegetable oil or olive oil
1 teaspoon sugar
Salt and freshly ground pepper

Avocado Cream:
2 large ripe avocados
2 tablespoon lemon juice
1 garlic clove, crushed
2 tablespoon grated onion
Parsley sprigs

Preheat oven to 350F (175C). In a small bowl, combine Italian seasoning, ginger, salt and pepper. Rub onto surface of pork. Place pork on a rack in a roasting pan. Bake 40 minutes per pound or until a thermometer inserted in thickest part registers 170F (75C). Remove cooked pork from oven; let cool to room temperature. Cover with foil; refrigerate until chilled.

To blanch vegetables, wash and trim fennel bulbs; cut each into 8 wedges. Cook in lightly salted water 8 minutes. Drain; set aside. Peel carrots; cut into 2" x 1/2" strips. Cook in lightly salted water 5 minutes. Drain; set aside. Wash leeks thoroughly to remove sand; cut into 2-inch pieces. Cook in lightly salted water 3 minutes. Drain; set aside. Cut celery into 2-inch pieces. Cook in lightly salted water 2 minutes. Drain; set aside. Peel cherry tomatoes, if desired; set aside.

To make marinade, in a small bowl, combine vinegar and oil. Beat until blended; beat in sugar. Season with salt and pepper.

To complete, arrange blanched vegetables and peeled cherry tomatoes in a shallow glass dish; pour marinade over top. Cover dish with foil; refrigerate 2 to 3 hours, occasionally spooning marinade over vegetables.

To make avocado cream, cut avocados in half; remove pits. Scoop flesh from 2 avocado halves. In a blender or food processor fitted with a metal blade, process scooped-out avocado flesh until pureed. Add lemon juice, garlic and onion. Process until smooth. Spoon Avocado Cream into remaining avocado halves.

To serve, slice roast pork; arrange on a serving dish. Surround with marinated vegetables. Garnish with parsley sprigs. Serve with Avocado Cream. Makes 8 servings.

Almond-Coated Chicken

4 chicken cutlets, page 117
Salt and freshly ground pepper
All-purpose flour
1 egg
3 tablespoons vegetable oil
1 to 1-1/2 cups finely chopped almonds
2 tablespoons butter or margarine

Lime Sauce:
1-1/4 cups dairy sour cream
1/4 cup lime juice
2 tablespoons dry vermouth or dry white wine
2 tablespoons chopped fresh mint leaves
1 tablespoon grated lime peel
2 tablespoons green peppercorns
Green salad
Mint leaves
Lime slices

Season chicken cutlets with salt and pepper; coat with flour. In a small bowl, combine egg and 1 tablespoon oil; stir until blended. Dip seasoned chicken into egg mixture; drain off excess egg mixture. Roll dipped chicken in chopped almonds. Heat butter or margarine and remaining 2 tablespoons oil in a large skillet; add coated chicken. Sauté coated chicken until browned on both sides, about 8 minutes. Drain on paper towels; set aside to cool.

To make sauce, spoon sour cream into a small bowl. Stir in lime juice, vermouth or wine, chopped mint and lime peel. Spoon into a small serving bowl.

To serve, garnish Lime Sauce with green peppercorns. Serve sautéed chicken with salad and Lime Sauce. Garnish with mint leaves and lime slices. Makes 4 servings.

Almond-Coated Chicken

For instructions on poaching chicken or turkey, see Poached Chicken Salad with Sherry Dressing, page 74, or Chicken Breasts with Caper-Tuna Dressing, page 120.

Baked Ham with Honey Glaze

Baked Ham with Honey Glaze

1 (6-lb.) boneless, fully cooked ham
Whole cloves, if desired
About 1 cup orange juice

Honey Glaze:
1 cup honey
1/2 cup orange juice
1 tablespoon prepared mustard
1/4 teaspoon ground cloves
1/4 teaspoon ground coriander

Apple-Apricot Chutney:
1/2 lb. cooking apples
8 oz. dried apricots
1/3 cup packed light-brown sugar
1/4 cup white-wine vinegar
1/4 cup water
Pinch of freshly ground nutmeg
5 green grapes

To serve:
1 to 2 tablespoon butter or margarine
8 to 10 green onions, if desired
Rosemary sprigs
Fresh figs
Applesauce, if desired
Double recipe Ginger & Curry Dressing, page 161

To bake ham, preheat oven to 325F (165C). Trim excess fat from ham; score top. Stud with cloves, if desired. Place ham on a rack in a roasting pan. Pour 1 cup orange juice over scored ham. Baste ham with orange juice and pan drippings during cooking, adding more orange juice as needed. Bake 25 minutes per pound or until a thermometer inserted in thickest part reaches 140F (60C).

To make glaze, in a small bowl, combine honey, orange juice, mustard, cloves and coriander. Stir until blended.

To make chutney, peel and finely chopped apples; finely chop apricots. In a medium saucepan, combine brown sugar, vinegar and water. Stir until blended; bring to a boil. Cook 2 minutes. Add chopped apples and apricots. Cook 10 minutes or until tender. Stir in nutmeg. Chill before serving. Garnish with green grapes.

To complete, about 20 minutes before ham is done, brush Honey Glaze over ham. When done, remove ham from oven; let cool to room temperature. Cover with foil; refrigerate until ready to serve.

To serve, heat butter or margarine in a medium skillet; add green onions. Sauté green onions until lightly browned. Garnish baked ham with rosemary sprigs. Serve with figs, applesauce, if desired, and sautéed green onions, if desired. Also serve with Ginger & Curry Dressing and Apple-Apricot Chutney. Makes 18 to 24 servings.

Grilled Turkey Breast

Picnic Chicken

1/4 cup all-purpose flour
1/4 cup cornflake crumbs
1/4 cup crushed seasoned stuffing mix
Salt and freshly ground pepper
1 (3-1/2- to 4-lb.) broiler-fryer, cut up
1/3 cup butter or margarine, melted

Preheat oven to 375F (190C). Grease a 13" x 9" baking dish; set aside. In a shallow bowl, combine flour, cornflake crumbs, stuffing mix, salt and pepper. Brush chicken pieces with butter or margarine; roll in flour mixture. Arrange coated chicken in greased baking dish. Bake 30 minutes. Using tongs, turn chicken pieces over; bake 30 minutes longer. Cool to room temperature. Cover with foil; refrigerate until chilled.

To serve, arrange chilled cooked chicken on a platter or serving plate. Makes 4 servings.

Grilled Turkey Breast

Salt
Paprika
1 (6- to 8-lb.) boneless turkey breast
Butter or margarine, melted
Cranberry sauce

Rub salt and paprika over surface of turkey breast. Insert rotisserie rod through center of turkey breasts; balance carefully. Place rod in holders over grill. Brush seasoned turkey with melted butter or margarine. Cook on grill 2-1/2 to 3 hours or until a thermometer inserted in thickest part reaches 185F (85C). Occasionally brush with butter or margarine. Remove rod; set grilled turkey breast aside to cool.

To serve, remove string; cut in thin slices. Serve with cranberry sauce. Makes 12 servings.

Variation

Substitute barbecue sauce for salt, paprika and butter or margarine. Brush turkey breast with barbecue sauce occasionally while grilling.

To Make Chicken or Turkey Cutlets

Place boned chicken or turkey breast halves on a flat surface. Cover with waxed paper or plastic wrap. Using the flat side of a meat mallet, pound each breast half until about 1/4 inch thick. If desired, make cutlets and freeze for future use. *To freeze cutlets,* arrange in a single layer on a baking sheet. Freeze until firm. Stack with waxed paper between frozen cutlets. Wrap in foil, folding to make airtight, or place in a plastic bag. Remove as much air from package as possible. Seal; freeze up to 2 months.

Cold Roast Duck

Cold Roast Duck

1 (4- to 5-lb.) duck
Salt and freshly ground pepper
1/4 cup water
Ginger ale
Salted iced water
Fresh figs
Firm Aspic, page 84, cut in cubes
Fresh herbs

Preheat oven to 450F (230C). Cut wing-tips off duck; remove giblets and neck from body cavity. Reserve for another use. Remove and discard any excess fat from duck. Wipe duck inside and out with a clean damp cloth. Sprinkle inside and out with salt and pepper. Prick duck skin all over to let fat drain during roasting. Place duck, breast-side up, on a rack in a roasting pan. Pour 1/4 cup water into roasting pan. If desired, insert a meat thermometer in center of inner-thigh muscle. Roast duck 20 minutes; reduce heat to 350F (175C). Basting occasionally with ginger ale, roast 1 hour to 1 hour 20 minutes or until thermometer reaches 180F to 185F (80C to 85C). Or roast until juices run clear when a knife is inserted between thigh and breast. Increase oven heat to 450F (230C) and brush duck with salted iced water 10 minutes before removing

duck from oven. This will crisp the skin. Remove from roasting pan; set aside to cool.

To serve, place cooled roasted duck on a platter. Surround with fresh figs, aspic cubes and fresh herbs. Makes 4 servings.

Peach-Garnished Chicken

4 chicken-leg quarters
Salt
Paprika
Lemon juice
Butter or margarine
Lettuce leaves
1 (16-oz.) can sliced peaches, drained
1 (11-oz.) can mandarin-orange sections, drained
Maraschino cherries
Firm Aspic, page 84, cut in cubes

Season chicken-leg quarters with salt, paprika and lemon juice. Place on a broiler rack; dot with butter or margarine. Broil until golden brown on both sides, about 35 minutes, occasionally basting with drippings. Set aside to cool.

To serve, arrange lettuce leaves on individual dishes. Add broiled chicken quarters. Arrange peach slices and mandarin-orange sections over chicken. Garnish with cherries and aspic cubes. Makes 4 servings.

Turkey Rolls on Ratatouille

16 large slices cooked turkey breast
Italian seasoning
3 tablespoons vegetable oil

Ratatouille:
2 small onions
2 red or green bell peppers
3 tomatoes
1 eggplant
2 zucchini
2 garlic cloves
About 1/3 cup olive oil
Italian seasoning
Salt and pepper
Chopped fresh parsley
Lemon wedges, if desired

Sprinkle turkey slices with Italian seasoning. Roll slices, jelly-roll style; tie with kitchen string. Heat vegetable oil in a large skillet. Add turkey rolls; sauté until browned on all sides, about 6 minutes. Drain on paper towels; set aside to cool. Cover with foil; refrigerate until ready to serve.
To make ratatouille, dice onions, bell peppers and tomatoes. Cube eggplant; slice zucchini. Mince garlic. Heat olive oil in a medium skillet; add diced

Turkey Rolls on Ratatouille

onions. Sauté onions until transparent. Add cubed eggplant, sliced zucchini, diced bell peppers and minced garlic. Season with Italian seasoning, salt and pepper. Add more olive oil, if needed. Stir well. Cover skillet; cook over medium heat, stirring occasionally, until vegetables are crisp-tender, 15 to 20 minutes. Gently stir in diced tomatoes; cook, uncovered, about 10 minutes. Adjust seasoning, if desired; spoon Ratatouille into a serving bowl. Cover with foil; refrigerate until chilled.
To serve, remove string from turkey rolls. Arrange turkey rolls over chilled Ratatouille. Garnish with chopped parsley. Serve with lemon wedges, if desired. Makes 8 servings.

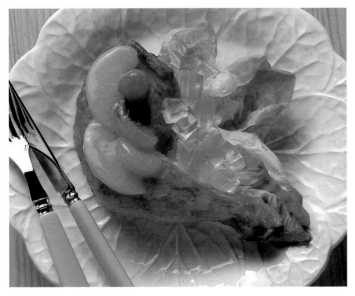

Peach-Garnished Chicken

Chicken & Endive Salad

2 kiwifruit
2 heads Belgian endive
1 lb. sliced, cooked, smoked or plain chicken breasts
1 (16-oz.) can sliced pineapple

Yogurt Dressing:
1/2 cup plain yogurt
1/4 cup mayonnaise
2 tablespoons prepared mustard
Salt and freshly ground pepper

Peel and slice kiwifruit. Separate and rinse endive leaves. Cut chicken into strips. Drain pineapple slices, reserving 2 tablespoons pineapple juice for dressing. Cut pineapple slices in half.

To make dressing, spoon yogurt into a small bowl. Stir in mayonnaise, mustard and 2 tablespoons reserved pineapple juice. Season with salt and pepper.

To serve, arrange rinsed endive leaves around edge of a serving plate, stem-ends toward center of plate. Arrange cut pineapple slices and kiwifruit slices over stem ends of endive leaves. Mound chicken strips over pineapple and kiwifruit. Serve with Yogurt Dressing. Makes 4 servings.

Variation

Substitute 1 pound sliced, cooked, smoked or plain turkey breast for chicken breasts.

Chicken & Endive Salad

Rabbit in Puff Pastry

Chicken Breasts with Caper-Tuna Dressing

1/2 cup dry vermouth or dry white wine
4 chicken cutlets, page 117
6 black peppercorns
2 parsley sprigs
1 garlic clove
1 celery stalk, cut in half
1 bay leaf

Caper-Tuna Dressing:
1 (6-1/2-oz.) can tuna, drained
1 cup mayonnaise
2 teaspoons lemon juice
1 tablespoon half and half
Salt and freshly ground pepper
2 tablespoons drained capers, chopped
Shredded lettuce
Paprika

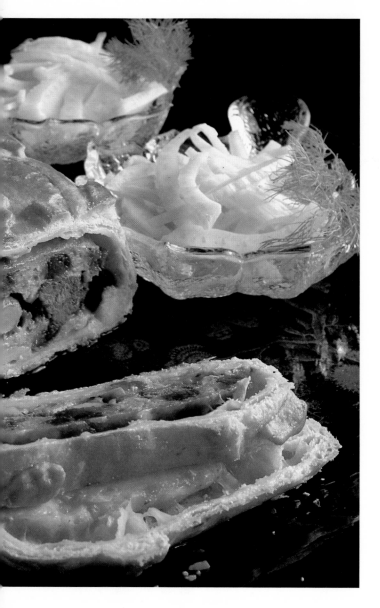

Rabbit in Puff Pastry

1-1/2 lbs. boneless rabbit or boneless turkey or
   chicken thighs
2 tablespoons vegetable oil
1 tablespoon lemon juice
1/2 teaspoon dried leaf thyme
1/2 teaspoon dried rosemary
Salt and freshly ground pepper
1/4 cup butter or margarine

Bratwurst Layer:
1/2 lb. bratwurst
10 pitted prunes
10 mushrooms
2 tablespoons brandy
1 tablespoon pistachios

Pastry:
1/2 (17-1/4-oz.) pkg. frozen puff pastry (1 sheet),
   thawed
1 egg yolk beaten with 1 tablespoon milk for glaze

To make filling, place rabbit, turkey or chicken in a glass or ceramic bowl. Sprinkle with oil, lemon juice, thyme and rosemary. Cover with foil; refrigerate 4 hours, turning meat occasionally. Drain marinated meat; season with salt and pepper. Melt butter or margarine in a medium skillet. Add drained meat; sauté on all sides. Set aside to cool.
To make bratwurst layer, remove casing from bratwurst. Slice bratwurst into a medium bowl. Dice prunes; slice 4 mushrooms. Add to sliced bratwurst. Stir in brandy and pistachios; set aside.
To prepare pastry, unfold puff-pastry sheet. Place on a lightly floured surface. Roll out pastry to a 12-inch square. Cut off 2 inches of pastry from 1 side, making a 12" x 10" rectangle. Cover and set aside 2-inch-wide pastry for decoration.
To complete, preheat oven to 400F (205C). Spread 1/2 of bratwurst mixture in a 4-inch strip lengthwise down center of pastry, leaving 4 inches of pastry on each side. Arrange sautéed meat over bratwurst mixture. Slice remaining mushrooms. Arrange over meat layer. Top with remaining bratwurst mixture. Fold both sides of pastry over top. Pinch seam and ends to seal. Place seam-side down on an ungreased baking sheet. Cut 2 or 3 small holes in pastry top for vents. Brush pastry with egg-yolk glaze. Cut decorations from reserved pastry. Brush bottom of decorations with egg-yolk glaze; arrange on top of pastry. Bake 35 to 40 minutes or until pastry is golden. Cool completely on baking sheet on a wire rack. Remove from baking sheet; place on a platter. Serve with a salad. Makes 6 to 8 servings.

Pour vermouth or wine into a large saucepan. Add chicken cutlets, peppercorns, parsley, garlic, celery, bay leaf and enough water to cover chicken. Simmer 6 to 8 minutes or until chicken is tender. Remove cooked chicken with a slotted spoon; set aside to cool.
To make dressing, in a blender or food processor fitted with a metal blade, process tuna until finely ground. Add mayonnaise, lemon juice and half and half. Season with salt and pepper. Process until smooth. Stir in capers.
To serve, arrange shredded lettuce on individual plates. Place 1 cooked chicken cutlet on each plate. Spoon Caper-Tuna Dressing over top; garnish with paprika. Makes 4 servings.

Breads

Frankfurter-Sauerkraut Bread

1 small onion
5 whole cloves
1 tablespoon butter or margarine
1 (27-oz.) can sauerkraut, drained
1 (16-oz.) pkg. white-yeast-bread mix
2 tablespoons caraway seeds
4 beef frankfurters

Stud onion with cloves; set aside. In a medium saucepan, melt butter or margarine. Add sauerkraut and studded onion; simmer 15 minutes, stirring occasionally. Discard onion and cloves; cool sauerkraut completely. Prepare bread mix according to package directions, adding caraway seeds with flour. On a lightly floured surface, knead dough until elastic, 8 to 10 minutes. Cover with bowl used for mixing; let stand 5 minutes.

To complete, grease a large baking sheet; set aside. Preheat oven to 375F (190C). Roll out dough to a 16" x 12" rectangle. Spoon 1/2 of sauerkraut lengthwise in a 3-inch-wide strip down center of dough. Arrange frankfurters in a double row, end to end and lengthwise of dough, over sauerkraut. Cover with remaining sauerkraut. Fold sides of dough over sauerkraut. Pinch seam to seal; tuck ends under. Place filled loaf, seam-side down, on greased baking sheet. Brush loaf with water. Bake in preheated oven 45 to 50 minutes or until bread sounds hollow when tapped on bottom. Remove from baking sheet; cool on a wire rack. Makes 1 filled loaf.

Frankfurter-Sauerkraut Bread

French Bread

Photo on pages 106 and 107.

2 cups warm water
1/2 teaspoon sugar
1 (1/4-oz.) pkg. active dry yeast (1 tablespoon)
2 teaspoons salt
2 tablespoons vegetable oil
4 to 4-1/2 cups all-purpose flour
2 tablespoons cornmeal

In a large bowl, combine water, sugar and yeast. Let stand until foamy, 5 to 10 minutes. Stir in salt, oil and 2-1/2 cups flour. Beat about 2 minutes. Stir in enough remaining flour to make a stiff sticky dough. Cover; let rise in a warm place, free from drafts, until doubled in bulk. Grease a large baking sheet; sprinkle with cornmeal. Stir down dough. Turn out 1/2 of dough onto a floured board. Sprinkle with flour; roll out to a 12-inch square. Roll up, jelly-roll style. Pinch edges to seal, tapering ends. Repeat with remaining dough. Place loaves, side by side, on prepared baking sheet. Use a sharp knife to cut 3 diagonal slashes across top of each loaf. Cover; let rise until almost doubled in bulk.

To complete, preheat oven to 425F (220C). Brush water over loaves. Bake 12 minutes. Reduce heat to 325F (165C). Brush tops of loaves with water. Bake 35 minutes or until crust is browned and firm. Cool on a wire rack. Makes 2 loaves.

On previous pages: Filled French Loaf, page 146

Poppy-Seed Pan Rolls

1 (16-oz.) loaf frozen white-bread dough, thawed
1 egg yolk beaten with 1 tablespoon water for glaze
Poppy seeds

Grease a medium bowl. Place dough in greased bowl, turning to coat all sides. Cover with a clean towel. Let rise in a warm place, free from drafts, until doubled in bulk. Grease a 9-inch-square baking pan. Punch down dough. Cut in half. Cut each half into 8 equal pieces. Shape each piece into a ball, pinching and tucking ends under. Brush rolls with egg-yolk glaze. Dip each glazed roll in poppy seeds. Arrange coated rolls in 4 rows in greased pan, allowing space between rolls for expansion. Cover; let rise until doubled in bulk and rolls touch.

To complete, preheat oven to 375F (190C). Sprinkle tops of raised rolls with additional poppy seeds, if desired. Bake in preheated oven 15 to 18 minutes or until deep golden brown. Remove from pan; cool on a wire rack. Makes 16 rolls.

Sausage-Filled Loaf

Soda Bread

About 4 cups all-purpose flour
1 tablespoon baking powder
1 teaspoon baking soda
1-1/2 teaspoons salt
1/4 cup butter or margarine, chilled
1-2/3 cups buttermilk

In a large bowl, blend 4 cups flour, baking powder, baking soda and salt. Use a pastry blender or 2 knives to cut in butter or margarine until mixture resembles coarse crumbs. Use a wooden spoon to stir in buttermilk, making a soft dough. Turn out dough onto a lightly floured surface. Knead until smooth, 8 to 10 strokes.
To complete, grease a large baking sheet. Preheat oven to 425F (220C). Shape dough into a round loaf. Using a sharp razor blade, cut a deep cross in top of loaf. Sprinkle lightly with flour. Bake in preheated oven 25 to 30 minutes or until bread is golden brown and sounds hollow when tapped on bottom. Remove from baking sheet; cool on a wire rack. Makes 1 loaf.

Sausage-Filled Loaf

1 (16-oz.) loaf frozen white-bread dough, thawed
Filling:
1-1/2 lbs. bulk pork sausage
1 green or red bell pepper, finely chopped
1 medium tomato, peeled, seeded, finely chopped
1 tablespoon chopped fresh parsley
2 eggs, beaten
Salt and freshly ground black pepper
2 tablespoons butter or margarine, melted

Grease a medium bowl. Place dough in greased bowl, turning to coat all sides. Cover with a clean towel. Let rise in a warm place, free from drafts, until doubled in bulk.
To make filling, while dough rises, in a large saucepan, cover sausage with water; bring to a boil. Cook until no longer pink; drain well. Place boiled sausage in a blender or food processor fitted with a metal blade; process until finely ground. In a large bowl, combine ground sausage, bell pepper, tomato, parsley and eggs. Season with salt and pepper. Blend well; set aside.
To complete, grease a large baking sheet; set aside. Punch down dough. On a lightly floured surface, roll out dough to a 12-inch square. Spoon sausage filling down center of dough in a 2-1/2-inch-wide strip. Brush edges of dough with water. Fold sides of dough over filling, pinch seam to seal; tuck ends under. Place filled loaf, seam-side down, on greased baking sheet. Cover; let rise 25 minutes. Preheat oven to 400F (205C). Lightly slash top of loaf, on a slight diagonal, with a sharp razor blade. Brush loaf with butter or margarine. Bake in preheated oven 60 to 70 minutes or until bread is golden brown and sounds hollow when tapped on bottom. Brush with butter or margarine several times during baking. Remove from baking sheet; cool on a wire rack. Makes 6 to 8 servings.

Rye & Salami Bread

Oatmeal-Honey Batter Bread

3/4 cup quick-cooking rolled oats
1/4 cup honey
1 teaspoon salt
1/4 cup butter or margarine
About 1 cup milk
1 (1/4-oz.) pkg. active dry yeast (1 tablespoon)
1 teaspoon sugar
1/4 cup warm water (110F, 45C)
1 egg
About 2-3/4 cups all-purpose flour

In a small bowl, combine oats, honey and salt; set aside. In a small saucepan, heat butter or margarine and 1 cup milk over low heat, stirring, until butter or margarine is melted. Pour over oats mixture; stir until blended. Set aside to cool. Grease a 9" x 5" loaf pan; set aside. In a large bowl, combine yeast, sugar and water. Let stand until foamy, 5 to 10 minutes. Stir in cooled oats mixture. Using an electric mixer, beat in egg and 2 cups flour. Beat on medium speed 2 minutes. Stir in enough remaining flour to make a soft dough. Place dough in greased pan. Cover with a clean towel. Let rise in a warm place, free from drafts, until doubled in bulk.
To complete, preheat oven to 375F (190C). Brush top of raised loaf with milk. Bake in preheated oven 40 to 50 minutes or until bread sounds hollow when tapped on bottom. Remove from pan; cool on a wire rack. Makes 1 loaf.

Rye & Salami Bread

1 (1/4-oz.) pkg. active dry yeast (1 tablespoon)
1 teaspoon sugar
1 cup warm water (110F, 45C)
2 tablespoons molasses
1 teaspoon salt
3 tablespoons butter or margarine, melted
1/3 lb. hard salami, finely chopped (about 1 cup)
1-1/2 cups medium rye flour
1-3/4 cups all-purpose flour

In a large bowl, combine yeast, sugar and water. Let stand until foamy, 5 to 10 minutes. In a small bowl, combine molasses, salt and butter or margarine. Stir into yeast mixture until blended. Stir in salami. Blend rye and all-purpose flours. Add 2-1/2 to 3 cups flour mixture to yeast mixture. Stir in, making a soft dough. Turn out dough onto a lightly floured surface. Knead in enough remaining flour mixture to make a stiff dough. Continue kneading until dough is smooth and elastic, 8 to 10 minutes. Clean and grease bowl. Place dough in greased bowl, turning to coat all sides. Cover with a clean towel. Let rise in a warm place, free from drafts, until doubled in bulk.
To complete, grease a large baking sheet. Punch down dough. Shape dough into a 12-inch-long oval loaf with tapered ends; place on greased baking sheet. Cover; let rise until almost doubled in bulk. Preheat oven to 400F (205C). Using a sharp razor blade, cut slashes, 2 inches apart, across top of loaf. Brush loaf with water. Bake in preheated oven 35 to 40 minutes or until bread sounds hollow when tapped on bottom. Brush bread with water several times during baking. Remove from baking sheet; cool on a wire rack. Makes 1 loaf.

Coriander Braid

1 (16-oz.) pkg. white-yeast-bread mix
1 tablespoon grated lemon peel or orange peel
1 teaspoon ground coriander
Water
All-purpose flour

Prepare bread mix according to package directions adding lemon peel or orange peel and coriander with flour. On a lightly floured surface, knead dough until smooth and elastic, 8 to 10 minutes. Cover dough with bowl used for mixing; let stand 5 minutes. Grease a large baking sheet; set aside.

To shape dough, cut into 2 pieces, making 1 piece 2/3 of dough. Cut larger piece of dough into 3 equal pieces. Shape each piece into a 16-inch rope. Braid ropes, pinching and tucking ends under. Place on greased baking sheet. Cut remaining small piece of dough into 3 equal pieces. Shape each piece into a 14-inch rope. Braid ropes, pinching and tucking ends under. Lightly brush large braid with water; place small braid on top. Cover with a clean towel; let rise 10 minutes.

To complete, preheat oven to 375F (190C). Brush raised dough with water; dust with flour. Bake in preheated oven 45 to 50 minutes or until bread sounds hollow when tapped on bottom. Remove from baking sheet; cool on a wire rack. Makes 1 loaf.

Health Bread

1-1/4 cups all-purpose flour
1 cup whole-wheat flour
3/4 cup regular or quick-cooking rolled oats
1/3 cup unprocessed bran or wheat germ
3/4 cup packed brown sugar
2-1/2 teaspoons baking powder
1 teaspoon baking soda
1 teaspoon salt
1 teaspoon ground cinnamon
1/2 teaspoon ground nutmeg
2 eggs, lightly beaten
2 tablespoons honey
1/2 cup vegetable oil
1 cup milk
1 cup raisins, if desired

Grease a 9" x 5" loaf pan. Preheat oven to 350F (175C). In a large bowl, blend flours, oats, bran or wheat germ, brown sugar, baking powder, baking soda, salt, cinnamon and nutmeg. Make a well in center of mixture. In a small bowl, beat eggs, honey, oil and milk until blended. Add to flour mixture; stir only until dry ingredients are moistened. Batter will be slightly lumpy. Stir in raisins, if desired. Pour into greased pan. Use a spoon to smooth top. Bake in preheated oven 65 to 75 minutes or until a wooden pick inserted in center comes out clean. Cool in pan on a wire rack 10 minutes. Remove from pan; cool completely on wire rack. Makes 1 loaf.

Coriander Braid

Gouda-Cheese Rolls

1 (1/4-oz.) pkg. active dry yeast (1 tablespoon)
1 tablespoon sugar
1/4 cup warm water (110F, 45C)
2 teaspoons salt
3 tablespoons vegetable oil
1 cup milk, scalded
1/2 teaspoon ground white pepper
1-1/2 cups finely shredded Gouda cheese (6 oz.)
About 3-1/4 cups all-purpose flour
1 egg yolk beaten with 1 tablespoon water for glaze

In a large bowl, combine yeast, sugar and water. Let stand until foamy, 5 to 10 minutes. Stir salt and oil into milk until blended. When cool, stir into yeast mixture. Beat in white pepper, 1 cup cheese and 2-1/2 cups flour. Stir in enough remaining flour to make a soft dough. Turn out dough onto a lightly floured surface. Knead until dough is smooth and elastic, 8 to 10 minutes. Clean and grease bowl. Place dough in greased bowl, turning to coat all sides. Cover with a clean towel. Let rise in a warm place, free from drafts, until doubled in bulk. Grease 2 medium baking sheets. Punch down dough.

To shape dough, divide into 12 equal pieces. Shape each piece into a ball. Slightly flatten each roll, pinching and tucking ends under. Place rolls, 3 inches apart, on greased baking sheets. Cover; let rise until almost doubled in bulk.

To complete, preheat oven to 400F (205C). Brush tops of rolls with egg-yolk glaze. Sprinkle with remaining 1/2 cup cheese. Bake in preheated oven 20 to 25 minutes or until rolls sound hollow when tapped on bottom. Remove from baking sheets; cool on wire racks. Serve warm or cold. Makes 12 rolls.

Zucchini Bread

3-1/4 cups all-purpose flour
1/2 cup granulated sugar
1/2 cup packed light-brown sugar
2-1/2 teaspoons baking powder
2 teaspoons ground cinnamon
1 teaspoon baking soda
1 teaspoon salt
1/2 teaspoon ground cloves
3 eggs, lightly beaten
1 teaspoon vanilla extract
1 cup vegetable oil
2 cups finely shredded zucchini, squeezed dry
3/4 cup coarsely chopped walnuts or pecans, if desired

Grease 2 (8" x 4") loaf pans. Preheat oven to 350F (175C). In a large bowl, blend flour, sugars, baking powder, cinnamon, baking soda, salt and cloves. Make a well in center of mixture. In a small bowl, beat eggs, vanilla and oil until blended. Add egg mixture and zucchini to flour mixture; stir only until dry ingredients are moistened. Batter will be slightly lumpy. Stir in nuts, if desired. Pour batter equally into greased pans. Use a spoon to smooth tops. Bake in preheated oven 60 to 65 minutes or until a wooden pick inserted in center comes out clean. Cool in pans on wire racks 10 minutes. Remove from pans; cool completely on wire racks. Makes 2 loaves.

Gouda-Cheese Rolls

Rolled Herb & Cheese Loaf

Rolled Herb & Cheese Loaf

1 (1/4-oz.) pkg. active dry yeast (1 tablespoon)
1 tablespoon sugar
1 cup warm water (110F, 45C)
1 egg
1 teaspoon salt
1/4 teaspoon ground white pepper
About 3 cups all-purpose flour

Filling:
1/4 cup butter or margarine
1 cup chopped onions
1 cup finely shredded Gouda cheese (4 oz.)
3 tablespoons chopped fresh parsley
2 tablespoons chopped fresh tarragon
2 tablespoons snipped fresh chives
1 egg
1 egg yolk beaten with 1 tablespoon water for glaze

In a large bowl, combine yeast, sugar and water. Let stand until foamy, 5 to 10 minutes. Beat in egg, salt, white pepper and 2-1/4 cups flour. Stir in enough remaining flour to make a soft dough. Turn out dough onto a lightly floured surface. Knead in enough remaining flour to make a stiff dough. Continue kneading until dough is smooth and elastic, 8 to 10 minutes. Clean and grease bowl. Place dough in greased bowl, turning to coat all sides. Cover with a clean towel. Let rise in a warm place, free from drafts, until doubled in bulk.

To make filling, melt 2 tablespoons butter or margarine in a small skillet. Add onions; sauté until transparent. Set aside to cool. When cool, stir in cheese, parsley, tarragon, chives and egg.

To complete, grease an 11" x 4" loaf pan; set aside. Punch down dough. On a lightly floured surface, roll out dough to a 16" x 12" rectangle. Spread remaining 2 tablespoons butter or margarine over dough. Spread herb-cheese filling over dough. Starting at a short end, roll up dough to center, jelly-roll style. Roll opposite end to center; pinch and tuck ends under. Lightly brush rolls with flour to keep from sticking together. Place rolled loaf, rolled-side up, in greased pan. Cover; let rise until doubled in bulk. Preheat oven to 375F (190C). Slash loaf down center to separate rolls, if necessary. Cut 1/2-inch-deep slashes in a zig-zag pattern lengthwise down top of each roll. Brush top with egg-yolk glaze. Bake in preheated oven 45 to 50 minutes or until bread sounds hollow when tapped on bottom. Remove from pan; cool on a wire rack. Makes 1 loaf.

Sesame-Seed Bread

flour to make a soft dough. Turn out dough onto a lightly floured surface. Knead in enough remaining flour to make a stiff dough. Continue kneading until dough is smooth and elastic, 8 to 10 minutes. Clean and grease bowl. Place dough in greased bowl, turning to coat all sides. Cover with a clean towel. Let rise in a warm place, free from drafts, until doubled in bulk.

To complete, grease a 9" x 5" loaf pan. Punch down dough. Shape dough into a loaf; place in greased pan. Cover; let rise until doubled in bulk. Preheat oven to 375F (190C). Brush top of raised loaf with egg-yolk glaze; sprinkle with sesame seeds. Bake in preheated oven 40 to 45 minutes or until bread sounds hollow when tapped on bottom. Remove from pan; cool on a wire rack. Makes 1 loaf.

Sesame-Seed Bread

1 (1/4-oz.) pkg. active dry yeast (1 tablespoon)
1 tablespoon sugar
1/4 cup warm water (110F, 45C)
2 tablespoons butter or margarine
1 teaspoon salt
1 cup milk, scalded
1 egg, lightly beaten
About 3-1/4 cups all-purpose flour
3 tablespoons sesame seeds, toasted
1 egg yolk beaten with 1 tablespoon water for glaze
Sesame seeds

In a large bowl, combine yeast, 1 teaspoon sugar and water. Let stand until foamy, 5 to 10 minutes. Stir butter or margarine, remaining 2 teaspoons sugar and salt into milk until blended. When cool, stir into yeast mixture. Beat in egg, 2-1/2 cups flour and toasted sesame seeds. Stir in enough remaining

Boston Brown Bread

1 cup rye flour
1 cup whole-wheat flour
1 cup yellow cornmeal
2 teaspoons baking soda
1 teaspoon salt
1 cup raisins
3/4 cup molasses
2 cups buttermilk

Generously grease 2 (1-pound) coffee cans. In a large bowl, blend flours, cornmeal, baking soda and salt. Add raisins; toss until thoroughly coated. In a medium bowl, combine molasses and buttermilk. Add to flour mixture; stir only until dry ingredients are moistened. Batter will be slightly lumpy. Pour batter into greased cans, filling 2/3 full. Butter 2 (6-inch) pieces of foil. Place over coffee cans, buttered-side down. Secure with kitchen string. Place filled coffee cans on a rack in a deep saucepan or Dutch oven. Pour in enough boiling water to come halfway up sides of cans. Cover pan or Dutch oven. Place over medium heat. Steam 3 hours, adding more boiling water to pan as necessary. Remove from water and place cans on a wire rack; remove foil. Let stand 10 minutes. Remove bread from cans; cool on rack. Makes 2 loaves.

Cheese-Soufflé Bread

Mexican Cheese Quick Bread

2 cups all-purpose flour
2-1/2 teaspoons baking powder
2 teaspoons chili powder
1 teaspoon salt
1/2 teaspoon dried leaf thyme
1/8 teaspoon pepper
2 eggs, lightly beaten
1 cup milk
1/4 cup vegetable oil
2 cups shredded Monterey Jack cheese (8 oz.)
Few drops hot-pepper sauce

Grease a 9" x 5" loaf pan. Preheat oven to 375F (190C). In a large bowl, blend flour, baking powder, chili powder, salt, thyme and pepper. Make a well in center of mixture. In a medium bowl, beat eggs, milk and oil until blended. Stir in cheese and hot-pepper sauce. Add to flour mixture; stir only until dry ingredients are moistened. Pour into greased pan. Use a spoon to smooth top. Bake in preheated oven 55 to 60 minutes or until a wooden pick inserted in center comes out clean. Cool in pan on a wire rack 10 minutes. Remove from pan; cool on rack. Makes 1 loaf.

Cheese-Soufflé Bread

1 (1/4-oz.) pkg. active dry yeast (1 tablespoon)
1 tablespoon sugar
1 cup warm water (110F, 45C)
About 2-3/4 cups all-purpose flour
1 teaspoon salt
1-1/2 cups finely shredded Swiss cheese (6 oz.)
1/2 cup cubed Swiss cheese (2 oz.)
1 egg yolk beaten with 1 tablespoon water for glaze

In a large bowl, combine yeast, sugar and water. Let stand until foamy, 5 to 10 minutes. Stir in 2 cups flour, salt and shredded cheese. Stir in enough remaining flour to make a soft dough. Turn out dough onto a lightly floured surface. Knead in enough remaining flour to make a stiff dough. Continue kneading until dough is elastic, 8 to 10 minutes. Clean and grease bowl. Place dough in greased bowl, turning to coat all sides. Cover with a clean towel. Let rise in a warm place, free from drafts, until doubled in bulk. Generously grease an 8-inch soufflé dish. Punch down dough. Shape dough into a round loaf; place in greased dish. Cut small slashes in top of dough; insert a cheese cube in each slit. Cover; let rise until almost doubled in bulk.

To complete, preheat oven to 400F (205C). Lightly brush top of bread with egg-yolk glaze. Bake in preheated oven 40 to 50 minutes or until bread is golden on top and loaf sounds hollow when tapped on bottom. Remove bread from soufflé dish. If cheese melts over side of dish, run tip of a sharp knife around inside edge of dish. Cool on a wire rack. Makes 1 loaf.

Spicy Corn Bread

1 cup yellow cornmeal
1 cup all-purpose flour
2 tablespoons sugar
1 tablespoon baking powder
1 teaspoon salt
1 teaspoon chili powder
1/2 teaspoon dried leaf thyme
1/4 teaspoon pepper
2 eggs, lightly beaten
1/4 cup butter or margarine, melted
1 cup milk
3/4 cup finely shredded sharp Cheddar cheese (3 oz.)
2 tablespoons diced green chilies
Hot-pepper sauce, if desired

Grease a 9-inch-square baking pan. Preheat oven to 400F (205C). In a medium bowl, blend cornmeal, flour, sugar, baking powder, salt, chili powder, thyme and pepper. Make a well in center of mixture. In a small bowl, beat eggs, butter or margarine and milk until blended. Add to cornmeal mixture; stir only until dry ingredients are moistened. Mixture will be slightly lumpy. Stir in cheese, green chilies and hot-pepper sauce, if desired. Pour into greased pan; use a spoon to smooth top. Bake in preheated oven 35 to 40 minutes or until a wooden pick inserted in center comes out clean. Cool in pan on a wire rack 15 minutes. Remove from pan; cool completely on wire rack. Makes 8 servings.

Herbed Whole-Wheat Bread

Cranberry-Nut Bread

2 cups all-purpose flour
1 cup sugar
1-1/2 teaspoons baking powder
1 teaspoon baking soda
1 teaspoon salt
1 cup fresh or frozen cranberries, coarsely chopped
1/2 cup coarsely chopped walnuts
1 egg, lightly beaten
1 cup orange juice
3 tablespoons vegetable oil

Grease a 9" x 5" loaf pan. Preheat oven to 350F (175C). In a large bowl, blend flour, sugar, baking powder, baking soda and salt. Stir in cranberries and walnuts; make a well in center of mixture. In a small bowl, beat egg, orange juice and oil until blended. Add to flour mixture; stir only until dry ingredients are moistened. Batter will be slightly lumpy. Pour batter into greased pan. Use a spoon to smooth top. Bake in preheated oven 60 to 65 minutes or until a wooden pick inserted in center comes out clean. Cool in pan on a wire rack 10 minutes. Remove from pan; cool completely on wire rack. Makes 1 loaf.

Variation

Reduce granulated sugar to 1/2 cup; add 1/2 cup packed light-brown sugar.

Herbed Whole-Wheat Bread

1 (1/4-oz.) pkg. active dry yeast (1 tablespoon)
1 tablespoon sugar
1/4 cup warm water (110F, 45C)
1 cup whole-wheat flour
About 2 cups all-purpose flour
1/3 cup unprocessed bran or wheat germ
3 tablespoons vegetable oil
3/4 cup milk, scalded
1 teaspoon salt
1 tablespoon Herbs de Provence or Italian seasoning

In a large bowl, combine yeast, sugar and water. Let stand until foamy, 5 to 10 minutes. Blend whole-wheat flour, 2 cups all-purpose flour and bran or wheat germ; set aside. Stir oil into milk. When cool, stir into yeast mixture. Stir in salt, Herbs de Provence or Italian seasoning and flour mixture, making a soft dough. Turn out dough onto a lightly floured surface; knead in enough all-purpose flour to make a stiff dough. Continue kneading until dough is elastic, 8 to 10 minutes. Clean and grease bowl. Place dough in greased bowl, turning to coat all sides. Cover with a clean towel. Let rise in a warm place, free from drafts, until doubled in bulk.

To complete, grease a large baking sheet. Punch down dough. Shape dough into a round loaf; place on greased baking sheet. Cover; let rise until doubled in bulk. Preheat oven to 400F (205C). Using a sharp razor blade, cut several slashes on top of loaf. Brush with water. Bake in preheated oven 40 to 45 minutes or until bread sounds hollow when tapped on bottom. Brush bread with water several times during baking. Remove from baking sheet; cool on a wire rack. Makes 1 loaf.

Dill Bread

1 (1/4-oz.) pkg. active dry yeast (1 tablespoon)
2 tablespoons sugar
1/4 cup warm water (110F, 45C)
8 oz. cottage cheese (1 cup), room temperature
2 tablespoons minced onion
1 teaspoon salt
1/4 teaspoon baking soda
1/4 cup chopped fresh dill or 1 tablespoon dried dill weed
2 tablespoons butter or margarine, melted
1 egg
About 2-3/4 cups all-purpose flour
1 egg yolk beaten with 1 tablespoon water for glaze

In a large bowl, combine yeast, 1 teaspoon sugar and water. Let stand until foamy, 5 to 10 minutes. Add cottage cheese, onion, salt, baking soda, dill, butter or margarine and remaining sugar. Stir until well blended. Beat in egg and 2 cups flour. Stir in enough remaining flour to make a soft dough. Turn out dough onto a lightly floured surface. Knead in enough remaining flour to make a stiff dough. Continue kneading until dough is smooth and elastic, 8 to 10 minutes. Clean and grease bowl. Place dough in greased bowl, turning to coat all sides. Cover with a clean towel. Let rise in a warm place, free from drafts, until doubled in bulk.

To complete, grease a 9" x 5" loaf pan. Punch down dough. Shape dough into a loaf; place in greased pan. Cover; let rise until doubled in bulk. Preheat oven to 375F (190C). Brush top of loaf with egg-yolk glaze. Bake in preheated oven 40 to 45 minutes or until bread sounds hollow when tapped on bottom. Remove from pan; cool on a wire rack. Makes 1 loaf.

Crusty Herb Rolls

dough onto a lightly floured surface. Knead in enough remaining flour to make a stiff dough. Continue kneading until elastic, 8 to 10 minutes. Clean and grease bowl. Place dough in greased bowl, turning to coat all sides. Cover with a clean towel. Let rise in a warm place, free from drafts, until doubled in bulk. Grease baking sheets; set aside. Punch down dough.

To shape dough, divide into 10 equal pieces. Shape each piece into a round ball, pinching and tucking ends under. Place rolls, 2-1/2 inches apart, on greased baking sheets. Using a sharp razor blade, cut a 1/2-inch-deep cross on top of each roll. Cover; let rise until doubled in bulk.

To complete, preheat oven to 400F (205C). Brush rolls with egg-yolk glaze. Bake in preheated oven 20 to 25 minutes or until rolls sound hollow when tapped on bottom. Remove from baking sheets; cool on wire racks. Makes 10 rolls.

Scones

2 cups all-purpose flour
1 teaspoon cream of tartar
1/2 teaspoon baking soda
1/2 teaspoon salt
3 tablespoons sugar
1/4 cup butter or margarine, chilled
About 2/3 cup milk

Grease 2 large baking sheets; set aside. Preheat oven to 425F (220C). In a medium bowl, blend flour, cream of tartar, baking soda, salt and sugar. Use a pastry blender or 2 knives to cut in butter or margarine until mixture resembles coarse crumbs. Stir in 2/3 cup milk, making a soft dough. Add more milk, if necessary. Turn out dough onto a lightly floured surface. Knead until dough is smooth, 10 to 12 strokes. Roll out dough until 3/4 inch thick. Cut dough with a floured 2-inch scalloped biscuit cutter. Place scones, 2 inches apart, on greased baking sheets. Brush tops of scones with milk. Bake in preheated oven 12 to 15 minutes or until golden brown. Remove from baking sheets; cool on wire racks. Makes 12 to 14 scones.

Variation

Whole-Wheat Scones: Substitute 1 cup all-purpose flour and 1 cup whole-wheat flour for 2 cups all-purpose flour. Substitute light-brown sugar for granulated sugar. Proceed as directed above.

Crusty Herb Rolls

1 (1/4-oz.) pkg. active dry yeast (1 tablespoon)
1 teaspoon sugar
1 cup warm water (110F, 45C)
3 tablespoons vegetable oil
2 teaspoons salt
1 egg
About 3 cups all-purpose flour
1/4 teaspoon pepper
2 tablespoons chopped fresh parsley
2 tablespoons snipped fresh chives
1 tablespoon chopped fresh dill
1 egg yolk beaten with 1 tablespoon water for glaze

In a large bowl, combine yeast, sugar and water. Let stand until foamy, 5 to 10 minutes. Stir in oil and salt until blended. Beat in egg, 2-1/4 cups flour, pepper, parsley, chives and dill. Stir in enough remaining flour to make a soft dough. Turn out

Wrapped Smoked Pork

Wrapped Smoked Pork

1 (16-oz.) loaf frozen white-bread dough, thawed
2 to 2-1/2 lbs. boneless, smoked pork-shoulder roast
Water
All-purpose flour

Grease a large bowl. Place dough in greased bowl, turning to coat all sides. Cover with a clean towel. Let rise in a warm place, free from drafts, until doubled in bulk. Grease a large baking sheet. Punch down dough. Roll out dough on a lightly floured surface to a rectangle twice the size of meat. Cut off about 1/4 of dough; reserve for decoration. Place meat in center of remaining rolled-out dough. Brush edges of dough with water. Fold dough over meat. Pinch seams to seal; tuck ends under.

To complete, place filled loaf, seam-side down, on greased baking sheet. Cut out decorations from reserved dough. Brush underside of decorations with water; place on top of loaf. Cover; let rise 20 minutes. Preheat oven to 350F (175C). Cut several small slashes in top of loaf to let steam escape. Brush loaf with water; lightly dust top with flour. Bake in preheated oven 70 to 80 minutes or until internal temperature of meat reaches 160F (70C) and bread is golden brown. Remove from baking sheet; cool on a wire rack. Makes 6 to 8 servings.

Potato Bread

1 (1/4-oz.) pkg. active dry yeast (1 tablespoon)
2 tablespoons sugar
1/4 cup warm water (110F, 45C)
3 tablespoons butter or margarine
1 teaspoon salt
1 cup milk, scalded
2 cups homemade or reconstituted instant
    mashed potatoes, room temperature
About 4 cups all-purpose flour
1 egg yolk beaten with 1 tablespoon water for glaze

In a large bowl, combine yeast, 1 teaspoon sugar and water. Let stand until foamy, 5 to 10 minutes. Stir butter or margarine, salt, and remaining sugar into milk until blended. When cool, stir into yeast mixture. Beat in mashed potatoes and 2-1/2 cups flour. Stir in enough remaining flour to make a soft dough. Turn out dough onto a lightly floured surface. Knead in enough remaining flour to make a stiff dough. Continue kneading until dough is smooth and elastic, 8 to 10 minutes. Clean and grease bowl. Place dough in greased bowl, turning to coat all sides. Cover with a clean towel. Let rise in a warm place, free from drafts, until doubled in bulk.

To complete, grease a 9" x 5" loaf pan. Punch down dough. Shape dough into a loaf; place in greased pan. Cover; let rise until almost doubled in bulk. Preheat oven to 375F (190C). Brush top of loaf with egg-yolk glaze. Bake in preheated oven 40 to 45 minutes or until bread sounds hollow when tapped on bottom. Remove from pan; cool on a wire rack. Makes 1 loaf.

Canadian Bacon en Croûte

1 (16-oz.) pkg. white-yeast-bread mix
2 lbs. unsliced Canadian-style bacon

Prepare bread mix according to package directions. On a lightly floured surface, knead dough until smooth and elastic, 8 to 10 minutes. Cover dough with bowl used for mixing; let stand 5 minutes. Grease a large baking sheet; set aside. Roll out dough to a rectangle twice the size of bacon. Cut off about 1/4 of dough; reserve for decoration. Place meat in center of remaining rolled-out dough; brush edges of dough with water. Fold dough over meat, pinch seams to seal; tuck ends under.

To complete, place filled loaf, seam-side down, on greased baking sheet. Cut out decorations or make twisted braid with reserved dough. Brush undersides of decorations with water; arrange on top of loaf. Cover; let rise 10 minutes. Preheat oven to 350F (175C). Cut several slashes in dough to let steam escape; brush loaf with water. Bake in preheated oven 65 to 70 minutes or until internal temperature of meat reaches 160F (70C) and bread is golden brown. Remove from baking sheet; cool on a wire rack. Makes 6 to 8 servings.

Canadian Bacon en Croûte

Whole-Wheat Muffins

1 cup all-purpose flour
3/4 cup whole-wheat flour
1 tablespoon baking powder
1/4 cup packed light-brown sugar
1 teaspoon salt
2 eggs, lightly beaten
3 tablespoons vegetable oil
3/4 cup milk

Grease a 12-cup muffin pan or line with paper baking cups. Preheat oven to 400F (205C). In a medium bowl, blend flours, baking powder, brown sugar and salt; make a well in center of mixture. In a small bowl, beat eggs, oil and milk until blended. Add to flour mixture; stir only until dry ingredients are moistened. Batter will be slightly lumpy. Spoon batter into prepared muffin cups, filling about 2/3 full. Bake in preheated oven 20 to 25 minutes or until a wooden pick inserted in center of a muffin comes out clean. Remove from pan; cool on a wire rack. Makes 12 muffins.

Bran Muffins

1 cup whole-wheat flour
1 cup wheat-bran-morsels cereal
1/3 cup packed light-brown sugar
1 tablespoon baking powder
1/2 teaspoon baking soda
1/2 teaspoon salt
1/2 cup raisins, if desired
1 egg, lightly beaten
1/4 cup vegetable oil
1 cup milk

Grease a 12-cup muffin pan or line with paper baking cups. Preheat oven to 400F (205C). In a medium bowl, blend flour, cereal, brown sugar, baking powder, baking soda and salt. Stir in raisins, if desired; make a well in center of mixture. In a small bowl, beat egg, oil and milk until blended. Add to cereal mixture; stir only until dry ingredients are moistened. Batter will be slightly lumpy. Spoon batter into prepared muffin cups, filling about 2/3 full. Bake in preheated oven 25 to 30 minutes or until a wooden pick inserted in center of a muffin comes out clean. Remove from pan; cool on a wire rack. Makes 12 muffins.

Bacon Bread

1/2 lb. lean bacon, diced
1 large onion, chopped
1 (16-oz.) pkg. white-yeast-bread mix
Water
All-purpose flour

In a medium skillet, sauté bacon until crisp. Remove bacon with a slotted spoon; drain on paper towels. Drain off all but 2 tablespoons drippings from pan. Add onion; sauté until transparent. Set aside to cool. Prepare bread mix according to package directions, adding cooked bacon and sautéed onion with flour. On a lightly floured surface, knead dough until elastic, 8 to 10 minutes. Cover dough with bowl used for mixing; let stand 5 minutes.

To complete, grease 2 medium baking sheets; set aside. Preheat oven to 375F (190C). Divide in half. Shape each half into a round loaf; place on greased baking sheets. Using a sharp razor blade, cut several 1/2-inch-deep slashes in top of each loaf. Brush loaves with water; dust with flour. Bake in preheated oven 45 to 50 minutes or until bread sounds hollow when tapped on bottom. Remove from baking sheets; cool on wire racks. Makes 2 loaves.

Bacon Bread

Pita Rounds

1 (1/4-oz.) pkg. active dry yeast (1 tablespoon)
1/2 teaspoon sugar
1-1/3 cups warm water (110F, 45C)
1/4 cup vegetable oil
2 teaspoons salt
3-1/2 to 4-1/2 cups all-purpose flour
Cornmeal

In a large bowl, combine yeast, sugar and water. Let stand until foamy. Add oil, salt and 2 cups flour; beat well. Stir in enough remaining flour to make a soft dough. Turn out dough onto a lightly floured surface. Knead 10 minutes or until smooth and elastic. Clean and grease bowl; place kneaded dough in greased bowl, turning to grease all sides. Cover; let rise in a warm place, free from drafts, until doubled in bulk.

To complete, punch down dough; divide into 12 pieces. Shape each into a smooth ball. Roll each ball to a 6-inch circle. Cover; let stand 10 minutes. Sprinkle 2 large baking sheets with cornmeal. Preheat oven to 500F (260C). Place 2 or 3 dough circles on each prepared baking sheet. Place 1 baking sheet on bottom rack in oven. Bake 5 minutes without opening oven. Move baking sheet to top rack; bake 3 minutes longer. Set aside to cool. Repeat with remaining dough rounds. When cool, wrap tightly; store in refrigerator or freezer. Makes 12 pita rounds.

Bread Ring

1 (16-oz.) loaf frozen white-bread dough, thawed
1 egg yolk beaten with 1 tablespoon water for glaze
Sesame seeds, poppy seeds, caraway seeds or
    a combination of seeds
Grated Parmesan cheese

Grease a large bowl. Place dough in greased bowl, turning to coat all sides. Cover with a clean towel. Let rise in a warm place, free from drafts, until doubled in bulk. Grease a large baking sheet. Punch down dough; divide into 10 equal pieces. Shape each piece into a ball, pinching and tucking ends under. Arrange balls in a circle, 1 inch apart, on greased baking sheet. Cover; let rise until doubled in bulk and balls touch each other.

To complete, preheat oven to 375F (190C). Brush ring with egg-yolk glaze; sprinkle with sesame seeds, poppy seeds or caraway seeds. Or sprinkle with a combination of seeds. Sprinkle with Parmesan cheese. Bake in preheated oven 30 to 35 minutes or until golden brown and bread sounds hollow when tapped on bottom. Remove from baking sheet; cool on a wire rack. Makes 1 loaf.

Buttermilk Bread

towel. Let rise in a warm place, free from drafts, until doubled in bulk.

To complete, grease a 9" x 5" loaf pan. Punch down dough. Shape dough into a loaf; place in greased pan. Cover; let rise until doubled in bulk. Preheat oven to 375F (190C). Slash top of loaf lengthwise with a sharp razor blade. Brush top with egg-yolk glaze. Bake in preheated oven 40 to 45 minutes or until bread sounds hollow when tapped on bottom. Remove from pan; cool on a wire rack. Makes 1 loaf.

Buttermilk Bread

1/4 cup butter or margarine
1 teaspoon salt
2 tablespoons honey
1 cup buttermilk
1 (1/4-oz.) pkg. active dry yeast (1 tablespoon)
1 teaspoon sugar
1/4 cup warm water (110F, 45C)
1/2 teaspoon baking soda
About 3-1/4 cups all-purpose flour
1 egg yolk beaten with 1 tablespoon water for glaze

In a small saucepan, combine butter or margarine, salt, honey and buttermilk. Stir over low heat until butter or margarine is melted. Cool until just warm. In a large bowl, combine yeast, sugar and water. Let stand until foamy, 5 to 10 minutes. Stir in cooled buttermilk mixture. Beat in baking soda and 2-1/2 cups flour. Stir in 1/2 cup flour or enough remaining flour to make a soft dough. Turn out dough onto a lightly floured surface. Let dough rest 5 minutes; clean and grease bowl. Knead dough, adding enough remaining flour to make a stiff dough. Continue kneading until dough is smooth and elastic, 8 to 10 minutes. Place dough in greased bowl, turning to coat all sides. Cover with a clean

Carrot-Nut Quick Bread

1-1/2 cups all-purpose flour
1 cup sugar
1 teaspoon baking powder
3/4 teaspoon baking soda
1/4 teaspoon salt
1/2 teaspoon ground cinnamon
1/4 teaspoon ground nutmeg
2 eggs, lightly beaten
3/4 cup vegetable oil
1 teaspoon vanilla extract
1 cup finely shredded carrots
1 cup finely chopped walnuts

Grease a 9" x 5" loaf pan. Preheat oven to 350F (175C). In a large bowl, blend flour, sugar, baking powder, baking soda, salt, cinnamon and nutmeg. Make a well in center of mixture. In a small bowl, beat eggs, oil and vanilla until blended. Add to flour mixture; stir only until dry ingredients are moistened. Batter will be lumpy. Fold in carrots and walnuts until blended. Pour batter into greased pan. Use a spoon to smooth top. Bake in preheated oven 45 minutes or until a wooden pick inserted in center comes out clean. Cool in pan on a wire rack 10 minutes. Remove from pan; cool on rack. Makes 1 loaf.

Blueberry Muffins

2 cups all-purpose flour
1/2 cup sugar
2-1/2 teaspoons baking powder
1/2 teaspoon baking soda
1/2 teaspoon salt
1 teaspoon grated lemon peel, if desired
1 egg, lightly beaten
1 cup buttermilk
1/2 cup butter or margarine, melted
1 cup fresh or frozen blueberries

Grease a 12-cup muffin pan or line with paper baking cups. Preheat oven to 400F (205C). In a large bowl, blend flour, sugar, baking powder, baking soda and salt. Stir in lemon peel, if desired. Make a well in center of mixture. In a small bowl, beat egg, buttermilk and butter or margarine until blended. Add to flour mixture; stir only until dry ingredients are moistened. Batter will be slightly lumpy. Fold in blueberries. Spoon batter into prepared muffin cups, filling 3/4 full. Bake in preheated oven 20 to 25 minutes or until golden. Remove from pan; cool on a wire rack. Makes 12 muffins.

Molasses-Currant Bread

1 cup all-purpose flour
1 cup medium rye flour
3/4 cup regular or quick-cooking rolled oats
1/2 cup packed light-brown sugar
1-1/2 teaspoons baking powder
1 teaspoon baking soda
1 teaspoon salt
1/4 cup molasses
1-1/4 cups buttermilk
1-1/2 cups currants

Grease a 9" x 5" loaf pan. Preheat oven to 350F (175C). In a large bowl, blend flours, oats, brown sugar, baking powder, baking soda and salt. Make a well in center of mixture. Add molasses and buttermilk; stir only until dry ingredients are moistened. Batter will be slightly lumpy. Stir in currants. Pour into greased pan. Use a spoon to smooth top. Bake in preheated oven 60 to 65 minutes or until a wooden pick inserted in center comes out clean. Cool in pan on a wire rack 10 minutes. Remove from pan; cool completely on wire rack. Makes 1 loaf.

Caraway-Rye Bread

1/4 cup butter or margarine
1/4 cup molasses
2 teaspoons salt
2 cups water
2 (1/4-oz.) pkgs. active dry yeast (2 tablespoons)
1 teaspoon sugar
1/4 cup warm water (110F, 45C)
2 tablespoons caraway seeds
2-1/2 cups medium rye flour
About 3 cups all-purpose flour
1 egg white beaten with 1 tablespoon water for glaze

In a medium saucepan, combine butter or margarine, molasses, salt and 2 cups water. Stir over low heat until butter or margarine is melted. Set aside to cool. In a large bowl, combine yeast, sugar and 1/4 cup water. Let stand until foamy, 5 to 10 minutes. Stir in cooled molasses mixture. Stir caraway seeds into rye flour. Add all-purpose flour and rye flour mixture alternately, beginning and ending with all-purpose flour, making a soft dough. On a lightly floured surface, knead in enough remaining all-purpose flour to make a stiff dough. Continue kneading until dough is elastic, 8 to 10 minutes. Clean and grease bowl. Place dough in greased bowl, turning to coat all sides. Cover with a clean towel. Let rise in a warm place, free from drafts, until doubled in bulk.

To complete, grease 2 medium baking sheets. Punch down dough. Divide dough in half. Shape each half into a round flat loaf. Place on greased baking sheets. Cover; let rise until doubled in bulk. Preheat oven to 400F (205C). Brush loaves with egg-white glaze. Bake in preheated oven 25 to 30 minutes or until bread sounds hollow when tapped on bottom. Remove from baking sheets; cool on wire racks. Makes 2 loaves.

Sandwiches & Canapés

French Luncheon Loaf

French Luncheon Loaf

1 loaf French bread

Filling:
1 cup butter or margarine, room temperature
1/4 lb. cooked ham, finely chopped
1/4 lb. cooked corned beef, finely chopped
2 hard-cooked eggs, finely chopped
1 tablespoon finely chopped green bell pepper
2 teaspoons drained capers, finely chopped
1/4 cup sliced pimento-stuffed olives
1 teaspoon Worcestershire sauce
Salt and freshly ground black pepper

Cut bread in half lengthwise, hollow out inside of top and bottom, leaving a 1-inch shell. Or, cut off ends; hollow out center, leaving a 1-inch-thick shell. In a blender or food processor fitted with a metal blade, process bread from center, making crumbs. Set crumbs aside.
To make filling, beat butter or margarine in a medium bowl until smooth. Stir in ham, corned beef, eggs, bell pepper, capers, olives and Worcestershire sauce. Stir in salt and black pepper to taste. Stir in reserved bread crumbs until evenly distributed. Mound filling on bottom half of bread; add bread top. Gently press loaf together. Or spoon filling into hollowed-out loaf. Wrap in foil; refrigerate until ready to serve. Cut into 1-inch slices. Makes 1 filled loaf.

Roquefort & Avocado Sandwiches

1 ripe avocado
4 oz. Roquefort cheese
1/2 cup butter or margarine, room temperature
Lemon juice
White pepper
4 large slices pumpernickel or other dark bread
2 large tomatoes
1 cup chopped radish sprouts, alfalfa sprouts
  or watercress
Lemon slices, if desired

Dice avocado. In a blender or food processor fitted with a metal blade, combine diced avocado, cheese and butter or margarine. Process until smooth. Season with lemon juice and white pepper. Spread a little avocado mixture on each bread slice. Slice tomatoes. Place 3 tomato slices in center of each sandwich. Arrange radish sprouts, alfalfa sprouts or watercress around tomatoes.
To serve, spoon remaining avocado mixture into a pastry bag fitted with a medium open-star tip. Pipe rosettes on each tomato slice. Garnish with lemon slices. Makes 4 open-faced sandwiches.

Roquefort & Avocado Sandwiches

On previous pages: Salmon & Caviar Sandwiches, page 150

Left to right: Carrot & Cottage-Cheese Sandwiches, Open-Faced Ham Sandwiches, Radish & Cream-Cheese Sandwiches

Carrot & Cottage-Cheese Sandwiches

8 oz. small-curd cottage cheese (1 cup)
2 cups finely shredded carrots
1 large apple, peeled, grated
2 tablespoons lemon juice
1 tablespoon apple juice
Butter or margarine, room temperature
4 slices white or whole-wheat bread
4 lemon curls, page 215
Alfalfa sprouts or watercress

Drain cottage cheese in a sieve; set aside. In a medium bowl, combine carrots, apple, lemon juice and apple juice; toss until evenly distributed. Spread butter or margarine on bread; cover each slice with 1/4 cup drained cottage cheese. Spoon 1/4 of carrot mixture onto each sandwich.

To serve, garnish each with a lemon curl and alfalfa sprouts or watercress. Makes 4 open-faced sandwiches.

Radish & Cream-Cheese Sandwiches

About 20 radishes
1 (8-oz.) carton whipped cream cheese,
   room temperature
1/4 cup milk
6 tablespoons finely chopped chives
Salt and freshly ground pepper
Butter or margarine, room temperature
4 slices white or whole-wheat bread

Finely chop 1/2 of radishes. Thinly slice remaining radishes; set aside. In a small bowl, combine cream cheese and milk; stir until blended. Stir in chopped radishes and 1/4 cup chives. Season with salt and pepper. Spread butter or margarine on bread. Top each slice with 1/4 of cream-cheese mixture. Arrange a row of sliced radishes on each sandwich.

To serve, garnish with remaining 2 tablespoons chives. Makes 4 open-faced sandwiches.

Open-Faced Ham Sandwiches

2 hard-cooked eggs
2 tomatoes
4 radishes
1 cucumber
Mayonnaise
4 slices white or whole-wheat bread
Boston lettuce
4 slices boiled ham
Dill sprigs

Slice hard-cooked eggs, tomatoes and radishes. Thinly slice cucumber. Spread mayonnaise on bread. Arrange lettuce on each sandwich so bread is covered. Top lettuce with ham. Arrange rows of sliced eggs, tomatoes, cucumber and radishes over ham.

To serve, garnish with dill sprigs. Makes 4 open-faced sandwiches.

Giant Sandwiches

Giant Sandwiches

4 large sandwich rolls
About 20 radishes
4 hard-cooked eggs
Mayonnaise
Boston lettuce
12 slices luncheon meat of choice
1/2 cup chopped fresh parsley, chives and dill, or
    other fresh herbs
4 slices Swiss cheese

Cut rolls in half horizontally. Slice radishes and hard-cooked eggs. Spread mayonnaise on cut sides of rolls. Place lettuce on bottom half of each roll. Roll up luncheon meat; place 3 luncheon-meat rolls on each sandwich. Arrange radish slices over meat rolls, overlapping slightly. Cover each with fresh herb mixture; top each with a cheese slice. Arrange egg slices over cheese. Cover each with top of roll. Makes 4 large sandwiches.

Piquant Chicken Spread

4 bacon slices
1 (7-oz.) can liver pâté
1 cup minced cooked chicken
1 garlic clove, crushed
1 tablespoon chopped fresh parsley
Salt and freshly ground pepper
Parsley sprigs
French bread

In a medium skillet, cook bacon until crisp. Cool slightly; crumble into fine pieces. In a medium bowl, combine crumbled bacon, liver pâté, chicken, garlic and chopped parsley. Season with salt and pepper. Spoon into a serving dish. Cover; refrigerate until chilled.
To serve, garnish with parsley sprigs; serve with French bread. Makes about 1-1/2 cups.

Piquant Chicken Spread

Orange & Cheese Stacks

BLT with Pineapple

4 bacon slices
2 canned pineapple slices
2 or 3 tomatoes
Mayonnaise
4 slices French bread
Boston-lettuce leaves
4 pimento-stuffed green olives

In a small skillet, cook bacon until most of fat is removed but bacon is still soft; drain on paper towels. Cut pineapple slices in half; slice tomatoes. Wrap 1 cooked bacon slice around each piece of pineapple; set aside. Spread mayonnaise on bread. Top each with lettuce and 3 tomato slices. Place 1 bacon-wrapped pineapple piece on each sandwich.
To serve, skewer olives on wooden picks. Use to garnish each sandwich. Makes 4 open-faced sandwiches.

Orange & Cheese Stacks

2 large oranges
8 slices whole-wheat bread
Butter or margarine, room temperature
8 oz. Roquefort cheese

Use a vegetable peeler to cut colored peel from 1 orange. Cut colored peel into thin strips; set aside. Use a sharp knife to cut white pith from orange. Cut colored peel and pith from remaining orange. Cut both ends from peeled oranges. Cut each peeled, trimmed orange into 4 slices. Cut bread to same size as orange slices. Spread butter or margarine on bread. Top each with an orange slice. Cut cheese into 8 slices. Top orange slices with cheese slices.
To serve, garnish with reserved orange-peel strips. Makes 8 open-faced sandwiches.

Pita Pockets

4 Pita Rounds, page 137, or bakery pita breads
Mayonnaise
Dijon-style mustard
4 to 6 thin ham slices, cut in shreds
2 tomatoes, chopped
1/2 head Boston lettuce, shredded
1 cup shredded Cheddar cheese (4 oz.)
1 ripe avocado, sliced
1 cup mung-bean sprouts
Salt and freshly ground pepper

Cut each pita round in half. Carefully separate each half into a pocket. Spread mayonnaise and mustard in each. Divide remaining ingredients among cut pocket rounds. Place 2 filled pita halves on each of 4 individual plates. Makes 4 servings.

BLT with Pineapple

Thuringer Supreme

Crabmeat Triangles

12 thin slices white bread
Butter or margarine, room temperature
1 (6-1/2-oz.) can crabmeat
1/2 cup finely chopped celery
1/2 teaspoon snipped chives
1/2 teaspoon lemon juice
1/2 teaspoon prepared horseradish
3 tablespoons dairy sour cream
Salt and freshly ground pepper
1/2 (13-oz.) can tomato aspic

Remove crusts from bread. Spread trimmed bread with butter or margarine. Drain crabmeat; flake and remove any cartilage. In a small bowl, combine flaked crabmeat, celery, chives and lemon juice; stir to blend. In another small bowl, combine horseradish and sour cream; stir into crabmeat mixture. Season with salt and pepper. Spread crabmeat mixture on 6 bread slices. Slice tomato aspic; place 1 slice on each sandwich. Cover with remaining 6 bread slices.
To serve, cut each sandwich in half diagonally; cut diagonally again, if desired. Makes 6 servings.

Thuringer Supreme

1/2 cup butter or margarine, room temperature
2 tablespoons prepared mustard
1 tablespoon prepared horseradish
4 slices pumpernickel bread
1/2 lb. Thuringer sausage
2 onions
1/4 cup beer
Salt and freshly ground pepper
4 slices boiled ham

To garnish:
4 sweet pickles
4 small white radishes
8 small red radishes
1 (3-1/2-oz.) jar cocktail onions, drained
4 miniature corn-on-the-cob, drained
Parsley sprigs
4 canned roasted red peppers, if desired, drained

In a small bowl, combine butter or margarine, mustard and horseradish; stir until blended. Spread on bread; set aside. Finely chop sausage and 1 onion; cut remaining onion into rings. In a medium bowl, combine chopped sausage, chopped onion and beer. Season with salt and pepper. Shape into 4 meatballs; place 1 meatball on each slice of bread. Roll up ham slices; place on bread. Partially slice pickles to form fans. Peel white radishes; cut in spirals, page 217.
To serve, garnish sandwiches with pickle fans, white-radish spirals, whole red radishes, onion rings, cocktail onions, miniature corn cobs, parsley sprigs and whole red peppers, if desired. Makes 4 open-faced sandwiches.

Filled French Loaf

Photo on pages 122 and 123.

1 small loaf French bread
Mayonnaise
Lettuce leaves
6 to 8 slices boiled ham
2 tomatoes, sliced
2 green bell peppers, cut in rings
2 onions, cut in rings
Sliced pickles
4 radishes, sliced
2 hard-cooked eggs, quartered
2 green onions, thinly sliced
Fresh herbs

Cut bread in half lengthwise. Spread mayonnaise on both halves. Arrange lettuce, ham, tomatoes, green-pepper rings, onion rings, pickles and radishes on bottom half of bread. Top with egg quarters; sprinkle with green onions.
To serve, garnish with fresh herbs. Cover with top half of bread. Slice to serve; serve immediately. Makes 1 small loaf or 3 to 4 servings.

Deluxe Vegetable Sandwich

Deluxe Vegetable Sandwich

1 (10-oz.) pkg. frozen mixed vegetables
2 frankfurters, cooked, diced, or
    1 cup chopped cooked ham
Mayonnaise
Salt and freshly ground pepper
1 round loaf French bread or Italian bread
1/4 cup coarsely chopped fresh parsley

Cook vegetables in lightly salted water until crisp-tender. Drain; refrigerate until chilled. Reserve 1/4 cup chilled cooked vegetables for garnish. In a medium bowl, combine remaining cooked vegetables, frankfurters or ham and about 2 tablespoons mayonnaise. Season with salt and pepper. Cut bread in half horizontally; spread with mayonnaise. Toast bread. Spread vegetable mixture over bottom of bread. Cover with top of bread.
To serve, in a small bowl, combine reserved vegetables and parsley. Spoon onto top of sandwich. Cut sandwich into slices. Makes 4 to 6 servings.

Roast-Beef & Cucumber Smorrebrod

1/4 cup mayonnaise
1 tablespoon prepared horseradish
4 slices whole-wheat or white bread
Lettuce
8 slices roast beef
1 small cucumber

In a small bowl, combine mayonnaise and horse-radish. Spread equally on bread slices; top each with lettuce. Arrange 2 slices roast beef on each slice of bread.
To serve, thinly slice cucumber; arrange cucumber slices over roast beef. Makes 4 open-faced sandwiches.

Variation

Roast-Beef & Asparagus Smorrebrod: Toast bread. Spread mayonnaise-horseradish mixture on toasted bread. Top with roast beef. Arrange 4 or 5 asparagus tips on each sandwich. Top each with a dollop of Creamy Mustard Dressing, page 160, and a mandarin-orange section. Garnish with parsley sprigs.

Camembert-Fruit Sandwiches

2 (4-oz.) pkgs. Camembert cheese
1/2 cup toasted sliced almonds
Butter or margarine, room temperature
8 slices French bread
Pineapple chunks, mandarin-orange sections or
  kiwifruit slices

Remove rind from Camembert cheese. Cut each Camembert round into 4 slices. Press almonds firmly onto cheese. Spread butter or margarine on bread slices. Place 1 cheese slice on each bread slice. **To serve,** garnish with pineapple chunks, orange sections or kiwifruit slices. Makes 8 open-faced sandwiches.

Camembert-Fruit Sandwiches

Shrimp-Salad Sandwiches

1 celery stalk
1 small onion
1/2 lb. cooked tiny shrimp
2 tablespoons chopped fresh parsley
Mayonnaise
Salt and freshly ground pepper
4 slices pumpernickel or other dark bread

Finely chop celery and onion. In a medium bowl, combine chopped celery and onion, shrimp, parsley and 1/4 cup mayonnaise; toss to blend. Season with salt and pepper. Spread a thin layer of mayonnaise on each bread slice. Spoon shrimp salad evenly on bread. Makes 4 open-faced sandwiches.

Roast-Beef & Caper Sandwiches

Mayonnaise
4 slices pumpernickel bread
8 large slices roast beef
Salt and pepper
Capers

Spread mayonnaise on bread. Place 1 slice roast beef on each slice of bread; season with salt and pepper. Fold meat corners toward center. Garnish with capers. Makes 4 open-faced sandwiches.

Roast-Beef & Caper Sandwiches

Shrimp Canapés

Ham & Kiwifruit Sandwiches

2 kiwifruit
Butter or margarine, room temperature
4 slices whole-wheat bread
Boston lettuce
1/2 lb. boiled ham, thinly sliced

Peel and slice kiwifruit. Spread butter or margarine on bread; top each with lettuce. Arrange kiwifruit and ham on top of lettuce. Makes 4 open-faced sandwiches.

Smoked-Salmon Canapés

1 (10- to 12-inch) loaf French bread
1/4 cup butter or margarine, room temperature
1 tablespoon lemon juice
1 tablespoon grated lemon peel
Salt and white pepper
5 slices smoked salmon
3 tablespoons prepared horseradish
Dill sprigs
Boston lettuce

Cut both ends from bread. Cut bread into 10 (1-inch-thick) slices. Using a fluted 2-inch cookie cutter, cut 10 rounds from sliced bread; set aside. Use end crusts and any remaining bread for another purpose. In a small bowl, beat butter or margarine, lemon juice and lemon peel until creamy; season with salt and white pepper. Spread on bread rounds. Cut salmon slices in half; roll up each half. Place 1 salmon roll on each buttered bread round.
To serve, top each canapé with a dollop of horseradish. Garnish each with a dill sprig. Arrange 10 lettuce leaves on a platter. Place 1 canapé on each lettuce leaf. Makes 10 canapés.

Shrimp Canapés

Butter or margarine, room temperature
2 slices dark bread such as pumpernickel
8 large slices bread-and-butter pickles
Finely chopped fresh dill
1/2 lb. cooked tiny shrimp
Dill sprigs

Spread butter or margarine on bread. Cut each slice into quarters. Place 1 pickle slice on each. Sprinkle with chopped dill. Arrange shrimp, pinwheel- style over pickles. Garnish with dill sprigs. Makes 8 canapés.

Shrimp & Radish Sandwiches

3/4 lb. cooked tiny shrimp
2 tablespoons lemon juice
Salt and freshly ground pepper
1 cucumber
About 20 radishes
Butter or margarine, room temperature
4 slices whole-wheat bread
Dill sprigs

Place shrimp in a medium bowl. Sprinkle with lemon juice; season with salt and pepper. Thinly slice cucumber and radishes. Spread butter or margarine on bread. On 2 opposite edges of each bread slice, arrange rows of cucumber slices and radish slices parallel to each other, leaving a space between rows. Arrange shrimp between rows of cucumber and radish slices on each sandwich.
To serve, garnish with dill sprigs. Makes 4 open-faced sandwiches.

Smoked-Salmon Canapés

Salmon & Apple Sandwiches

Salmon & Caviar Sandwiches

Photo on pages 140 and 141.

1 large white radish
1/2 pint whipping cream (1 cup)
2 teaspoons prepared horseradish
Salt
Sugar
8 slices smoked salmon
Dill Butter, page 166
4 slices French bread
1 (3-1/2-oz.) jar red lumpfish caviar
Dill sprigs
Watercress sprigs

Peel radish, if desired; cut into thin lengthwise slices. In a small bowl, beat cream until stiff peaks form. Fold in horseradish. Season with salt and sugar. Spoon whipped-cream mixture into a pastry bag fitted with a medium open-star tip. Pipe some of whipped-cream mixture onto each salmon slice; roll up. Spread Dill Butter over bread. Top each buttered bread slice with 2 filled salmon rolls. Garnish with radish strips, caviar, dill and watercress. Makes 4 open-faced sandwiches.

Salmon & Apple Sandwiches

Prepared horseradish sauce
8 slices white bread
Lettuce
8 slices smoked salmon
2 large apples
Lemon juice
Dill sprigs
4 lemon twists, if desired, page 215

Spread a very thin layer of horseradish over each bread slice. Place lettuce on 4 slices of bread, covering completely. Top each sandwich with a salmon slice. Peel and core 1 apple. Cut both apples in horizontal slices. Sprinkle lemon juice on both sides of each cored apple slice. Place 1 cored apple slice on each sandwich.

To serve, top each sandwich with a dill sprig and remaining bread. Cut each sandwich in half diagonally. Serve with remaining apple slices and lemon twists on lettuce leaves. Makes 4 sandwiches.

Party Sandwiches

Apple-Liverwurst Canapés

Party Sandwiches

4 large slices white bread
Boston lettuce
1/2 cup whipping cream
1 to 2 tablespoons prepared horseradish
8 slices smoked salmon
8 slices hearts of palm
4 artichoke hearts
4 lemon slices
2 pimento-stuffed green olives, sliced
4 teaspoons red lumpfish caviar
Alfalfa sprouts or watercress

Toast bread; remove crusts. Top each toasted bread slice with lettuce, covering 1/2 of bread. Beat cream until stiff peaks form. Stir in horseradish. Spread whipped-cream mixture evenly on salmon slices; roll up. Place 2 salmon rolls, 2 slices hearts of palm, 1 artichoke heart, 1 lemon slice and 1 olive slice on each toasted bread slice.
To serve, spoon 1 teaspoon caviar onto each artichoke heart. Garnish with alfalfa sprouts or watercress. Makes 4 open-faced sandwiches.

Apple-Liverwurst Canapés

2 large apples
Juice of 1 lemon
8 (1/4-inch) liverwurst slices
4 pitted green olives
8 almond slivers
Parsley sprigs

Peel and core apples. Cut 8 (1/4-inch) slices from peeled apples. Sprinkle lemon juice over both sides of each apple slice. Place 1 liverwurst slice over each apple slice. Use a deep, round, fluted, 3-inch cookie cutter to cut liverwurst and apple slices.
To serve, cut olives in half lengthwise. Place 1/2 olive, cut-side down, on each canapé. Garnish each by inserting almond slivers in hollow centers of olives. Add a parsley sprig to each canapé. Makes 8 canapés.

Beef Canapés with Special Toppings

Avocado-Sardine Surprise

2 (3-3/4-oz.) cans sardines in mustard sauce
1 small onion
1 ripe avocado
Lemon juice
4 slices pumpernickel bread
1/4 cup mayonnaise

Drain sardines, reserving mustard sauce; set aside. Cut onion into rings; slice avocado. Sprinkle avocado slices with lemon juice. Cut bread slices in half diagonally. In a small bowl, combine reserved mustard sauce and mayonnaise. Spread on bread triangles. Arrange avocado slices on bread. Top with reserved sardines and onion rings. Makes 4 servings.

Cheese Canapés

1/4 lb. Edam cheese
1/4 cup finely chopped peanuts
1/4 cup finely chopped walnuts
1 to 2 tablespoons mayonnaise
1 tablespoon dairy sour cream
10 slices cocktail bread
Walnut halves

Dice cheese. In a medium bowl, combine diced cheese, peanuts and chopped walnuts. In a small bowl, combine mayonnaise and sour cream; stir into cheese mixture. Spread on bread. Garnish each with a walnut half. Makes 10 canapés.

Beef Canapés with Special Toppings

Photo on opposite page.

1 (3-lb.) beef-round eye round
Wine Aspic, page 89
Toppings, below

Preheat oven to 325F (165C). Roast beef about 1 hour or until a meat thermometer inserted in center registers 160F (70C). Cool thoroughly before cutting in 1/4-inch-thick slices. Prepare toppings; make beef canapés, as topping directs. Prepare Wine Aspic; refrigerate until aspic has consistency of unbeaten egg whites.
To top with aspic, place prepared canapés on wire racks set over serving trays. Spoon partially set aspic over each. Refrigerate until set. Pour remaining aspic into a small baking dish with a flat bottom; refrigerate until firm. Place a large platter or serving plate in freezer to chill.
To serve, cut firm aspic in cubes. Place completed canapés and cubed aspic on chilled platter or plate. Makes 36 to 48 canapés.

Apricot Topping:
1 (16-oz.) can apricot halves, drained
6 slices cooked beef-round eye round
3 maraschino cherries, halved
Mint leaves

Place 2 apricot halves, rounded-sides down, on each beef slice. Place 1 cherry half on center of each apricot half. Cover with aspic as directed; refrigerate until set. Garnish with mint leaves. Makes 6 canapés.

Avocado-Cheese-Caviar Topping:
1/2 ripe avocado
1 (3-oz.) pkg. cream cheese, room temperature
6 slices cooked beef-round eye round
1 (2-oz.) jar red lumpfish caviar
Parsley leaves

In a blender or food processor fitted with a metal blade, process avocado and cream cheese until pureed. Spoon pureed mixture into a pastry bag fitted with a medium open-star tip. Pipe onto beef slices. Top each with a little caviar. Cover with aspic as directed; refrigerate until set. Garnish each with parsley leaves. Makes 6 canapés.

Mango Topping:
1/2 ripe mango
6 slices cooked beef-round eye round
Walnut halves

Peel mango; cut into 12 slices. Cross 2 mango slices on each beef slice, as shown. Garnish each with a walnut half. Cover with aspic as directed; refrigerate until set. Makes 6 canapés.

Liverwurst & Orange Topping:
3 thick liverwurst slices
6 slices cooked beef-round eye round
12 mandarin-orange sections
Pistachios

Cut liverwurst slices in half; place each half on a beef slice. Top each with 2 orange sections. Garnish each with pistachios. Cover with aspic as directed; refrigerate until set. Makes 6 canapés.

Liver-Pâté Topping:
1/2 lb. chicken livers
2 tablespoons butter or margarine
Salt and pepper
2 teaspoons mayonnaise
1 tablespoon Madeira
6 slices cooked beef-round eye round
1 hard-cooked egg, sliced
2 or 3 pimento-stuffed olives, sliced

In a medium skillet, sauté chicken livers in butter or margarine until liver is no longer pink. Season with salt and pepper. In a blender or food processor fitted with a metal blade, process cooked liver and pan drippings until pureed. Add mayonnaise and Madeira; process until blended. Spoon into a pastry bag fitted with a medium open-star tip. Pipe liver puree onto beef slices, covering completely. Slice hard-cooked egg and olives. Place 1 hard-cooked-egg slice and 1 olive slice on each puree-topped beef slice. Cover with aspic as directed; refrigerate until set. Makes 6 canapés.

Orange Topping:
1 (10-1/2-oz.) can mandarin-orange sections, drained
6 slices cooked beef-round eye round
Chopped pistachios

Arrange orange sections evenly on beef slices. Cover with aspic as directed; refrigerate until set. Garnish with chopped pistachios. Makes 6 canapés.

Cream-Cheese & Radish Canapés

2 (3-oz.) pkgs. cream cheese, room temperature
2 tablespoons half and half or milk
1 shallot
Salt and freshly ground pepper
12 slices cocktail bread
6 radishes, sliced
Mint leaves

Place cream cheese in a small bowl; stir until smooth. Add half and half or milk; stir until blended. Mince shallot; stir into cheese mixture. Season with salt and pepper. Spoon cheese mixture into a pastry bag fitted with a plain tip; pipe onto bread, covering completely. Top each canapé with 3 radish slices. Garnish each canapé with mint leaves. Makes 12 canapés.

Chicken Canapés

3 tablespoons mayonnaise
1 teaspoon Dijon-style mustard
10 slices cocktail bread
20 small slices cooked chicken
Salt and freshly ground pepper
Pistachios

In a small bowl, combine mayonnaise and mustard. Spread on bread, using about 1/3 of mayonnaise mixture. Top each bread slice with 1 chicken slice. Season with salt and pepper. Spread 1/2 of remaining mayonnaise mixture evenly over seasoned chicken slices. Top each with a second chicken slice. Season with salt and pepper. Spoon remaining mayonnaise evenly over tops. Garnish with pistachios. Makes 10 canapés.

Ham & Honeydew Canapés

Mayonnaise
10 slices cocktail bread
5 thin slices boiled ham
1/2 small honeydew melon
Freshly ground pepper

Spread mayonnaise on bread. Cut ham slices in half. Curl ham pieces onto each bread slice. Using a melon baller, scoop out 10 melon balls; place 1 ball on each canapé. Sprinkle each with pepper. Makes 10 canapés.

Canapés by rows from top: Cream-Cheese & Radish, Roast-Beef; Roast-Beef, Cream-Cheese & Radish; Cream-Cheese & Kiwifruit, Ham & Honeydew; Ham & Honeydew, Pâté & Olive; Pâté & Cranberry, Chicken.

Pâté & Olive Canapés

Butter or margarine, room temperature
Cocktail bread
About 12 small lettuce leaves
1 (7-oz.) can liver pâté
2 tablespoons Madeira
Pitted ripe olives or 1 black truffle

Spread butter or margarine on bread. Top each with a lettuce leaf. Spoon pâté into a small bowl. Add Madeira; stir until blended. Spoon pâté mixture into a pastry bag fitted with a medium open-star tip. Pipe onto each lettuce leaf, covering completely. Cut olives or truffle into thin strips. Use to garnish canapés. Makes about 12 canapés.

Herring Canapés

Cream-Cheese & Kiwifruit Canapés

2 (3-oz.) pkgs. cream cheese, room temperature
2 tablespoons half and half or milk
Grated peel of 1 lemon
Cocktail bread
2 kiwifruit

Place cream cheese in a small bowl; stir until smooth. Add half and half or milk and lemon peel; stir until blended. Spoon cheese mixture into a pastry bag fitted with a plain tip; pipe onto bread, covering completely. Peel kiwifruit; cut each into 6 slices. Press kiwifruit slices vertically into cream cheese. Makes about 12 canapés.

Herring Canapés

1 (8-oz.) jar herring fillets in red-wine sauce
1 small red onion
4 large slices pumpernickel
Butter or margarine, room temperature
5 to 6 tablespoons snipped chives
Freshly ground pepper

Drain herring; cut drained herring into small pieces. Cut onion into rings. Remove crusts from bread, if desired. Spread butter or margarine on trimmed bread. Sprinkle chives evenly over buttered bread slices; cut each slice into quarters. Arrange herring pieces on top of each quarter; top each with onion rings. Sprinkle with freshly ground pepper. Makes 16 canapés.

Pâté & Cranberry Canapés

Butter or margarine, room temperature
Cocktail bread
1 (7-oz.) can liver pâté
2 tablespoons brandy
Cooked cranberries

Spread butter or margarine on bread. Place pâté in a medium bowl. Add brandy; stir until blended. Spoon into a pastry bag fitted with a medium open-star tip; pipe onto bread, covering completely. Garnish with cranberries. Makes about 12 canapés.

Roast-Beef Canapés

Mayonnaise
10 slices cocktail bread
5 thin slices roast beef
1 hard-cooked egg yolk

Spread mayonnaise on bread. Cut roast beef slices in half. Curl beef slices onto each bread slice. Press egg yolk through a sieve; sprinkle evenly over canapés. Makes 10 canapés.

Sauces, Dips & Butters

From top: Herbal Dressing, Rémoulade Sauce, Horseradish Cream; carafe holds Vinegar

Herbal Dressing

2/3 cup dairy sour cream
3 tablespoons ketchup
2 teaspoons Italian seasoning
1 teaspoon sugar
1/4 teaspoon paprika
Salt and freshly ground pepper

In a small bowl, combine sour cream, ketchup, Italian seasoning, sugar and paprika; stir until blended. Stir in salt and pepper to taste. Serve over salad or as a dip. Makes about 1 cup.

Horseradish Cream

1/2 pint whipping cream (1 cup)
3 tablespoons prepared horseradish
1/4 cup lemon juice
1 tablespoon sugar
Salt

In a small bowl, whip cream until stiff peaks form. Stir in horseradish, lemon juice, sugar and salt to taste. Serve with ham or boiled beef. Makes about 2-1/4 cups.

Rémoulade Sauce

2 small sweet pickles
1 or 2 anchovy fillets
1 cup mayonnaise
1 teaspoon Dijon-style mustard
1 tablespoon drained capers
1 teaspoon chopped green bell pepper
2 teaspoons Italian seasoning

Chop pickles and anchovies. In a small bowl, combine all ingredients; stir until blended. Serve as a dip or sauce with cold meat, poultry or shellfish. Makes about 1-1/4 cups.

Tartar Sauce

1/2 cup mayonnaise
1/2 cup dairy sour cream
1 hard-cooked egg
1/2 cup sweet-pickle relish
1 teaspoon chopped fresh parsley
Salt and freshly ground pepper

Spoon mayonnaise into a small bowl. Stir in sour cream until blended. Press hard-cooked egg through a sieve into mayonnaise mixture. Stir in relish. Refrigerate until ready to serve. Stir in chopped parsley. Season with salt and pepper.

Mustard Cream with Dill

2/3 cup dairy sour cream
1/4 cup finely chopped fresh dill
1 to 2 tablespoons prepared mustard
Salt and freshly ground pepper
1 teaspoon gin, if desired

In a small bowl, combine sour cream, dill and mustard. Stir in salt and pepper to taste. Stir in gin, if desired. Serve with poultry or fish. Makes about 1 cup.

On previous pages: Mayonnaise, page 163.

Aioli Sauce

1/2 cup mayonnaise
4 garlic cloves, minced
1/2 teaspoon lemon juice
Pinch red (cayenne) pepper
Salt and freshly ground black pepper

In a small bowl, combine mayonnaise, garlic, lemon juice and red pepper; stir until blended. Stir in salt and black pepper to taste. Serve with fish or barbecued meat. Makes about 1/2 cup.

Aioli Sauce

Piquant Mustard Mayonnaise

1 egg yolk
2 tablespoons Dijon-style mustard
1 tablespoon lemon juice
Salt and freshly ground pepper
1 cup olive oil
1/4 cup whipping cream
2 tablespoons chopped fresh parsley
Parsley sprig

In a medium bowl, combine egg yolk, mustard and lemon juice. Add salt and pepper to taste. Beat with a whisk until blended. Add oil in a slow steady stream, beating constantly, until all oil has been added and sauce has thickened. Stir in cream and parsley. Adjust seasoning; spoon into a small serving bowl. Garnish with parsley sprig. Serve with salad or as a meat sauce. Makes about 1-1/2 cups.

Basil Sauce

4 tomatoes
16 oz. plain yogurt (2 cups)
1/2 pint whipping cream (1 cup)
2 to 3 tablespoons chopped fresh basil
Freshly ground pepper
Basil sprig

Peel and coarsely chop tomatoes. In a blender or food processor fitted with a metal blade, process chopped tomatoes until pureed. Add yogurt, cream, chopped basil and pepper to taste; process until thick and creamy. Spoon into a medium serving bowl. Garnish with basil sprig. Serve with fish or meat. Makes about 3 cups.

Clockwise from top: Basil Sauce, Piquant Mustard Mayonnaise, Walnut Sauce

Walnut Sauce

1 orange
1/2 cup dairy sour cream
1/2 cup mayonnaise
1/4 cup chopped walnuts
1 tablespoon lemon juice
Salt and freshly ground pepper

Cut 1/4 of orange peel into very thin strips; set aside. Grate remaining peel. Squeeze orange juice into a small bowl. Add grated orange peel, sour cream, mayonnaise, 3 tablespoons chopped walnuts and lemon juice. Stir in salt and pepper to taste. Spoon into a small serving bowl; garnish with reserved orange-peel strips and remaining chopped walnuts. Serve with fish or poultry. Makes about 1-1/2 cups.

Sherry & Cream Sauce

1 egg yolk
1 tablespoon sugar
2 tablespoons dry sherry
1 tablespoon lemon juice
2 tablespoons dairy sour cream or plain yogurt
1 tablespoon finely chopped almonds

In a small bowl, beat egg yolk. Add sugar; beat until thick and lemon-colored. Stir in sherry and lemon juice. Fold in sour cream or yogurt. Spoon into a small bowl; garnish with almonds. Serve with a citrus-fruit salad. Makes about 1/2 cup.

Creamy Roquefort Dressing

1/3 cup crumbled Roquefort cheese
    (1-1/2 oz.), room temperature
1/2 pint dairy sour cream (1 cup)
1 tablespoon lemon juice
Salt and freshly ground pepper
2 thin slices Roquefort cheese (1 oz.)

In a blender or food processor fitted with a metal blade, process 1/3 cup crumbled Roquefort cheese until smooth. Add sour cream; process until creamy. Add lemon juice; add salt and pepper to taste. Blend well; spoon into a small serving bowl. Garnish with sliced Roquefort cheese. Serve with a green salad. Makes about 1-1/2 cups.

Top to bottom: Creamy Mustard Dressing, Creamy Roquefort Dressing, Sherry & Cream Sauce

Creamy Mustard Dressing

1/2 pint whipping cream (1 cup)
2 teaspoons prepared mustard
1 tablespoon lemon juice
Salt and freshly ground pepper
Lemon peel strips
Lemon slice

In a medium bowl, beat cream until slightly thickened. Stir in mustard and lemon juice. Stir in salt and pepper to taste. Spoon into a small bowl. Garnish with lemon peel and lemon slice. Serve with a green salad or as a dip with raw vegetables. Makes about 1 cup.

Almond-Yogurt Dip

16 oz. plain yogurt (2 cups)
2 teaspoons Dijon-style mustard
2 tablespoons olive oil
3 hard-cooked eggs, chopped
1/2 cup ground almonds
1 teaspoon sugar
Salt and freshly ground pepper

In a medium bowl, combine yogurt, mustard and oil. Add eggs, almonds and sugar. Stir in salt and pepper to taste. Serve as a dip with raw vegetables. Makes about 3 cups.

Apricot Sauce with Curry

1/2 cup apricot jam
1/2 cup mayonnaise
1 to 2 teaspoons curry powder

In a small bowl, combine jam and mayonnaise; stir until blended. Add curry powder; mix well. Serve with poultry. Makes about 1 cup.

Ginger & Curry Dressing

2 teaspoons ground ginger
1 teaspoon curry powder
1 teaspoon Dijon-style mustard
1/2 teaspoon ground coriander
Pinch of ground cinnamon
8 oz. plain yogurt (1 cup)
Salt

In a small bowl, combine ginger, curry powder, mustard, coriander and cinnamon. Stir in yogurt until blended. Stir in salt to taste. Serve with a green salad or as a sauce with meat. Makes about 1 cup.

Apricot Sauce with Curry

Clockwise from top right: Ginger & Curry Dressing, Herbed Yogurt Dip, Almond-Yogurt Dressing

Herbed Yogurt Dip

Photo on page 18.

1-1/2 cups plain yogurt
3 tablespoons lemon juice
3 tablespoons olive oil
2 large shallots, minced
1 garlic clove, minced
1 tablespoon chopped fresh dill
1 tablespoon chopped fresh parsley
1 tablespoon chopped fresh basil
1 teaspoon sugar
Salt and freshly ground pepper

In a medium bowl, combine yogurt, lemon juice and oil. Add shallots, garlic, dill, parsley, basil and sugar. Stir in salt and pepper to taste. Serve as a dip with raw vegetables. Makes about 2 cups.

Piquant Vinaigrette

Piquant Vinaigrette

6 tablespoons vegetable oil or olive oil
3 tablespoons white-wine vinegar
1 teaspoon prepared mustard
1 small onion, diced
1 or 2 hard-cooked eggs, chopped
3 or 4 sweet pickles, minced
2 tablespoons chopped fresh parsley
1/4 teaspoon drained capers
Salt and freshly ground pepper

In a medium bowl, beat together oil and vinegar. Beat in mustard. Stir in onion, eggs, pickles, parsley and capers. Stir in salt and pepper to taste. Spoon into a medium serving bowl. Serve with a salad. Makes about 2 cups.

Spicy Ham Dip

1/4 lb. cooked ham
1 small green chili
1 (8-oz.) carton whipped cream cheese
4 to 5 tablespoons half and half
2 tablespoons chopped fresh basil
Salt and freshly ground pepper

Dice ham; set aside. To handle fresh chili, cover your hands with rubber or plastic gloves. After handling, do not touch your face or eyes. Cut chili in thin strips; discard seeds. Finely chop chili. In a medium bowl, combine cream cheese and half and half; beat well. Add basil, diced ham and chopped chili. Stir in salt and pepper to taste. Makes about 1-1/2 cups.

Crème Fraîche

1 cup whipping cream
1 teaspoon buttermilk

In a small saucepan, combine cream and buttermilk. Over low heat, heat until warm (110F, 45C). Let stand at room temperature (60F to 85F, 15C to 30C) until thick, about 1 hour. Stir well; chill before serving. Will keep in refrigerator up to 1 week. Makes 1 cup.

Caraway Dip

1 (8-oz.) carton whipped cream cheese
1/4 cup half and half
1 tablespoon caraway seeds
2 drops hot-pepper sauce
Salt
Caraway seeds

In a medium bowl, combine cream cheese and half and half, stirring until blended. Add 1 tablespoon caraway seeds, hot-pepper sauce and salt to taste; stir until combined. Spoon into a small serving bowl. Garnish with caraway seeds. Makes about 1-1/2 cups.

Chive Dip

1 (8-oz.) carton whipped cream cheese
1/4 cup dairy sour cream
2 tablespoons snipped chives
1 tablespoon chopped fresh parsley
2 drops hot-pepper sauce
Salt to taste

In a medium bowl, combine cream cheese and sour cream, stirring until blended. Add remaining ingredients; stir until well blended. Spoon into a small serving bowl. Makes about 1-1/2 cups.

Tomato Dip

1/4 cup milk
2 tablespoons tomato paste
1 (8-oz.) carton whipped cream cheese
1/2 cup minced onion
2 teaspoons dried leaf basil
1/4 teaspoon sugar
Salt to taste

In a medium bowl, combine milk and tomato paste, stirring until smooth. In a medium bowl, stir milk mixture into cream cheese until blended. Add remaining ingredients; stir to combine. Spoon into a small serving bowl. Makes about 1-1/2 cups.

Clockwise from top: Chive Dip, Caraway Dip, Tomato Dip

Herb Dip

2 tomatoes
10 pimento-stuffed green olives
3 anchovy fillets
1 egg yolk
1 teaspoon prepared spicy mustard
1 to 2 tablespoons vinegar
Salt and freshly ground pepper
3/4 cup vegetable oil or olive oil
3 to 4 tablespoons Italian seasoning
1 tablespoon capers, drained

Peel and dice tomatoes. Chop olives and anchovies; set aside. In a blender or food processor fitted with a metal blade, combine egg yolk, mustard and vinegar. Add salt and pepper to taste; process until smooth. Add oil in a slow steady stream, processing until creamy; spoon into a medium bowl. Stir in diced tomatoes, chopped olives, chopped anchovies, Italian seasoning and capers. Serve as a dip with raw vegetables. Makes about 1-1/2 cups.

Mayonnaise

Photo on pages 156 and 157.

1 egg
2 drops hot-pepper sauce
1/2 teaspoon Dijon-style mustard
1/4 teaspoon salt
2 tablespoons white-wine vinegar
1 cup vegetable oil

In a blender or food processor fitted with a metal blade, combine egg, hot-pepper sauce, mustard, salt and vinegar. Process on high speed until blended. With machine running, very slowly pour in oil. Store in refrigerator. Makes 2-1/2 cups.

Note: If mayonnaise fails to combine, pour mixture into a medium bowl. Add 1 egg yolk to blender or food processor. Turn machine on; slowly pour mayonnaise into bowl through feed tube.

Clockwise from top right: Ham & Cheese Dip, Cream-Cheese Dip, Cranberry-Cheese Dip

Ham & Cheese Dip

1 (8-oz.) carton whipped cream cheese
1/4 cup buttermilk or half and half
1/4 lb. cooked ham, diced
1 tablespoon Italian seasoning
Snipped chives
Garlic salt
Freshly ground pepper

In a medium bowl, combine cream cheese and buttermilk or half and half, stirring until blended. Add ham, Italian seasoning and chives, reserving a few chives for garnish. Stir in garlic salt and pepper to taste. Spoon into a medium serving bowl; sprinkle with reserved chives. Makes about 2 cups.

Cream-Cheese Dip

1 small tomato
1 (8-oz.) carton whipped cream cheese
1/4 cup buttermilk or half and half
2 tablespoons chopped green olives
1 anchovy fillet, diced
2 teaspoons minced onion
Salt and freshly ground pepper
Dried leaf thyme

Peel tomato; cut in quarters. Remove and discard seeds and soft pulp; dice tomato. In a medium bowl, combine cream cheese and buttermilk or half and half, stirring until blended. Add diced tomato, olives, anchovy and onion. Stir in salt and pepper to taste. Spoon into a small serving bowl; sprinkle with thyme. Makes about 1-1/2 cups.

Milano Dip

2/3 cup dairy sour cream
2 oz. Genoa salami, diced
1 medium onion, diced
Salt
Paprika
Potato chips
Cocktail rye bread

Spoon sour cream into a small bowl. Add salami and onion; stir in salt and paprika to taste. Spoon into a serving bowl; serve with potato chips or cocktail bread. Makes about 1 cup.

Cranberry-Cheese Dip

1/3 cup fresh or frozen cranberries
1 (8-oz.) carton whipped cream cheese
1/4 cup half and half
2 tablespoons prepared mustard
Salt
Sugar

Wash cranberries; discard badly bruised or very soft cranberries. In a blender or food processor fitted with a metal blade, combine cream cheese and half and half; process until smooth. Add cleaned cranberries, reserving a few for garnish. Add mustard; season with salt and sugar to taste. Process until blended. Spoon into a small serving bowl; garnish with reserved cranberries. Makes about 1-1/2 cups.

Milano Dip

Anchovy Butter

1/2 cup butter, room temperature
2 anchovy fillets, minced
1 teaspoon anchovy paste
2 teaspoons minced onion

In a small bowl, beat butter until creamy. Add remaining ingredients; beat until blended. Spoon into a small serving bowl, making peaks with back of a spoon. Cover; refrigerate 2 hours. Makes about 3/4 cup.

Chive Butter

1/2 cup butter, room temperature
2 tablespoons snipped chives
Salt, if desired
White pepper to taste

In a small bowl, beat butter until creamy. Add remaining ingredients; beat until blended. Spoon into a small serving bowl, making peaks with back of a spoon. Cover; refrigerate 2 hours. Makes about 1/2 cup.

From left: Curry Butter, Paprika Butter

Paprika Butter

1/2 cup butter, room temperature
1 tablespoon paprika
Salt, if desired

In a small bowl, beat butter until creamy. Add paprika and salt to taste; beat until blended. Shape into balls or a round or square log. Wrap in waxed paper; refrigerate 2 hours. Score balls with tines of a fork or cut log with a waffle-edged cutter. Makes about 1/2 cup.

Horseradish Butter

1/2 cup butter, room temperature
3 tablespoons prepared horseradish
Salt, if desired

In a small bowl, beat butter until creamy. Add remaining ingredients; beat until blended. Spoon into a small serving bowl, making peaks with back of a spoon. Cover; refrigerate 2 hours. Makes about 3/4 cup.

Curry Butter

1/2 cup butter, room temperature
1 tablespoon curry powder
Salt, if desired

In a small bowl, beat butter until creamy. Add curry powder and salt, if desired; beat until blended. Shape into balls or a round or square log. Wrap in waxed paper; refrigerate 2 hours. Score balls with tines of a fork or cut log with a waffle-edged cutter. Makes about 1/2 cup.

Dill Butter

1/2 cup butter, room temperature
2 tablespoons chopped fresh dill
1/4 teaspoon dried leaf thyme
Salt, if desired
Freshly ground pepper to taste

In a small bowl, beat butter until creamy. Add remaining ingredients; beat until blended. Spoon into a small serving bowl, making peaks with back of a spoon. Cover; refrigerate 2 hours. Makes about 3/4 cup.

Onion Butter

1/2 cup butter, room temperature
1/4 cup diced red onion
Salt, if desired
White pepper to taste

In a small bowl, beat butter until creamy. Add remaining ingredients; beat until blended. Shape into a 2-inch-thick log; wrap in waxed paper or foil. Refrigerate 2 hours. Cut into slices. Scallop slices by cutting with a round fluted cookie cutter, if desired. Makes about 3/4 cup.

Onion Butter

Mustard Butter

1/2 cup butter, room temperature
2 teaspoons prepared mustard
Juice of 1/2 lemon
Salt, if desired

In a small bowl, beat butter until creamy. Add remaining ingredients; beat until blended. Spoon into a small serving bowl, making peaks with back of a spoon. Cover; refrigerate 2 hours. Makes about 1/2 cup.

Lemon Butter

1/2 cup butter, room temperature
Peel of 1 lemon

In a small bowl, beat butter until creamy. Remove any white pith from lemon peel; finely mince peel. Stir minced peel into creamed butter until blended. Spoon into a small serving bowl, making peaks with back of a spoon. Cover; refrigerate 2 hours. Makes about 1/2 cup.

Herb Butter

1/2 cup butter, room temperature
2 teaspoons chopped fresh parsley
1 teaspoon minced onion
1 teaspoon lemon juice
1 teaspoon dry white wine or dry vermouth
1/2 teaspoon Worcestershire sauce
1/4 teaspoon dried leaf tarragon
1 garlic clove, crushed
Salt, if desired

In a small bowl, beat butter until creamy. Stir in remaining ingredients until blended. Shape into a 2-inch-thick log; wrap in waxed paper. Refrigerate 2 hours. Slice with a waffle-edged cutter. Makes about 3/4 cup.

Fruit

Fruit Platter with French Toast

Fruit Platter with French Toast

1 mango
1 papaya
3 to 4 tablespoons orange-flavored liqueur
2 tablespoons honey
2 pints strawberries, sweet cherries, raspberries,
  blackberries, blueberries, red currants or
  yellow plums, or combination (4 cups)
1 egg
1/4 cup milk
1 teaspoon sugar
1 teaspoon vanilla extract
3 to 4 tablespoons butter or margarine
8 slices small French bread or baguette
Ground cinnamon
About 1/4 cup sparkling white wine or orange juice

Peel, halve and remove pits of mango and papaya. Place mango and papaya fruit in a blender or food processor fitted with a metal blade. Add liqueur and honey; process until pureed. Refrigerate until chilled. Clean remaining fruit. In a medium bowl, beat egg; stir in milk, sugar and vanilla. Melt butter or margarine in a large skillet. Quickly dip bread slices in egg mixture. Do not leave in egg mixture or bread will become soggy and hard to remove. Place coated bread in skillet; brown on both sides. Sprinkle with cinnamon.

To serve, arrange cleaned fruit around edge of platter. Stir wine into reserved puree; spoon into center of platter. Top with French-toast slices. Makes 4 servings.

On previous pages: Fruity Breakfast Treat, page 178

Melon Surprise

1 (6.5-oz.) can mandarin-orange sections
1 honeydew melon
2 apples
2 bananas
2 to 3 tablespoons lemon juice
2 tablespoons honey
Chopped walnuts or pecans

Drain mandarin oranges; set aside. Peel melon; cut in half. Remove seeds; cut fruit into 3/4-inch pieces. Peel, core and chop apples. Peel bananas; cut in 1/4-inch slices. Place prepared fruit in a large bowl; sprinkle with lemon juice to prevent browning. Drizzle honey over top of fruit; stir gently.
To serve, spoon into 4 individual serving dishes; sprinkle with nuts. Makes 4 servings.

Autumn Fruit Bowl

1/2 cup fresh or frozen cranberries
1 lb. small red prunes
1 lb. seedless green grapes
1 cup red-currant jelly
1/4 cup cherry-flavored liqueur
2 tablespoons powdered sugar
1/4 teaspoon ground cinnamon

Sweet Yogurt Dressing:
2 egg yolks
1/2 cup granulated sugar
3/4 cup plain yogurt
1/2 cup whipping cream
16 walnut halves

Wash cranberries; discard badly bruised or very soft cranberries. Cut prunes in half; remove pits. Cut grapes in half. In a small saucepan, bring jelly to a boil; reduce heat until jelly just simmers. Add cleaned cranberries; simmer 2 to 3 minutes. Using a slotted spoon, remove cooked berries from jelly; place in a small bowl. Refrigerate until chilled. Boil jelly until slightly thick and syrupy. Cool slightly; stir in 2 tablespoons liqueur. Refrigerate jelly mixture until chilled. Blend powdered sugar and cinnamon. In a medium bowl, combine halved prunes and grapes. Sprinkle with powdered-sugar mixture and remaining 2 tablespoons liqueur; stir gently. Add chilled cooked cranberries; refrigerate.
To make dressing, in a medium bowl, beat egg yolks and granulated sugar until thick and lemon colored. Stir in yogurt. In a small bowl, beat cream until soft peaks form; fold into yogurt mixture.
To serve, spoon fruit mixture into 4 individual serving dishes. Top each with a dollop of Sweet Yogurt Dressing; spoon jelly syrup over each. Garnish each serving with 4 walnut halves. Makes 4 servings.

Crispy Baked Apples

1/4 cup raisins
3 tablespoons rum
4 large firm tart apples
1/4 cup chopped walnuts
1/4 cup packed brown sugar
1/2 cup water
Half and half, if desired

In a small bowl, combine raisins and rum; let stand 15 minutes. Preheat oven to 350F (175C). Cut a slice off top of each apple. Remove cores to within 1/2 inch of bottom of each apple. Remove 1 inch of skin from around top of each apple. Stir walnuts into raisin mixture. Spoon mixture evenly into hollowed centers of apples. Spoon brown sugar onto top of each. Arrange filled apples in a small baking dish. Pour water into baking dish until about 1/2 inch deep. Bake apples in preheated oven about 45 minutes or until tender. Cool slightly; refrigerate until chilled. Serve with half and half, if desired. Makes 4 servings.

Autumn Fruit Bowl

Raspberry Granola

4 cups granola or muesli
1 pint raspberries (2 cups)
1 teaspoon grated lemon peel
Sugar
1/2 cup whipping cream
1 teaspoon vanilla extract

Pour 1 cup granola or muesli into each of 4 individual serving bowls. Top each serving with 1/2 cup raspberries; sprinkle with lemon peel and sugar to taste. In a medium bowl, beat cream until slightly thickened. Add vanilla; beat until soft peaks form. Spoon over raspberries. Makes 4 servings.

Variation

Substitute plain yogurt or dairy sour cream for whipping cream. Omit vanilla.

Raspberry Granola

Cantaloupe Cups

Cantaloupe Cups

4 small cantaloupe
1 mango
4 candied kumquats
1 cup drained canned lychee nuts
Juice of 1 lemon
2 tablespoons cherry-flavored liqueur
1/4 cup brandy
1 teaspoon vanilla extract
1 to 2 tablespoons powdered sugar
4 maraschino cherries for garnish

Cut off melon tops in a zig-zag pattern. Scoop out seeds; scoop out flesh, leaving a 1/4-inch layer. Reserve shells in refrigerator; chop scooped-out cantaloupe flesh. Peel and chop mango. Drain kumquats; coarsely chop. Combine chopped cantaloupe, mango and kumquats in a large bowl. Add lychee nuts. In a small bowl, combine lemon juice, liqueur, brandy and vanilla. Stir in powdered sugar until dissolved. Pour over fruit. Cover; refrigerate at least 1 hour.

To serve, stir fruit mixture; spoon into chilled cantaloupe shells. Top each filled cantaloupe shell with a maraschino cherry. Makes 4 servings.

Fruity Muesli

2 oranges
4 medium apples
2 bananas
1 cup muesli or granola
1/2 cup chopped walnuts, pecans or almonds
Honey or sugar
Half and half

Peel and section oranges. Peel, core and coarsely chop apples. Slice bananas. Divide muesli among 4 individual serving bowls. Top with chopped apples, sliced bananas, orange sections and nuts. Season with honey or sugar to taste. Serve with half and half. Makes 4 servings.

Spiced Pears

4 large or 8 small very firm pears with stems attached
1 lemon
1-1/2 cups sugar
1/2 cup water
4 whole cloves
1 (3-inch) cinnamon stick
1-1/2 cups sweet red wine

Peel pears, leaving stems attached. Thinly slice lemon. In a saucepan large enough to hold pears upright, combine sugar, water, cloves, cinnamon and sliced lemon. Stirring constantly, bring liquid to a boil; continue stirring until sugar dissolves. Place peeled pears upright in pan. Cover pan; simmer 15 minutes. Remove pan cover; pour wine over partially cooked pears. Simmer uncovered 20 minutes or until pears are barely tender. Using a slotted spoon, place cooked pears upright in a serving dish with a rim. Strain sauce; return to saucepan. Boil sauce until reduced and syrupy; spoon over pears. Let stand until cool, occasionally spooning syrup over pears. Refrigerate until thoroughly chilled. Makes 4 servings.

Fruity Muesli

Green-Grape Cocktail

1/2 lb. seedless green grapes
1/2 cup vanilla-flavored yogurt
1/2 cup dairy sour cream
1 tablespoon sugar, if desired
1 cup granola or muesli

Slice grapes or leave whole. Divide sliced or whole grapes among 4 tall glasses. In a small bowl, combine yogurt, sour cream and sugar, if desired; stir until smooth. Spoon over grapes. Top with granola or muesli. Makes 4 servings.

Green-Grape Cocktail

Apple Fluff

1/4 cup water
1 (1/4-oz.) envelope unflavored gelatin (1 tablespoon)
2 egg whites
1/4 cup superfine sugar
1 cup applesauce
1 teaspoon lemon juice
Sweetened whipped cream

In a medium saucepan, sprinkle gelatin over water; let stand 5 minutes. Place saucepan over low heat; stir until gelatin dissolves. Cool slightly. In a medium bowl, beat egg whites until soft peaks form. Add sugar slowly, beating until stiff peaks form. Pour applesauce into a medium bowl. Stir in gelatin mixture and lemon juice. Fold in egg-white mixture. Refrigerate until thoroughly chilled. Serve with sweetened whipped cream. Makes 4 servings.

Ambrosia

1/2 cup raisins
1/2 cup orange juice
2 navel oranges
2 bananas
1/4 cup powdered sugar
1-1/2 cups shredded coconut
Mint leaves

In a small bowl, combine raisins and orange juice; set aside. Peel and section oranges; slice bananas. In a medium bowl, combine orange sections and sliced bananas. Sprinkle powdered sugar over oranges and bananas; stir gently. Stir in coconut and raisin mixture. Refrigerate until thoroughly chilled.
To serve, spoon chilled mixture into 4 individual serving dishes. Decorate with mint leaves. Makes 4 servings.

Tropical Delight

Fruit with Cream Sherry

1 (8-1/4-oz.) can chunk pineapple
1/2 pint strawberries (1 cup)
2 peaches
3 kiwifruit
1 banana
1/2 lb. seedless green grapes
1 tablespoon sugar
1/4 cup cream sherry
1 tablespoon finely chopped pistachios

Drain pineapple; use syrup for another purpose. Hull strawberries. Peel and slice peaches, kiwifruit and banana. In a large bowl, combine drained pineapple, hulled strawberries and sliced peaches, kiwifruit and banana. Add grapes; toss to distribute fruit. Sprinkle with sugar. Pour sherry over top; toss gently. Refrigerate 30 minutes.
To serve, spoon fruit mixture into 4 or 6 individual serving bowls. Sprinkle each serving with pistachios. Makes 4 to 6 servings.

Tropical Delight

1 mango
2 kiwifruit
2 nectarines or peaches
2 bananas
1 tablespoon lemon juice
Sugar
1/2 pint dairy sour cream or plain yogurt (1 cup)
1 cup muesli or granola

Peel and slice mango, kiwifruit, nectarines or peaches and bananas. Combine sliced fruit in a large bowl. Sprinkle with lemon juice and sugar to taste. Toss gently to distribute. Gently stir in sour cream or yogurt.
To serve, spoon fruit mixture into 4 individual serving bowls; top with muesli or granola. Makes 4 servings.

Berry Delight

Berry Delight

**2 pints mixed strawberries, blueberries, blackberries,
   raspberries and red currants (4 cups)**
6 to 8 tablespoons powdered sugar or to taste
1/4 teaspoon ground cinnamon
2 tablespoons lemon juice
1 tablespoon orange-flavored liqueur
1/2 pint whipping cream (1 cup)
1 pint vanilla ice cream

Clean and hull berries; place hulled berries and
currants in a large bowl. Blend powdered sugar and
cinnamon. Stir in lemon juice and liqueur. Sprinkle
over fruit mixture; stir gently. Cover; let stand 30
minutes. In a small bowl, beat cream until soft
peaks form. Set 1 cup fruit aside; fold whipped
cream into remaining fruit.
To serve, spoon fruit-and-whipped-cream mixture
into 4 stemmed glasses. Cut ice cream into small
cubes; arrange evenly on top of mixture in glasses.
Spoon reserved fruit on top. Makes 4 servings.

Mixed Fruit Salad

**1-1/2 to 2 lbs. mixed oranges, apples, bananas,
   seedless green grapes, strawberries and red currants**
1/2 cup orange juice
2 tablespoons kirsch or other cherry-flavored liqueur

Clean fruit. Peel and section oranges; chop sections.
Peel, core and chop apples. Peel bananas; cut in
1/4-inch slices. Slice grapes and strawberries, if
desired. Combine prepared fruit in a large bowl.
Sprinkle orange juice and liqueur over fruit; stir
gently. Refrigerate at least 1 hour.
To serve, spoon into 4 individual serving dishes.
Makes 4 servings.

Mixed Fruit Salad

Orange Muesli Crunch

5 small oranges
1/4 cup honey
2 cups muesli or granola
Mint leaves

Peel 4 oranges; cut in small pieces. Slice remaining orange. In a medium bowl, combine orange pieces and honey; let stand 15 minutes. Add muesli or granola.

To serve, spoon into individual serving dishes. Garnish with orange slices and mint leaves. Makes 4 servings.

Variation

After adding muesli, stir in 1/2 pint (1 cup) vanilla-flavored yogurt.

Granola & Yogurt

Granola & Yogurt

4 medium apples
2 cups muesli or granola
1 cup raisins
Sugar
Plain yogurt

Peel, core and chop apples. In a medium bowl, combine chopped apples, muesli or granola and raisins. Sprinkle with sugar; mix well.

To serve, spoon into 4 individual serving bowls. Top each serving with a dollop of yogurt. Makes 4 servings.

Orange Muesli Crunch

Fruity Breakfast Treat

Fruity Breakfast Treat

Photo on pages 168 and 169.

1 pint strawberries (2 cups)
1 pint red currants or raspberries (2 cups)
2 cups muesli or granola
Sugar
Milk or half and half

Wash fruit; hull strawberries. Divide hulled strawberries among 4 individual cereal bowls. Add currants or raspberries; top with muesli or granola. Sprinkle with sugar; serve with milk or half and half. Makes 4 servings.

Grapefruit Crunch

2 grapefruit
2 peaches
8 oz. plain yogurt (1 cup)
2 to 4 tablespoons sugar or to taste
1 cup muesli or granola
4 maraschino cherries

Cut each grapefruit in half; carefully remove flesh. Cut out and discard white pith from grapefruit shells; reserve shells. Cut grapefruit flesh into small pieces; place in medium bowl. Peel and chop peaches; add to grapefruit pieces. In a small bowl, combine yogurt and sugar. Stir into fruit mixture. Stir in muesli or granola.
To serve, spoon fruit mixture into grapefruit shells; top each with a cherry. Makes 4 servings.

Grapefruit Crunch

Fruit-Filled Crepes

1 pint strawberries (2 cups)
1/2 pint raspberries or red currants (1 cup)
Sugar

Crepes:
1/2 cup all-purpose flour
2 tablespoons sugar
2 eggs, lightly beaten
2/3 cup milk
2 tablespoons butter, melted
Butter or margarine

Wash and hull strawberries. Reserve 6 to 8 strawberries for decoration. Cut remaining strawberries in half; place in a medium bowl. Place raspberries or red currants in a small bowl. Sprinkle cut strawberries and raspberries or red currants with sugar to taste. Toss lightly to coat; set aside.

To make crepes, in a medium bowl, blend flour and 2 tablespoons sugar. In a small bowl, beat eggs and milk until blended. Gradually add egg mixture to flour mixture, beating constantly. Continue beating until mixture is completely smooth. Stir in melted butter until blended. Pour batter into a pitcher; cover and refrigerate at least 1 hour. Over medium heat, melt about 1 teaspoon butter or margarine in a 6- or 7-inch crepe pan or skillet. Stir batter; pour about 2 tablespoons batter into heated pan or skillet. Tip pan to distribute batter evenly over bottom. Batter should cover bottom of pan in a thin layer. Cook over medium heat 1 to 1-1/2 minutes or until small bubbles begin to form on surface of crepe. Turn crepe over; cook 1 to 1-1/2 minutes or until bottom is golden brown. Slide crepe onto a flat plate. Cook remaining batter, making 12 crepes. Add more butter or margarine to pan or skillet as needed.

To serve, spoon sugar-coated strawberries and raspberries or currants onto crepes; roll into cornets. Sprinkle with sugar; decorate with reserved strawberries. Makes 6 servings.

Fruit-Filled Crepes

Desserts

Almond-Custard Ring

Almond-Custard Ring

Almond Praline:
2 tablespoons butter or margarine
1/4 cup sugar
2/3 cup chopped almonds

Custard Ring:
2 (3-oz.) pkgs. golden-egg-custard mix
4 teaspoons unflavored gelatin powder
1 qt. milk (4 cups)
2 egg yolks, beaten
1 teaspoon vanilla extract

Apricot Sauce:
1 (16-oz.) can apricot halves packed in heavy syrup
Water
Peel of 1/2 orange, cut into julienne strips
1 to 2 tablespoons orange-flavored liqueur
Sweetened whipped cream

To make praline, grease a baking sheet; set aside. In a medium skillet, melt butter or margarine. Add sugar; stir constantly until sugar is dissolved and syrup is caramel in color. Stir in almonds. Pour mixture onto greased baking sheet; quickly spread out. Let stand at room temperature until completely cooled. Remove from baking sheet; crush with a rolling pin. Set aside.

To make custard ring, in a medium saucepan, combine custard mix and gelatin. Gradually stir in milk and egg yolks until blended. Over low heat, cook, stirring constantly, until mixture thickens. Remove from heat; cool slightly. Stir in vanilla. Rinse a 6-cup ring mold with water; drain. Pour custard mixture into rinsed mold; refrigerate until set.

To make sauce, drain apricots, reserving syrup in a 1-cup measure. Add water to make 1 cup. Refrigerate apricots. Pour syrup mixture into a small saucepan; add orange peel. Bring to a boil over medium heat. Boil steadily until mixture is reduced by 1/3. Pour into a serving dish; stir in liqueur.

To serve, run tip of a knife around edge of molded custard. Invert custard onto a platter or serving plate; remove mold. Press crushed almond praline over surface of custard ring. Spoon reserved apricots into center of ring; decorate with sweetened whipped cream. Serve with Apricot Sauce. Makes 6 to 8 servings.

Mocha-Chip Delight

1/4 cup chocolate syrup
1/4 cup coffee-flavored liqueur
1 pint mocha-chip ice cream
Sweetened whipped cream
Shaved chocolate, page 189

In a small bowl, combine chocolate syrup and liqueur; stir until blended. Pour into 4 chilled dessert dishes. Scoop ice cream into small balls; place in glasses. Decorate with sweetened whipped cream and shaved chocolate. Makes 4 servings.

On previous pages: Fruity Sorbets, page 191

Raspberry & Sour-Cream Mousse

Raspberry & Sour-Cream Mousse

1 (8-oz.) pkg. cream cheese, room temperature
1/3 cup sugar
2 tablespoons lemon juice
1/2 pint dairy sour cream (1 cup)
1/2 cup cold water
1 (1/4-oz.) envelope unflavored gelatin
1 pint fresh raspberries (2 cups), cleaned
Mint leaves or raspberry leaves

In a medium bowl, combine cream cheese and sugar; beat until light and fluffy. Add lemon juice and sour cream; beat until barely blended. Pour water into a small saucepan. Sprinkle gelatin over top; let stand 5 minutes. Stir over low heat until gelatin is dissolved. Cool slightly. Gradually stir cooled gelatin into cheese mixture until thoroughly blended. Refrigerate 20 minutes. Gently fold 1/2 of raspberries into cheese mixture. Reserve remaining raspberries for decoration. Rinse a 4-cup decorative mold with water; drain. Spoon cheese mixture into rinsed mold; smooth top. Refrigerate 3 to 4 hours or until set. Place a platter or serving plate in freezer to chill.

To serve, invert mold onto chilled platter or serving plate. Wet a dish towel in hot water; wring dry. Place hot wet towel around mold. Leave 5 to 10 seconds; remove mold and cloth. Decorate with reserved 1/2 pint raspberries and mint leaves or raspberry leaves. Makes 6 servings.

Blueberry Bavarian

Blueberry Bavarian

1 (3-oz.) pkg. blackberry-flavored gelatin
1 (1/4-oz.) envelope unflavored gelatin
1 cup boiling water
1 cup cold water
1 pint fresh or frozen blueberries, thawed (2 cups)
1/2 cup powdered sugar
2 tablespoons lemon juice
1 pint whipping cream (2 cups)
Sweetened whipped cream

In a medium bowl, combine blackberry-flavored gelatin and unflavored gelatin. Stir in boiling water until gelatins are completely dissolved. Stir in cold water; cool to room temperature. In a blender or food processor fitted with a metal blade, process 1-1/2 cups blueberries, powdered sugar and lemon juice until pureed. Fold blueberry puree into cooled gelatin mixture. Refrigerate until mixture mounds when dropped from a spoon. In a medium bowl, beat cream until stiff peaks form. Fold into blueberry mixture. Pour into a 6- or 7-cup decorative mold; smooth top. Refrigerate 3 to 4 hours or until set.

To serve, invert mold onto a platter or serving plate. Wet a dish towel in hot water; wring dry. Place hot wet towel around mold. Leave 5 to 10 seconds; remove mold and cloth. Serve with reserved blueberries and sweetened whipped cream. Makes 6 to 8 servings.

Orange-Cream Baskets

3 large navel oranges

Orange Cream:
1/4 cup cold water
1 (1/4-oz.) envelope unflavored gelatin
1 tablespoon lemon juice
3 eggs, separated
1/2 cup sugar
1/4 cup warm water
1/2 cup whipping cream
Chocolate-dipped slivered almonds, if desired

Cut oranges in half. Gently press out juice, reserving juice in a 1-cup measure and keeping orange halves in shape. Hollow out orange halves; discard pulp. Set orange shells aside.

To make orange cream, measure 2/3 cup juice; set aside. Use remaining juice for another purpose. Pour 1/4 cup cold water into a small saucepan. Sprinkle gelatin over top; let stand 5 minutes. Stir over low heat until gelatin is dissolved. Stir in reserved 2/3 cup orange juice and lemon juice. Set aside to cool. In a medium bowl, combine egg yolks, sugar and 1/4 cup warm water. Beat until foamy. Gradually beat in cooled gelatin mixture. Continue beating until light and fluffy. Refrigerate 30 to 45 minutes or until mixture mounds when dropped from a spoon. In a small bowl, beat cream until stiff peaks form. Fold whipped cream into gelatin mixture. Beat egg whites until stiff but not dry; fold into gelatin mixture. Spoon or pipe orange cream into reserved orange shells. Refrigerate 2 hours or until set.

To serve, decorate each orange basket with chocolate-dipped slivered almonds. Makes 6 servings.

Orange-Cream Baskets

Hazelnuts with a Cool Kiss

Hazelnuts with a Cool Kiss

1 (6-oz.) jar chocolate-fudge topping
Whole hazelnuts
1 to 1-1/2 pints vanilla-and-chocolate-ribbon ice cream
Sweetened whipped cream
Maraschino cherries
Mandarin-orange sections
Mint leaves

Open jar of fudge topping; place in a small saucepan. Pour water in pan until half way up side of jar. Bring water to a simmer; stir until topping is soft and warmed through.

To serve, spoon topping into 4 to 6 dessert dishes. Add whole hazelnuts. Cut ice cream into thin slices. Place 2 slices in each dish. Decorate with sweetened whipped cream, cherries, orange sections and mint leaves. Serve immediately. Makes 4 to 6 servings.

Marble Cake a la Mode

4 slices marble cake
1 pint cherry-vanilla or black-cherry ice cream
Cherry ice-cream topping
Sweetened whipped cream
Toasted slivered almonds
Chopped maraschino cherries

Place 1 cake slice in each of 4 chilled dessert dishes. Scoop ice cream into small balls; place an equal number on each serving. Spoon cherry topping over ice cream. Decorate with sweetened whipped cream, almonds and cherries. Makes 4 servings.

Raspberry Pudding with Cream

1 (4-3/4-oz.) pkg. Danish-style raspberry pudding-
  and-pie-filling mix
2 tablespoons granulated sugar
2 cups cold water
1 (10-oz.) pkg. frozen raspberries, thawed, drained
1/2 cup whipping cream
1 tablespoon powdered sugar
1/2 teaspoon vanilla extract
12 to 18 fresh raspberries, if desired

In a medium saucepan, combine pudding-and-pie-filling mix and granulated sugar. Gradually stir in water until blended. Over medium heat, cook, stirring constantly, until mixture comes to a boil. Boil 1 minute. Pour into a medium bowl; cool to room temperature. Fold in thawed raspberries. Refrigerate until mixture mounds when dropped from a spoon.

To serve, in a medium bowl, beat cream until soft peaks form. Add powdered sugar and vanilla; beat until stiff peaks form. Spoon raspberry pudding into dessert dishes. Top each with a dollop of whipped cream. Decorate each with 3 fresh raspberries, if desired. Makes 4 to 6 servings.

Raspberry Pudding with Cream

Sweet Strawberry-Cheese Dessert

Fruit-Garden Sundaes

8 scoops assorted ice cream
8 scoops assorted sherbet
Sweetened whipped cream
Pineapple chunks
Kiwifruit slices, quartered
Mandarin-orange sections
Maraschino cherries
Shaved chocolate, page 189
Rolled cookies

Place 2 scoops ice cream and 2 scoops sherbet in each of 4 chilled dessert dishes. Decorate with sweetened whipped cream, pineapple, kiwifruit, orange sections, maraschino cherries and shaved chocolate. Serve with cookies. Makes 4 servings.

Sweet Strawberry-Cheese Dessert

1-1/2 pints strawberries (3 cups)
8 oz. ricotta cheese (1 cup)
1 (3-oz.) pkg. cream cheese, room temperature
1/3 cup granulated sugar
1/2 pint whipping cream (1 cup)
2 tablespoons powdered sugar
1 teaspoon vanilla extract, if desired

Wash and hull strawberries. Reserve 1/2 pint hulled strawberries for decoration. In a blender or food processor fitted with a metal blade, process remaining 1 pint strawberries to a smooth puree. Using back of a wooden spoon, press strawberry puree through a fine sieve to remove seeds; set aside. In a medium bowl, beat ricotta, cream cheese and granulated sugar until light and fluffy. Stir in strawberry puree until thoroughly blended. Refrigerate 1 hour. In a small bowl, beat cream until soft peaks form. Add powdered sugar and vanilla; beat until stiff peaks form. Fold whipped cream into strawberry-cheese mixture. Refrigerate until thick and creamy.

To serve, spoon into dessert dishes; decorate with reserved strawberries. Makes 6 servings.

Fruit-Garden Sundaes

Black Forest Cherry Cream

1 (3-1/4-oz.) pkg. vanilla pudding-and-
pie-filling mix
2 teaspoons unflavored gelatin powder
3-1/4 cups milk
3 tablespoons cherry-flavored liqueur
1/2 pint whipping cream (1 cup)
1 tablespoon powdered sugar
1 (16-oz.) can pitted dark sweet cherries, drained
Shaved chocolate, page 189

In a medium saucepan, combine pudding-and-
pie-filling mix and gelatin. Gradually stir in milk;
continue stirring until blended. Over low heat,
cook, stirring constantly, until mixture thickens and
comes to a boil. Pour into a large bowl. Place a sheet
of waxed paper over surface of pudding to prevent a
skin from forming. Cool completely. Stir in liqueur.
In a small bowl, beat cream until soft peaks form.
Add powdered sugar; beat until stiff peaks form.
Reserve about 2/3 cup whipped cream; refrigerate.
Fold remaining whipped cream into pudding.
Refrigerate 3 to 4 hours or until thoroughly chilled.
To serve, spoon 3 or 4 tablespoons pudding mixture
into 4 dessert dishes. Reserve 4 cherries for
decoration. Spoon remaining cherries evenly over
pudding in each dish. Top with remaining pudding.
Spoon reserved whipped cream into a pastry bag
fitted with a small rosette tip. Pipe a swirl of
whipped cream on top of each dessert. Decorate
with reserved cherries and chocolate. Refrigerate
until ready to serve. Makes 4 servings.

Black Forest Cherry Cream

Walnut & Orange Cream

1/2 cup milk
1 (1/4-oz.) envelope unflavored gelatin
2 eggs, separated
1/3 cup granulated sugar
2 tablespoons hot water
1 cup orange juice
3 tablespoons orange-flavored liqueur
1/2 pint whipping cream (1 cup)
2 tablespoons powdered sugar
1/2 cup finely chopped walnuts
4 to 6 walnut halves

Pour milk into a small saucepan. Sprinkle gelatin
over top; let stand 5 minutes. Stir over low heat
until gelatin is dissolved. Set aside to cool. In a
medium bowl, combine egg yolks, granulated sugar
and hot water; beat until foamy. Add orange juice
and liqueur; beat until blended. Gradually beat in
cooled gelatin mixture until thoroughly blended.
Refrigerate 30 to 40 minutes or until mixture
mounds when dropped from a spoon. In a medium
bowl, beat cream until soft peaks form. Add
powdered sugar; beat until stiff peaks form.
Reserve 3/4 cup whipped cream; refrigerate. Fold
remaining whipped cream into orange-juice
mixture. In a medium bowl, beat egg whites until
stiff but not dry. Fold beaten egg whites and
chopped walnuts into orange cream. Spoon orange
cream into 4 to 6 dessert dishes or wine glasses;
refrigerate 2 to 3 hours or until thoroughly chilled.
To serve, spoon reserved whipped cream into a
pastry bag fitted with a rosette tip. Pipe whipped
cream decoratively on each dessert; decorate with
walnut halves. Makes 4 to 6 servings.

Caribbean Dreams

2 ripe mangos
1 pint pistachio-cherry ice cream
1/4 cup orange-flavored liqueur
Sweetened whipped cream
Chopped pistachios

Wash and dry mangos. Cut each mango in half lengthwise; carefully remove pits. Place mango halves, cut-side up, in 4 dessert dishes. Scoop ice cream into mango halves. Spoon 1 tablespoon liqueur over each serving. Decorate with sweetened whipped cream and pistachios. Serve immediately. Makes 4 servings.

Special Strawberry Ice-Cream Treat

Special Strawberry Ice-Cream Treat

1 pint strawberries (2 cups)
2 to 3 tablespoons sugar
4 to 5 tablespoons orange-flavored liqueur
1 pint strawberry ice cream
Sweetened whipped cream
Pistachios
Rolled cookies

Wash and hull strawberries. Slice 2 or 3 hulled strawberries; reserve for decoration. Place remaining strawberries in a small bowl. Sprinkle with sugar and liqueur; toss gently to coat. Let stand at room temperature 1 hour. Spoon strawberries and liquid that has formed into 4 chilled sherbet glasses. Scoop strawberry ice cream into small balls; place scoops on top of strawberries in sherbet glasses. Store in freezer until ready to serve.

To serve, decorate with sweetened whipped cream, reserved sliced strawberries and pistachios. Serve immediately with cookies. Makes 4 servings.

Frozen Strawberry Cream

1 pint fresh strawberries (2 cups), washed, hulled
1/2 cup sugar
1/2 cup cold water
2 (1/4-oz.) envelopes unflavored gelatin
4 eggs, separated
1/2 cup milk
Mint leaves

Wash and hull strawberries. Slice hulled strawberries; reserve 1/2 of sliced strawberries for decoration. In a blender or food processor fitted with a metal blade, process remaining sliced strawberries and sugar until pureed. Set aside. Pour water into a small saucepan. Sprinkle gelatin over top; let stand 5 minutes. Stir over low heat until gelatin is dissolved; set aside. In top of a double boiler, combine egg yolks and milk; beat until blended. Over simmering water, cook, stirring constantly, until thickened. Gradually beat in gelatin mixture. Pour into a medium bowl. Add strawberry puree; stir until blended. Cool to room temperature. In another medium bowl, beat egg whites until stiff peaks form; fold into strawberry mixture. Pour into a rigid freezer container; freeze 2 to 3 hours or until firm.

To serve, place in refrigerator 30 minutes to soften. Scoop frozen mixture into small balls. Place balls in individual serving dishes. Decorate with reserved sliced strawberries and mint leaves. Makes 6 to 8 servings.

Individual Sherry Charlottes

1/4 cup cold water
1 (1/4-oz.) envelope unflavored gelatin
3 egg yolks
1 tablespoon orange juice
1/2 cup sugar
1/2 cup sweet cream sherry
1/2 pint whipping cream (1 cup)
16 sponge cookies or ladyfingers
Maraschino cherries

Pour water into a small saucepan. Sprinkle gelatin over top; let stand 5 minutes. Stir over low heat until gelatin is dissolved; set aside. In a medium bowl, combine egg yolks, orange juice and sugar. Set bowl over, but not in, a pan of simmering water. Beat egg-yolk mixture until foamy; remove bowl from heat. Stir in gelatin mixture; beat until blended. Stir in 1/4 cup sherry. Refrigerate until mixture has consistency of unbeaten egg whites, about 25 minutes. In a small bowl, beat cream until stiff peaks form. Reserve 1/2 cup whipped cream; refrigerate.

Individual Sherry Charlottes

To serve, fold remaining whipped cream into egg-yolk mixture. Sprinkle remaining 1/4 cup sherry over sponge biscuits or ladyfingers. Spoon whipped-cream mixture into each of 4 dessert dishes or wine glasses. Place 4 sherry-laced biscuits or ladyfingers in dishes or glasses. Spoon reserved whipped cream into a pastry bag fitted with a small rosette tip. Pipe small swirls of whipped cream on top of each charlotte. Decorate each with a maraschino cherry. Refrigerate until ready to serve. Makes 4 servings.

Frozen Strawberry Cream

Shaved Chocolate

Melt 6 ounces sweet-chocolate pieces over hot water. Do not let water boil. Stir until smooth. Spread melted chocolate on a cold marble slab. When set, using a metal spatula, carefully slide spatula between marble and chocolate. As chocolate is loosened, it will roll.

Frozen Coffee Parfait

2 tablespoons instant coffee powder
1 tablespoon boiling water
6 egg yolks
3/4 cup granulated sugar
2 to 3 tablespoons coffee-flavored liqueur
1 pint whipping cream (2 cups)
3 to 4 tablespoons powdered sugar

Dissolve coffee powder in boiling water; set aside. In a medium bowl, combine egg yolks and granulated sugar; beat until foamy. Add dissolved coffee and liqueur; beat until blended. In a large bowl, beat cream until soft peaks form. Add powdered sugar; beat until stiff peaks form. Spoon 1 cup whipped cream; refrigerate. Fold remaining whipped cream into coffee mixture. Spoon coffee cream into 4 to 6 sherbet glasses or dessert dishes; freeze until firm.
To serve, spoon reserved whipped cream into a pastry bag fitted with a small rosette tip. Pipe whipped-cream rosettes decoratively on top of each parfait. Makes 4 to 6 servings.

Mocha Mousse

Mocha Mousse

5 oz. semisweet chocolate, broken into pieces
4 eggs
3 tablespoons sugar
2 tablespoons coffee-flavored liqueur
1 teaspoon instant coffee powder
3/4 cup whipping cream

Melt chocolate in a small saucepan over hot water, stirring until smooth. Set aside to cool. In a medium bowl, combine 1 egg, sugar, liqueur and instant coffee powder. Separate remaining 3 eggs. Add 3 egg yolks to sugar mixture; stir to blend. Set bowl over, but not in, a pan of simmering water. Beat with a whisk 5 minutes or until mixture is foamy. Remove bowl from heat; beat 5 minutes longer or until mixture forms stiff peaks. Fold in cooled melted chocolate. In a small bowl, beat cream until soft peaks form. Fold whipped cream into chocolate mixture. In a medium bowl, beat egg whites until stiff but not dry. Fold beaten egg whites into chocolate mixture. Spoon into dessert dishes; refrigerate 3 to 4 hours or until thoroughly chilled. Makes 4 to 6 servings.

Red-Wine Cream

1 (4-3/4-oz.) pkg. Danish-style raspberry
   pudding-and-pie-filling mix
1/3 cup granulated sugar
1 cup red wine
1 cup boiling water
1/2 pint whipping cream (1 cup)
2 tablespoons powdered sugar

In a medium saucepan, combine pudding-and-pie-filling mix, granulated sugar and red wine; stir until blended. Stir in boiling water until sugar is dissolved. Over low heat, cook, stirring constantly, until mixture comes to a boil. Reduce heat; simmer 1 minute. Pour into a large bowl; cool to room temperature, stirring occasionally. In a small bowl, beat cream until soft peaks form. Add powdered sugar; beat until stiff peaks form. Reserve about 1 cup whipped cream; refrigerate. Fold remaining whipped cream into red-wine pudding. Spoon into 6 dessert dishes or wine glasses. Refrigerate 3 to 4 hours or until thoroughly chilled.
To serve, spoon reserved whipped cream into a pastry bag fitted with a small rosette tip. Pipe whipped cream decoratively on each dessert. Makes 6 servings.

Fruity Sorbets

Fruity Sorbets

Photo on pages 180 and 181.

Assorted Iced Berries, see below
4 scoops lemon sorbet
4 scoops black-currant sorbet
4 scoops strawberry sorbet
Mint leaves

Prepare Iced Berries. Place 1 scoop of each kind of sorbet in each of 4 chilled dessert dishes. Decorate with Iced Berries and mint leaves. Makes 4 servings.

Iced Berries: Rinse berries under cold running water; drain well. Place in single layer on a baking sheet; freeze until firm. Let berries stand at room temperature 3 to 5 minutes before serving.

Note: Black-currant sorbet is available in some gourmet ice-cream shops.

Flaming Kiwifruit Heidelberg

1 pint eggnog-flavored ice cream
4 kiwifruit
2 tablespoons butter or margarine
1/4 cup finely chopped blanched almonds
3 tablespoons sugar
2 tablespoons orange juice
1/8 teaspoon ground cinnamon
1/4 cup apple-flavored brandy or cognac
Fan-shaped cookies or rolled cookies

Scoop ice cream into small balls; arrange in 4 chilled dessert dishes. Return to freezer until ready to serve. Peel kiwifruit; cut into thick slices. In a medium skillet, melt butter or margarine. Add almonds; stir constantly until lightly browned. Sprinkle with sugar; cook, stirring constantly until sugar is dissolved and caramel in color. Stir in orange juice and cinnamon. Add reserved kiwifruit slices; simmer until orange juice has almost evaporated. Remove from heat.
To serve, in a small saucepan, heat brandy or cognac. Add to kiwifruit mixture; carefully ignite. Quickly spoon over ice cream. Serve immediately with cookies. Makes 4 servings.

Peaches & Cream

2 (3-oz.) pkgs. cream cheese, room temperature
2 tablespoons milk
1 teaspoon almond extract
1/2 pint whipping cream (1 cup)
2 tablespoons powdered sugar
1/3 cup finely ground blanched almonds
12 canned peach halves, well drained
Strawberry ice-cream topping

Place 6 dessert plates in freezer to chill. In a medium bowl, combine cream cheese, milk and almond extract; beat until fluffy. In another medium bowl, beat cream until soft peaks form. Add powdered sugar; beat until stiff peaks form. Fold whipped cream into cream-cheese mixture. Fold in ground almonds. Spoon mixture into a pastry bag fitted with a rosette tip. Place 2 peach halves, cut-side up, on each chilled plate. Pipe cream-cheese mixture decoratively into peach cavities. Refrigerate until ready to serve.
To serve, spoon strawberry topping over each serving. Makes 6 servings.

Kiwi Dreams

Kiwi Dreams

1 qt. vanilla ice cream
1 pint banana-rum or eggnog flavored ice cream
4 to 6 kiwifruit
Honey
Toasted chopped hazelnuts
Sweetened whipped cream
Rolled cookies

Place vanilla ice cream in a medium bowl; let stand at room temperature 10 minutes to soften. Wet a large spoon; use to stir softened vanilla ice cream. Spoon 1/3 of softened ice cream into a small bowl; place in freezer. Pack remaining softened vanilla ice cream into an 8" x 4" loaf pan, spreading ice cream over bottom and 2/3 up sides of pan, making a shell. Freeze until firm. Spoon banana-rum or eggnog-flavored ice cream into a medium bowl; let stand at room temperature 10 minutes to soften. Wet a large spoon; use to stir softened ice cream. Pack softened ice cream into center of frozen vanilla shell; smooth top. Freeze until firm. Remove reserved vanilla ice cream from freezer; let stand at room temperature 5 minutes to soften. Spread over top of firm-frozen ice cream, sealing to sides of shell and covering completely. Cover with foil; freeze 3 to 4 hours or until firm. Place a platter or serving plate in freezer to chill. Invert loaf pan onto chilled platter or serving plate. Wet a dish towel in hot water; wring dry. Place hot wet towel around mold. Leave 5 to 10 seconds; remove mold and cloth. Return to freezer until ready to serve.

To serve, peel and slice kiwifruit. Cut ice-cream loaf into 12 slices. Place 1 slice on each of 6 dessert dishes. Top with kiwifruit slices. Drizzle honey over kiwifruit slices; sprinkle with chopped hazelnuts. Top each with a second ice-cream slice. Decorate with sweetened whipped cream. Serve immediately with cookies. Makes 6 servings.

Cherry-Orange Delight

1 pint cherry-vanilla or black-cherry ice cream
1/2 cup whipping cream
1 tablespoon powdered sugar
1 to 2 tablespoons cherry-flavored liqueur
12 orange slices, peeled
12 maraschino cherries
Chopped pistachios

Scoop ice cream into small balls. Place ice-cream balls in 4 chilled dessert dishes; place in freezer. In a small bowl, beat cream until soft peaks form. Add powdered sugar and liqueur; beat until stiff peaks form.

To serve, place 3 orange slices in each dish with ice cream. Decorate with whipped cream, cherries and pistachios. Makes 4 servings.

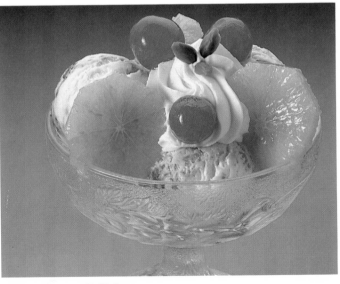

Cherry-Orange Delight

Château Royale Sundaes

10 tablespoons chocolate sauce
1/4 cup brandy or coffee-flavored liqueur
1/4 cup whipping cream
1 to 2 tablespoons finely chopped crystallized ginger
1 pint vanilla ice cream
1 pint coffee-flavored ice cream
Sweetened whipped cream
Banana slices
Mandarin-orange sections
Maraschino cherries
Chopped pistachios
Fancy cookies

In a small bowl, combine chocolate sauce, brandy or liqueur, whipping cream and ginger; stir until blended. Pour mixture into 6 to 8 chilled sherbet glasses. Scoop vanilla and coffee-flavored ice cream into small balls. Divide evenly among glasses. Place in freezer until ready to serve.

To serve, decorate each portion with sweetened whipped cream, bananas, orange sections, cherries and pistachios. Serve with cookies. Makes 6 to 8 servings.

Château Royale Sundaes

Pineapple Sherbet Aloha

1 large ripe mango
3 to 4 tablespoons dark rum
1 pint pineapple sherbet
1 pint praline or caramel-fudge ice cream
Chopped macadamia nuts

Peel mango; remove pit. Cut mango flesh into cubes; place mango cubes in a small bowl. Sprinkle with rum; toss gently. Cover and refrigerate at least 2 hours. Cover a baking sheet with waxed paper. Scoop sherbet and ice cream into small balls. Place ice cream and sherbet balls on lined baking sheet. Return to freezer; freeze until firm.

To serve, arrange ice-cream and sherbet balls in 6 to 8 chilled dessert dishes. Decorate with mango cubes and macadamia nuts. Makes 6 to 8 servings.

Maple-Nut Sundaes

1 pint maple-nut ice cream
4 to 6 tablespoons crème de cacao

To decorate:
Sweetened whipped cream
Chopped walnuts
4 maraschino cherries

Scoop ice cream into small balls. Place ice-cream balls in 4 chilled dessert dishes or sherbet glasses. Spoon 1 to 1-1/2 tablespoons crème de cacao over each serving. Decorate with sweetened whipped cream and chopped walnuts. Top each with a maraschino cherry. Serve immediately. Makes 4 servings.

Chocolate-Rum Box

Chocolate-Rum Box

1 qt. chocolate ice cream
1 pint rum-raisin ice cream
4 or 5 bananas
Lemon juice
Sweetened whipped cream
Maraschino cherries
Shaved chocolate, page 189
Lychee nuts, if desired

Place chocolate ice cream in a medium bowl; let stand at room temperature 10 minutes to soften. Wet a large spoon; use to stir softened chocolate ice cream. Spoon 1/3 of softened ice cream into a small bowl; place in freezer. Pack remaining softened chocolate ice cream into an 8" x 4" loaf pan, spreading ice cream over bottom and 2/3 up sides of pan, making a shell. Freeze until firm. Place rum-raisin ice cream in a medium bowl; let stand at room temperature 10 minutes to soften. Wet a large spoon; use to stir softened rum-raisin ice cream. Pack softened rum-raisin ice cream into center of frozen chocolate shell; smooth top. Freeze until firm. Remove reserved chocolate ice cream from freezer; let stand at room temperature 5 minutes to soften. Spread over top of rum-raisin ice cream, sealing to sides of shell, covering completely. Cover with foil; freeze 3 to 4 hours or until firm. Place a platter or serving plate in freezer to chill 15 minutes. Invert loaf pan onto chilled platter or serving plate. Wet a dish towel in hot water; wring dry. Place hot wet towel around mold. Leave 5 to 10 seconds; remove mold and cloth. Return frozen mixture to freezer until ready to serve.

To serve, slice bananas diagonally; sprinkle all sides with lemon juice. Arrange on 6 dessert plates as shown. Cut ice-cream loaf into 12 slices. Place 2 slices over bananas in each dish. Decorate with sweetened whipped cream, maraschino cherries, shaved chocolate and lychee nuts, if desired. Serve immediately. Makes 6 servings.

Blackberry Delight

1/2 pint fresh blackberries (1 cup)
2 to 3 tablespoons sugar
1 pint vanilla ice cream
Blackberry syrup
Sweetened whipped cream

Wash blackberries; drain well. Place drained blackberries in a small bowl. Sprinkle with sugar; toss lightly to distribute sugar. Refrigerate until ready to serve.

To serve, scoop small balls of ice cream into 4 sherbet glasses. Spoon blackberry syrup over ice cream. Decorate with sweetened whipped cream and sugared blackberries. Serve immediately. Makes 4 servings.

Blackberry Delight

Exotic Magic

Exotic Magic

**4 ice-cream rolls of desired flavors, such as hazelnut,
  butter crunch, toasted almond, from
  Aladdin's Magic Lamp, page 198**
1/2 cup whipping cream
1 tablespoon powdered sugar
1/2 teaspoon vanilla extract
4 kiwifruit
Toasted coconut
Mint leaves

Prepare and freeze ice-cream rolls according to
directions. Place a platter and 4 serving dishes in
freezer to chill. Remove ice-cream rolls from juice
containers. Cut each roll into 4 slices. Place on
chilled platter; return to freezer. In a small bowl,
beat cream until soft peaks form. Add powdered
sugar and vanilla; beat until stiff peaks form. Peel
and slice kiwifruit.
To serve, arrange ice-cream slices and kiwifruit
alternately on chilled dessert dishes. Spoon whipped
cream on top of ice-cream slices. Sprinkle with
toasted coconut; decorate with mint leaves. Makes
4 servings.

Note: These are large servings. Cut servings in half,
if desired.

Banana-Ginger Ice Cream

2 eggs
2 tablespoons sugar
3 tablespoons honey
2 tablespoons syrup from stem ginger preserved in syrup
2 tablespoons lemon juice
3 ripe bananas, mashed
1/2 pint half and half (1 cup)
1/2 pint whipping cream (1 cup)
**5 or 6 whole stem ginger preserved in syrup, drained,
  coarsely chopped**
Chocolate sauce

In a medium bowl, beat eggs until foamy. Add
sugar, honey and ginger syrup; beat until
thoroughly blended. Stir in lemon juice, bananas,
half and half, whipping cream and ginger. Pour into
an ice-cream canister. Freeze in an ice-cream maker
according to manufacturer's directions.
To serve, scoop ice cream into 6 to 8 dessert dishes.
Serve with chocolate sauce. Makes 6 to 8 servings.

Apple-Grape Sorbet

2 cups white-grape juice
1/4 cup lemon juice
1/2 cup sugar
3 tablespoons light corn syrup
1 Golden Delicious apple
Seedless red and green grapes

In a medium saucepan, combine grape juice, lemon juice, sugar and corn syrup; stir until blended. Over low heat, cook, stirring constantly, until sugar is completely dissolved. Pour into a medium bowl. Peel, core and grate apple. Add grated apple to grape-juice mixture; stir until blended. Cool to room temperature. Freeze until ice crystals form around edge of bowl. Remove from freezer; beat vigorously with a fork or whisk. Return to freezer; freeze 2 to 3 hours.

To serve, scoop sorbet into small balls; place in 6 to 8 dessert dishes. Decorate with grapes. Makes 6 to 8 servings.

Ice-Cream Fondue

Ice-Cream Fondue

6 ice-cream rolls in assorted flavors, from Aladdin's Magic Lamp, page 198

Assorted toppings:
Sweetened whipped cream
Grated or shaved chocolate, page 189
Chocolate sprinkles
Multi-colored sprinkles
Strawberry, cherry or fudge ice-cream topping
Almond Praline from Almond-Custard Ring, page 182

Prepare and freeze ice-cream rolls according to directions. Remove ice-cream rolls from juice containers; cut each in half. Arrange on a platter or serving plate. Return to freezer until ready to serve.

To serve, place assorted toppings in separate small bowls. Fill a shallow bowl with cracked ice; place platter or plate with ice-cream rolls over ice. Surround with small dishes of assorted toppings. Makes 6 to 12 servings.

Apple-Grape Sorbet

Cassis Summer Bombe

1 pint Cassis or other black-currant sorbet
1/2 pint whipping cream (1 cup)
1 tablespoon powdered sugar
1 to 2 tablespoons black-currant-flavored liqueur
Shaved chocolate, page 189

Place a platter or serving plate in freezer 30 minutes. Let sorbet stand at room temperature 5 to 10 minutes to soften. Cut container with sharp scissors, keeping sorbet in 1 solid piece. Place on chilled platter or plate; return to freezer. Freeze until firm. In a medium bowl, beat cream until soft peaks form. Add powdered sugar and liqueur; beat until stiff peaks form. Spoon whipped cream into a pastry bag fitted with a medium open-star tip. Pipe whipped cream in circles around sorbet starting at bottom and covering sorbet completely. Freeze 1 hour.

To serve, decorate with shaved chocolate. Dipping a sharp knife in hot water, cut decorated sorbet into 4 wedges. Makes 4 servings.

Note: Sorbet should be in a round container. If it is not, spoon softened sorbet into a 2- to 3-inch-deep, round container. Freeze until firm. Remove from container in a solid piece. Decorate as directed above.

Tropical Neapolitan

Maraschino cherries
Banana slices
Mandarin-orange sections
Honeydew or cantaloupe cubes
Strawberry syrup
1/2 gallon brick Neapolitan ice cream

Place 12 dessert dishes in freezer to chill. Thread cherries, bananas, orange sections and melon cubes onto 12 to 24 (4-inch) wooden picks; set aside. Spoon 2 tablespoons syrup into each chilled dish.
To serve, let ice cream stand at room temperature 5 to 10 minutes to soften. Cut ice-cream brick in half lengthwise. Cut each half into 6 slices. Place 1 slice in each dessert dish. Decorate each ice-cream slice with 1 or 2 fruit picks. Makes 12 servings.

Tropical Neapolitan

Flaming Ice-Cream-Filled Crepes

Flaming Ice-Cream-Filled Crepes

6 ice-cream rolls made with vanilla ice cream, from
   Aladdin's Magic Lamp, opposite
6 crepes from Fruit-Filled Crepes, page 179
Shredded or flaked coconut
1/2 cup dark or light rum

Prepare and freeze ice-cream rolls according to directions. Place a platter in freezer to chill. Remove ice-cream rolls from juice containers. Place on chilled platter; return to freezer. Prepare crepes according to directions. Sprinkle crepes with coconut.
To serve, place 1 ice-cream roll on center of each coconut-covered crepe; roll up. Place filled crepes, seam-side down, on a wire rack set over a shallow flameproof tray. Warm rum in a small saucepan over low heat. Pour warm rum over crepes; carefully ignite. Serve while still flaming. Makes 6 servings.

Aladdin's Magic Lamp

Ice-Cream Rolls:
1 qt. strawberry ice cream

Wine Cream:
1 egg
2 tablespoons sugar
1 teaspoon cornstarch
1/2 cup sweet white wine
3 strawberries

To make ice-cream rolls, spoon ice cream into a medium bowl. Let stand at room temperature 10 minutes to soften. Rinse a large spoon with water; use to stir ice cream. Spoon softened ice cream into 6 (6-ounce) empty frozen-juice cans, leaving about 1/3-inch headspace at top of each container. Place filled containers on a small baking sheet; freeze until very firm, 4 to 5 hours. Place a dessert dish or platter in freezer 30 minutes before ice-cream rolls are to be unmolded. Dip containers, 1 at a time, into a small bowl of hot water. Invert onto chilled dish or platter. Use a can opener to remove bottom of container. Use can bottom to push out ice-cream roll. Repeat with remaining ice-cream rolls. Return to freezer until ready to serve.

To make wine cream, in a small bowl, combine egg, sugar, cornstarch and wine; stir until blended. Set bowl over a pan of simmering water. Beat with electric mixer until thick and foamy. Do not let mixture come to a boil. Remove from heat.

To serve, spoon Wine Cream over ice-cream rolls. Cut strawberries in half. Top each ice-cream roll with a strawberry half. Makes 6 servings.

Note: These make 5-1/2-ounce servings. If desired, cut ice-cream rolls in half. Slice strawberries into 12 pieces.

Pistachio-Apricot Scoops

Pistachio-Apricot Scoops

1 pint pistachio ice cream
12 canned apricot halves, well drained
Raspberry or strawberry syrup
Sweetened whipped cream
Toasted slivered almonds
Rolled cookies

Scoop ice cream into 12 small balls. Place 3 ice-cream balls in each of 4 chilled dessert dishes. Top each ice-cream ball with an apricot half. Spoon syrup over apricots.

To serve, decorate with sweetened whipped cream and almonds. Serve with cookies. Makes 4 servings.

Aladdin's Magic Lamp

Amaretto Sundaes

Amaretto Sundaes

1/4 cup chocolate syrup
1/4 cup amaretto liqueur
1 pint amaretto-nut or caramel-nut ice cream
Sweetened whipped cream
Whole almonds
Rolled cookies

In a small bowl, combine chocolate syrup and liqueur; stir until blended. Pour into 4 chilled sherbet glasses. Scoop ice cream into small balls; place in glasses. Return to freezer until ready to serve.
To serve, decorate with sweetened whipped cream and almonds. Serve with cookies. Makes 4 servings.

Cardinal Peaches & Ice Cream

1 pint caramel-nut, butter-pecan or praline ice cream
4 canned peach halves, drained
Raspberry or strawberry syrup
Toasted almond slivers
Sweetened whipped cream
Fan-shaped cookies

Scoop ice cream into small balls; place in 4 chilled dessert dishes. Return to freezer until ready to serve.
To serve, top each serving with a peach half. Spoon syrup over top; sprinkle with toasted almonds. Top with a dollop of sweetened whipped cream. Serve with cookies. Makes 4 servings.

Sherbet & Grape Sundaes

1 lb. seedless red grapes
1 pint raspberry sherbet
1 pint orange sherbet
Pecan ice-cream topping
Sweetened whipped cream
Toasted coconut
Chopped pecans

Rinse and dry grapes. Scoop raspberry and orange sherbets into small balls. Place an equal number in each of 6 to 8 chilled sherbet glasses. Return to freezer until ready to serve.
To serve, add grapes; spoon topping over each serving. Decorate with sweetened whipped cream, coconut and pecans. Makes 6 to 8 servings.

Cardinal Peaches & Ice Cream

Chocolate-Coated Ice Cream Petits Fours

Chocolate-Coated Ice Cream Petits Fours

6 ice-cream rolls made with vanilla or chocolate ice cream, from Aladdin's Magic Lamp, page 198

Chocolate Coating:
5 oz. semisweet chocolate, broken into pieces
3 tablespoons vegetable shortening

To decorate:
Sweetened whipped cream
Maraschino cherries
Blackberries
Red currants
Whole hazelnuts
Walnut halves
Chopped pistachios
Chocolate-coated coffee-bean candies

Prepare and freeze ice-cream rolls according to directions. Remove ice-cream rolls from juice containers; cut each in half. Place on a platter or large plate; return to freezer until ready to serve.

To make chocolate coating, in a small saucepan, melt chocolate and shortening over low heat, stirring until smooth. Set aside to cool.

To complete, remove ice-cream rolls from freezer. Using a short metal skewer, pierce 1 roll on top. Holding skewer, dip roll into cooled chocolate mixture, coating bottom and side. After chocolate sets on ice-cream roll, remove from skewer, being careful not to touch coating. Place chocolate-coated ice-cream roll in a small dessert dish, coated-end up; return to freezer. Repeat with remaining ice-cream rolls. Freeze until ready to serve.

To serve, decorate with sweetened whipped cream, fruit, nuts and candies. Makes 12 coated ice-cream rolls.

Beverages

Frozen Daiquiri

1 (6-oz.) can frozen limeade concentrate
5 jiggers white rum
Ice cubes
6 to 8 lime slices

In a blender, combine limeade and rum. Fill container with ice cubes. Process until ice is crushed and mixture is frothy. Pour into 6 to 8 large wine glasses. Garnish each with a lime slice. Makes 6 to 8 servings.

Variation

Frozen Non-Alcoholic Daiquiri: Omit rum. Combine 1 cup daiquiri mix and 1/3 cup sugar with limeade. Process as above.

Gin Fizz

2 jiggers gin
1 tablespoon superfine sugar
1 jigger lemon juice
1/2 jigger lime juice
3 to 4 ice cubes
Club soda

In a drink shaker, combine gin, sugar, lemon juice, lime juice and ice cubes. Shake vigorously; strain into a tall chilled drinking glass. Fill with club soda. Makes 1 serving.

Variation

Sloe Gin Fizz: Substitute 1 jigger gin and 1 jigger sloe gin for 2 jiggers gin.

Vermouth Cocktail

Vermouth Cocktail

Ice cubes
2 jiggers dry vermouth
1/2 jigger lemon juice
Mint leaves

Place ice cubes in a cocktail glass. Add vermouth and lemon juice. Garnish with mint. Makes 1 serving.

Party Scotch Sours

1 (6-oz.) can frozen lemonade
3/4 cup scotch
3/4 cup water
Ice cubes
6 maraschino cherries
6 orange slices

In a blender, combine frozen lemonade, scotch and water. Fill with ice cubes. Process on high until ice is crushed and mixture is frothy. Pour into 6 glasses. Garnish each with a cherry and an orange slice. Makes 6 servings.

On previous pages: Tequilla Splash, page 206

Rum-Watermelon Cocktail

Rum-Watermelon Cocktail

1 (1-1/2- to 2-lb.) watermelon
Juice of 1 lemon
1/2 cup white rum
1 lime, cut in 6 slices

Scoop out 12 melon balls; set aside. Cut remaining melon flesh into small pieces. Process in a blender or food processor fitted with a metal blade until pureed. Pour into a large bowl; stir in lemon juice and rum. Cover; refrigerate 1 hour. Pour into 6 drinking glasses. Garnish each cocktail with 2 melon balls and 1 lime slice. Makes 6 servings.

Eggnog

2 jiggers brandy
1 cup milk
1 egg
1 tablespoon superfine sugar
1 teaspoon vanilla extract
1/2 cup crushed ice
Ground nutmeg

In a drink shaker, combine brandy, milk, egg, sugar, vanilla and ice; shake vigorously. Strain into a tall drinking glass. Sprinkle with nutmeg. Makes 1 serving.

Variation

Non-Alcoholic Eggnog: Omit brandy.

Eggnog

Spiked Citrus Punch

2 lemons, thinly sliced
2 oranges, thinly sliced
1 lb. seedless green grapes
Ice cubes
3 jiggers gin
3 jiggers dry vermouth
1 (1-liter) bottle dry white wine
1 (1-liter) bottle lemon-lime soda

Place lemons, oranges, grapes and ice cubes in a punch bowl. Add gin and vermouth. Slowly pour wine and soda into bowl at the same time. Stir gently. Makes 32 servings.

Spiked Citrus Punch

Orange Piña Colada

Southern Delight

Orange Piña Colada

1 cup cream of coconut
1-1/2 cups pineapple juice
1/2 cup orange juice
1-1/2 cups white rum
Ice cubes
Mint sprigs, maraschino cherries or pineapple sticks,
   if desired

In a blender, combine cream of coconut, pineapple juice, orange juice and rum. Fill with ice cubes. Process on high until ice is crushed and mixture is thick and frothy. Pour into 4 large wine glasses; garnish with mint, cherries or pineapple sticks, if desired. Makes 4 servings.

Tequila Splash

Photo on pages 202 and 203.

2 ice cubes
1 lime slice
2 maraschino cherries
2 jiggers tequila
Lemonade

Combine ice cubes, lime, and cherries in a tall, slender drinking glass. Add tequila. Fill glass with lemonade. Makes 1 serving.

Southern Delight

1 lemon
4 ice cubes
2 jiggers orange-flavored liqueur
Tonic water

Cut 2 long strips of lemon peel. Remove white pith from peel. Squeeze juice from lemon; reserve juice. Place ice cubes in 2 tall drinking glasses. Pour 1 jigger liqueur and 2 teaspoons lemon juice over ice in each glass. Fill with tonic water; garnish with lemon peel. Makes 2 servings.

Strawberry-Champagne Punch

1 pint strawberries (2 cups)
6 tablespoons superfine sugar
1/2 cup strawberry liqueur or brandy
1 (750 ml) bottle champagne or sparkling wine, chilled

Wash and hull strawberries. Cut each in half; place in a punch bowl. Sprinkle with sugar; toss to coat. Pour strawberry liqueur or brandy over berries; let stand 1 hour. Slowly pour champagne or wine into punch bowl. Ladle into punch glasses. Makes about 8 servings.

Exotic Punch

1 small honeydew melon
8 pitted dates
2 jiggers brandy
2 kiwifruit
3 (750-ml) bottles white wine, chilled
1 (750-ml) bottle champagne or sparkling wine

Scoop out melon balls; place in punch bowl. Slice dates; add to punch bowl. Add brandy; toss to distribute. Cover; let stand 1 hour. Peel and slice kiwifruit. Add sliced kiwifruit and 1 bottle white wine to punch bowl; let stand 1 hour. Add remaining white wine and champagne or sparkling wine when punch is served. Makes about 40 servings.

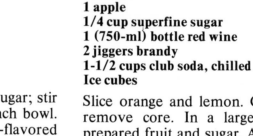

Exotic Punch

Champagne Punch

3 cups lemon juice
1 cup superfine sugar
1 (6-inch-square) ice block
1 cup cherry-flavored liqueur
1 (500-ml) bottle curaçao
1 (500-ml) bottle brandy
2 (750-ml) bottles champagne, chilled
1 (1-liter) bottle club soda
Fruit in season

In a large bowl, combine lemon juice and sugar; stir until sugar is dissolved. Place ice in a punch bowl. Pour sugar mixture over ice. Add cherry-flavored liqueur, curaçao and brandy. Slowly pour champagne and club soda into bowl at the same time. Stir gently. Decorate with fruit. Makes about 40 servings.

Sangria

1 orange
1 lemon
1 apple
1/4 cup superfine sugar
1 (750-ml) bottle red wine
2 jiggers brandy
1-1/2 cups club soda, chilled
Ice cubes

Slice orange and lemon. Cut apple into 8 wedges; remove core. In a large glass pitcher, combine prepared fruit and sugar. Add wine and brandy; stir well. Refrigerate several hours. To serve, add club soda and ice. Makes about 8 servings.

Aperitif Kir

2 jiggers chilled dry white wine
1/2 jigger crème de cassis

Pour wine into a chilled wine glass. Stir in crème de cassis. Makes 1 serving.

Crème de Menthe Glow

Photo on page 211.

1 jigger crème de menthe
1 jigger vodka
3 tablespoons frozen orange-juice concentrate, thawed
Lemonade

Combine crème de menthe, vodka and orange-juice concentrate in a tall drinking glass. Stir to blend. Fill glass with lemonade. Makes 1 serving.

Aperitif Kir

Virgin Island Champagne

1/2 teaspoon banana-flavored liqueur or brandy
1/2 teaspoon white rum
Dash Angostura Bitters
Chilled champagne
1 banana slice

Combine liqueur or brandy, rum and bitters in a chilled champagne glass; stir gently. Fill glass with champagne; top with banana slice. Makes 1 serving.

Blue Angel

1/2 jigger blue curaçao
Chilled champagne or sparkling wine

Pour curaçao into a chilled champagne glass. Fill glass with champagne or wine. Makes 1 serving.

Apricot Blossom

1/2 jigger apricot-flavored liqueur
Chilled champagne or sparkling wine
Dash Angostura Bitters

Pour apricot liqueur into a chilled champagne glass. Fill glass with champagne or wine. Add bitters; stir gently. Makes 1 serving.

Black Velvet

1/2 cup dark beer
Chilled champagne

Slowly pour beer into a chilled champagne glass. Slowly fill with champagne. Makes 1 serving.

Note: This mixture must be poured very carefully to prevent foaming.

Frosty Chocolate Shake

About 2 cups milk
About 1 pint chocolate ice cream
1/2 teaspoon vanilla extract

In a blender, combine 2 cups milk, 1 pint ice cream and vanilla. Process until blended, thick and smooth. Add more milk or ice cream as desired. Makes 4 servings.

From left to right: Virgin Island Champagne, Blue Angel, Apricot Blossom, Black Velvet, Sparkling Kirsch Champagne, Champagne Kir

Sparkling Kirsch Champagne

1 teaspoon grenadine
1/2 jigger kirsch
1/2 jigger orange juice
Chilled champagne or sparkling wine

In a chilled champagne glass, combine grenadine, kirsch and orange juice. Fill with champagne or wine. Makes 1 serving.

Champagne Kir

1 jigger crème de cassis or cassis syrup
Chilled champagne

Pour liqueur or syrup into a chilled champagne glass. Fill with champagne. Makes 1 serving.

California Punch

1 (6-oz.) can frozen lemonade concentrate
1 (6-oz.) can frozen limeade concentrate
1 (6-oz.) can frozen grapefruit-juice concentrate
Water
About 24 ice cubes
1 lemon, sliced

In a punch bowl, combine frozen concentrates. Add water to reconstitute. Stir until concentrates are thawed. Add ice; float lemon slices on top of punch. Makes 10 to 12 servings.

Three-Juice Cocktail

1 lime
Sugar
1 cup pineapple juice
1/2 cup unsweetened grapefruit juice
1/2 cup pear nectar
8 ice cubes

Cut 4 slices from center of lime. Use remaining lime to moisten rims of 4 glasses. Dip glass rims in sugar. In a large bowl, combine pineapple juice, grapefruit juice and pear nectar; stir well. Place 2 ice cubes in each of 4 cocktail glasses. Pour juice mixture over ice. Garnish each glass with a lime slice. Serve with straws. Makes 4 servings.

Variation

Add 3 jiggers white rum with fruit juices.

Three-Juice Cocktail

Spiced Cider

2 tablespoons whole cloves
2 (3-inch) cinnamon sticks
2 whole allspice or 1 teaspoon ground allspice
1 gal. apple cider
1 orange, sliced
1 lemon, sliced
Ice cubes

Tie cloves, cinnamon and whole allspice in a piece of cheesecloth. Pour cider into a 6-quart pot. Add spice bag. Add orange, lemon and ground allspice, if used. Bring to a simmer. Cover; set aside to steep 2 hours. Remove and discard spice bag. Refrigerate until thoroughly chilled. Serve over ice. Makes 32 (1/2-cup) servings.

Cardinal Punch

1 cup cranberry juice
1/2 cup orange juice
1/4 cup lemon juice
8 to 10 ice cubes
Ginger ale

In a blender, combine juices and ice cubes. Process until ice is broken and mixture is frothy. Pour into 4 drinking glasses or goblets. Fill glasses with ginger ale. Makes 4 servings.

Shirley Temple

1/2 cup passion-fruit juice
1 cup pineapple juice
8 to 10 ice cubes
Lemonade
4 pineapple sticks or slices
4 maraschino cherries

In a blender, combine juices and ice cubes. Process until ice is broken and mixture is frothy. Pour into 4 highball glasses or short drinking glasses. Fill glasses with lemonade. Spear each cherry with a wooden pick. Press other end of each pick into a pineapple stick or slice; use to decorate glasses. Makes 4 servings.

Orange Flip

1 cup orange juice
2/3 cup whipping cream
Sugar to taste
Orange slice, if desired

In a blender, combine orange juice, cream and sugar; process until thick and smooth. Pour into a tall glass. Garnish with an orange slice, if desired. Makes 1 serving.

Frozen-Strawberry Milkshake

1 pint milk or half and half (2 cups)
1/3 cup sugar or honey
1/2 teaspoon vanilla extract
1 (20-oz.) pkg. frozen whole strawberries

In a blender or food processor fitted with a metal blade, combine milk or half and half, sugar or honey and vanilla. With machine running, drop strawberries through feed tube, 1 or 2 at a time, until mixture is frothy and thickens. Makes 4 servings.

Cranberry-Sherbet Punch

2 pints raspberry sherbet
1 (16-oz.) can frozen cranberry-juice-cocktail concentrate, thawed
1/2 cup lemon juice
3 cups orange juice
3/4 cup sugar
2 (28-oz.) bottles ginger ale or lemon-lime soda, chilled

Soften 1 pint sherbet. Reconstitute cranberry-juice cocktail. In a punch bowl, combine softened sherbet, lemon juice, orange juice and sugar. Stir until sugar is dissolved. Stir in reconstituted cranberry-juice cocktail. Refrigerate until ready to serve. To serve, add ginger ale or lemon-lime soda. Spoon or scoop remaining sherbet into pieces or balls; float on top of punch. Makes about 30 (1/2-cup) servings.

Strawberry Milkshake

Strawberry Milkshake

1 pint strawberries (2 cups)
3 tablespoons superfine sugar
1 pint half and half (2 cups)
1 pint milk (2 cups)
4 teaspoons finely chopped walnuts

Wash and hull strawberries. Cut 2 strawberries in half; reserve for garnish. Process remaining strawberries in a blender or food processor fitted with a metal blade until pureed. Add sugar, half and half and milk; process until combined. Pour into 4 decorative drinking glasses. Garnish each with 1 teaspoon chopped walnuts and 1/2 strawberry. Serve immediately. Makes 4 servings.

Drivers' Fizz

4 ice cubes
2 eggs
3 tablespoons powdered sugar
1 teaspoon vanilla extract
1 cup milk
Club soda
Ground nutmeg

In a blender, combine ice cubes, eggs, powdered sugar, vanilla and milk. Process until ice is crushed and mixture is frothy. Pour into 4 mugs or glasses. Fill each with club soda. Sprinkle each with nutmeg. Garnish with shamrocks. Makes 4 servings.

Cucumber Drink

1 cucumber
1 tablespoon half and half
2 to 3 ice cubes
Salt and freshly ground pepper
1 dill sprig

Peel cucumber; cut a slice from center. Reserve cucumber slice. Remove seeds from remaining cucumber pieces. Cut seeded cucumber into chunks. In a blender, combine cucumber chunks, half and half, ice cubes. Season with salt and pepper. Process until smooth. Pour into a tall drinking glass; garnish with cucumber slice and dill sprig. Makes 1 serving.

Fruit Flip

1 cup orange juice
2 cups grape juice
1 cup carbonated orange drink
1 tablespoon lemon juice
4 thin lemon-peel strips
2 orange slices, cut in half

Pour orange juice into 1/2 of an ice-cube tray to make 8 orange-juice cubes. Place in freezer until frozen. In a drink shaker, combine orange-juice ice cubes, grape juice, carbonated orange drink and lemon juice; shake vigorously. Pour into 4 drinking glasses. Garnish each with a lemon-peel strip and 1/2 orange slice. Makes 4 servings.

Left to right: Tomato Drink, Cucumber Drink, Crème de Menthe Glow

Left to right: Fruit Flip, Driver's Fizz

Tomato Drink

2 tomatoes
1/2 cup cubed honeydew melon
1 teaspoon lemon juice
Dash Worcestershire sauce
2 to 3 ice cubes
Salt
Red (cayenne) pepper
2 tablespoons dairy sour cream
Paprika

Peel and quarter tomatoes; remove seeds. In a blender, combine tomato quarters, melon, lemon juice, Worcestershire sauce and ice cubes. Process until smooth. Add salt and red pepper to taste. Pour into 2 tall glasses; garnish each with 1 tablespoon sour cream. Sprinkle each with paprika. Makes 2 servings.

Helpful Hints

Helpful Hints

BE READY FOR UNEXPECTED GUESTS

Unexpected guests can appear on your doorstep at any time. Be ready to offer something good—something cold. Some foods must be stored in your refrigerator or freezer, while others can be stored at room temperature or at least in a cool, dry place. Canned goods keep well and offer a wide variety.

To make it easy on your pocketbook, add a few items to your storage each time you go shopping. Everything won't be used in a single meal, but should be rotated periodically. For example, when you use a can of water chestnuts, buy another to replace it. If not used for company, treat your family or neighbors to a cold meal from your stock of canned, refrigerated and frozen foods. Those things that were purchased first should be used first.

Following are some ingredients to help you arrange a cold buffet quickly. You probably already have many of them. Add other things as you desire. With stored foods, you will enjoy preparing a surprise meal for your surprise guests.

Cupboard storage is ideal for noodles and other pasta, rice, crackers, packaged pastries, coffee, tea, nuts and sauces, such as horseradish or barbecue sauce. Pudding mixes, basic baking mixes and cake and pie mixes are also possible storage items. Canned foods for storage might include milk, meats, spices, vegetables, tomato sauce, tomato puree, pickles, olives, fish, shellfish, fruit, fruit juices, vegetable juices and soups.

Refrigerator-storage items include those things you usually keep there, such as eggs, butter, milk, mayonnaise and salad dressing. Ketchup, mustard and Worcestershire sauce may be stored in the cupboard or refrigerator. Also keep on hand fresh meat, firm cheese, sweet or sour cream, yogurt, cottage cheese, sausage, fresh vegetables and fresh fruit.

Freezer space can be used to store most foods. Be sure to include vegetables, fruit, fruit juices, meat, fish and poultry. Plan ahead for cold meals using shrimp, lobster, crab, sausages, smoked salmon, game, bread, cream, butter, nuts, ice cream and whipped topping. When time allows, prepare terrines and freezable spreads. After freezing terrines, remove them from their baking pan and wrap them in freezer wrap. Place them back in their baking pans for easy thawing.

Beverages can also be stored in your cupboard, refrigerator or freezer. Be sure to have canned or bottled juices. Your freezer supply of fruit juices will give you something to offer hot or weary guests. Soft drinks are a possible storage item, and you may also want to have wine, brandy or liqueur on hand.

Make guests feel at ease by having a nicely decorated home, lovely music and an inviting array of appetizers and other cold foods.

There are several ways you can serve your guests. Use the one that best fits the occasion and is most convenient for you. Serving cold cuisine is easy, because everything can be done ahead of time.

Buffet service lets you arrange food on the table before guests arrive. Then you are free to mingle and talk. Place all food on one or two tables. If the group is large, arrange serving tables so guests can serve themselves from either side. If space is small, have the food on one table and the drinks and desserts on another table. Arrange food so the normal flow of traffic takes your guests from one course to the next. Place plates, silver and napkins at the beginning course.

With buffet service, guests serve themselves, choosing those foods they desire. After filling their plates, they can sit at tables you have set up, or they can sit on couches or chairs placed around the room.

Table service lets everyone be seated at a single table where food is passed and guests help themselves. For only a few guests, this is an easy service and can be very cozy and friendly.

A variation of table service is serving plates from the kitchen. You or a helper prepare plates in the kitchen and bring them out one or two at a time. Some foods may still be placed on the table for guests to serve themselves.

Table decorations should be low so guests can see over them and conversation is not difficult between guests who sit opposite each other.

Combination service lets you serve appetizers buffet-style, then serve dinner with guests seated. You may want to follow dinner with dessert or coffee in the living room.

An attractive service will please and delight guests as they anticipate eating the delicious-looking food. Colors of tablecloth, flowers and dishes should harmonize with each other and with the food. Think about how the food will look on the table—when it is full and as food is removed. Large trays are hard to keep full and looking good. It is better to have smaller plates or trays that can be replaced with full ones.

Never crowd food on serving plates or on the table. Some foods, such as sandwiches or pieces of meat, can be stacked or slightly overlapped. If guests will pick them up with their hands, leave room so no other food will be touched. If possible, supply serving pieces, such as tongs, forks or spoons.

Attractive garnishes make food more appealing. Use some of the following ideas, or garnish very simply with watercress, parsley, endive, cherry tomatoes or sprigs of dill or other herbs.

On previous pages: Caviar Appetizer, page 37

GARNISHES

Garnishing is really the art of leaving out—that is, never overdoing. The garnish should never mask the food, but should enhance and underline its appetizing appearance. Most garnishes are easily done. Radish rosettes, tomato roses and lemon wheels are made quickly. They can add eye and taste appeal, and in no way detract from the meal. Garnishes can help you make magic!

Butter or margarine should be refrigerated until it is shaped.
• Cut the butter into even slices or cubes with a serrated decorating knife.
• Fill a dish with soft butter. Refrigerate until firm. Cut curls by pulling a butter curler through the butter from the outside of the dish to the center, so that a flower forms in the center. Garnish with a little parsley.

From top: lemon curls, shredded peel, scored lemon with sprouts, slashed half-moon of lemon peel, lemon slices with scalloped edges.

• To make balls, cut cold butter into cubes. Shape into balls by gently rolling between two wet, ribbed, wooden boards. Leave plain, or roll butter balls in sweet paprika, chopped herbs or coarsely ground pepper.
• Curls are easily made with the butter curler.
• Herb butter is made by mixing chopped herbs and seasonings with soft butter. Shape into a log, then wrap in foil. Refrigerate until cold and firm. Cut into slices.
• Butter must be almost room temperature for motifs to be stamped with a press or for butter to be shaped in wooden molds. Soak the molds in cold water 30 minutes before pressing the butter into them. Pressed butter, whether with motifs or pressed in molds, should be placed in or on ice immediately.

Lemons make excellent garnishes.
• Cut lemon into slices. Notches may be cut into the peel before slicing.
• Cut lemon in slices, then slash slices from center to outside edge. Twist to make a curl, or fit two slices into each other at slashes.
• Cut strips of lemon peel using a citrus zester. The citrus zester can be used to cut small notches in the peel. Citrus zesters have five tiny, very sharp cutting holes that scrape off threads of peel.
• Use a citrus scorer to cut thicker pieces of lemon peel. This tool has a single-pronged cutting edge.
• Using a citrus scorer, cut three deep notches in the peel of a half lemon. Fill the notches with fine alfalfa sprouts or parsley.
• Cut notches into a half-moon piece of lemon peel.

Top: serrated butter slices, butter flower; center: butter balls rolled in paprika, herbs and ground pepper; butter curls; lower right: butter press and stamped butter; lower left: sliced herbed butter.

Clockwise from top left: tomato flower, red-and-white garnish, tomato roses, whole tomato, tomato crescents.

Tomatoes are popular for garnishing because they add bright red color. Combined with white radishes and green herbs they have an even fresher effect.

• For tomato flowers, begin on bud end and cut into 12 even wedges, without cutting through stem end. The resulting pointed leaf-like segments produce a flower when every other segment is bent outwards. Insert parsley or alfalfa sprouts into center.

• To make a red-and-white garnish, cut tomato in half lengthwise. Lay one half cut-side down. Cut about halfway through, into six wedges. Fill cuts with slices of white radish, turnip or jicama that have been cut with a fluted cookie cutter.

• Crescents are made by cutting seedless tomato quarters almost to the stem end. Gently pull apart to make double crescents.

• Using a vegetable peeler, peel firm-skinned tomatoes in a single strip. Peel should have a little flesh on it. Loosely roll the peel as shown, making a rose. Add smooth parsley for leaves. Tomato roses enhance the appearance of cold platters and salads. Use the remaining tomato flesh as a salad ingredient.

Carrots can be used in many ways. If carrot slices are cooked, they must be slightly thicker than when raw.

• To make cutout shapes, use hors d'oeuvre cutters to make tiny hearts, flowers and clover leaves. Use carrot cutouts and slices with cutouts removed to garnish salads or a cold platter. Also place cutouts on slices of unpeeled cucumber. The contrast is even greater when a little parsley is added.

• Carrot curls are made from raw carrots. When possible, use thick carrots. Slice in half lengthwise; let come to room temperature. Using a vegetable peeler, cut into long, thin lengthwise slices. It is almost like shaving a piece off. Roll carrot pieces and secure with wooden picks. Place in iced water. When chilled, remove wooden picks. (not shown)

• Carrot slices, sloping rectangles and cubes, cooked or raw, are attractive when cut with a scalloped decorating knife.

• Core a 3- to 4-inch piece of a medium to large carrot. Make crosswise cuts, 1/8 inch thick, not quite all the way through. Carefully spread slices apart; shape into a circle. Garnish center with dill or another green herb.

Clockwise from top left: cored and partially sliced carrot arranged in a circle, round and rectangular carrot slices, cutouts with cutters, cutouts on a cucumber slice, carrot cubes.

Radishes have been popular as garnishing vegetables since grandmother's time. The red-skinned variety with white centers are popular because they are so fresh looking. However, white radishes can be prepared in ways other radishes cannot. After cutting any radish garnish, place it in iced water to help it spread and become crisp and firm.

• Slice the radish, then cut the edges into scallops. Top with tomato or red-radish roses. (not shown)

• Cut in thin slices, then slash slices from center to outside edge. Twist to make a curl, or fit two slices into each other at slashes. Place on green lettuce leaves.

• Make long radish spirals. Use a radish-spiral cutter, available in many household stores. Follow package directions for using the cutter. The spiral will open up as shown.

• Slice radish. Lay around edge of plate so slices overlap. (not shown)

• Make flowers by cutting the radish in eight wedges, not cutting all the way through at bottom. Or, cut into four wedges, not cutting all the way through. Place in iced water until radishes open up into flowers, about ten minutes. Top with a parsley sprig. Serve them as a side dish or as a garnish.

• Using a knife or radish-rosette cutter, cut radish roses as shown. Cut the skin in pointed sections almost to the root.

• For rustic platters, rinse radishes but do not remove leaves. Arrange the cleaned radishes around a salt cellar on a platter. To eat, hold them by the leaves; dip them in salt. They are delicious with liver pâté sandwiches. (not shown)

• Leave bunch of radishes tied together. Rinse and trim off any blemishes. Place in a small bowl, leaf-side down. You now have a bowl of radish flowers ready to serve. Radishes with their leaves are pulled from the bunch, one at a time. (not shown)

Clockwise from top right: white-radish curl, thick red-radish slices, white-radish spiral.

Red-radish roses

Red-radish flowers

Rye & Salami Bread, page 126.

BREAD—BASIC FOR COLD CUISINE

For interesting cold sandwiches or accompaniments to cold soups or salads, use a variety of bread of different sizes, shapes and textures. When serving a smorgasbord or buffet, serve at least three types of bread. Consider including white, whole-wheat and rye. Add other breads to complement the flavors and textures of other foods being served.

Interesting Specialty Breads—There is a broad range of fragrant breads flavored with buttermilk, onions, caraway seeds, sesame seeds and nuts. They all make interesting cold-cuisine breads. Make sure the flavor of the bread blends and enhances the flavors of the meat, fish, poultry, vegetables or fruit that will top or be served with it. Some recipes are included in this book. See *Breads* in the index.

White bread is mild-flavored and may be soft- or firm-textured.

Mild-flavored rye bread is light in color and has a mild rye flavor and moist texture.

Strong-flavored rye bread is dark in color and has a more assertive rye flavor.

Whole-wheat bread has a mild, slightly sweet, nutty flavor.

Whole-grain bread includes the husk, germ and endo-sperm of the grain. It has a stronger flavor than whole-wheat bread. It may be topped with flakes of the same grain that it is made from.

Graham bread has a loose texture, a strong nutty flavor and is often served as a diet bread.

Pumpernickel bread has a typical dark appearance, with a malty sweet-strong flavor and moist texture.

Onion rolls have fresh chopped or slivered onion pressed onto the unbaked dough. After baking, the onions make a crisp topping.

Sesame rolls have sesame seeds sprinkled on their surface, giving the rolls a rich nut-like flavor.

Kaiser rolls are sprinkled with poppy seeds.

Small hard rolls have firm crusts with soft centers.

French bread or rolls are also breads with firm crusts. Thick slices are often spread with a garlic-butter mixture and lightly toasted.

Potato rolls have a soft texture and soft crust. Their mild flavor will not detract from mild-flavored spreads.

Whole-wheat rolls may be mild- or strong-flavored, depending on the ingredients. Molasses or dark honey will give a more distinct flavor than white sugar.

Nut quick breads are usually mild-flavored and complement cream-cheese or other mild-flavored fillings.

English muffins have a dense texture and are best toasted.

Muffins are very tender. They make excellent accompaniments to salads or soups.

Cheese twists may be made from a quick-bread dough or a yeast dough.

Garlic bread is a traditional yeast bread for use with strong-flavored fillings.

Pastries may also be served as sweet accompaniments.

Pita or pocket bread makes interesting salad-sandwiches. They let you hold your salad in your hand.

Tortillas have become a popular bread the world over. They are like soft flat pancakes but not as tender. Wrap them around meats or vegetables or use as a bread.

Bagels are a heavy bread that is cooked in water or baked or both. They are excellent served with cream cheese or cream-cheese mixtures.

Matzo are unleavened bread similar to crackers. They can be used as the base for appetizers and canapés.

Lavash is matzo-like Armenian cracker bread. This crisp bread can be used as crackers in appetizers and canapés or can be served with soups and salads.

CANAPÉS, SANDWICHES & SMORREBROD

Canapés are bread tidbits with toppings. They should be just large enough for a single mouthful. Canapés are usually served as snacks. They are seldom served as entrees or before a meal. Plain or toasted white, delicate rye or whole-wheat bread is cut into squares, triangles, strips, diamonds or circles. The pieces are not much bigger than the diameter of an egg slice. The bread is always spread with butter or a butter mixture. Top them with the best filling available—caviar, smoked salmon, pieces of lobster or oyster, or delicious but delicate cheese, meat or vegetable toppings. Allow about six canapés per person.

Sandwiches are probably as old as bread. They come in all sizes, shapes and styles, made from all kinds of breads and with all kinds of fillings. They may be served as appetizers, snacks, breakfasts, lunches, main dishes and desserts. No matter what they are made from or how, they are best eaten fresh.

Sandwiches may have the traditional two slices of bread, may be open-faced or made with several layers. Bread should always be spread with something to keep the filling from soaking through and making the sandwich soggy. This is usually butter or margarine. If sandwiches are made ahead, add lettuce, tomato slices, sprouts or other moist ingredients at serving time.

Smorrebrod are Danish open-faced sandwiches. They are usually more dainty and colorful than regular sandwiches. Use compact breads that hold their shape when cut. Day-old bread is better than fresh-baked bread. Slice or have the bread sliced 1/4 to 3/8 inch thick. Slice French bread 1/2 inch thick. Remove the crusts from most breads. Do not remove the crusts from French bread. Butter the bread, covering completely to edges. Toppings may be salmon or other fish, lobster, crabmeat, scrambled or hard-cooked eggs, thinly sliced meat, poultry, sausage, cheese or delicate salads. Typically, smorrebrod have fresh lettuce leaves on them. They are never made without an interesting garnish, such as dill, parsley or other herbs; sprouts; tomato slices or wedges; onion rings; cucumber twists; or orange or lemon twists.

from the Pacific Chinook or coho species. Cold-smoking does not cook the fish. *Lox* is mildly brined, cold-smoked salmon. *Nova* or *Nova Scotia salmon* is a type of cold-smoked salmon.

Lobster is one of the most popular shellfish for use in cold cuisine. It tastes delicious cold and is wonderfully suited for cocktails and salads as well as for sandwich fillings.

Caviar is a must for those who like it. Use small quantities to garnish canapés and salads.

Smoked herring and smoked mackerel are not common, but are nice in cold cuisine.

Smoked halibut is a delicacy with tender, moist flesh. It is excellent in any fish buffet, but is also tasty on bread and in fish salads.

Mushrooms are good in salads and can also be used in sandwich fillings or as garnishes.

Shrimp are especially delicious. They are used for salads, cocktails, with bread, in creams and as garnishes.

Canned fish, from crabmeat to herring in tomato sauce, from lobster tails to mussels, make exciting fish platters and interesting bread toppings, smorrebrod and salads. All are readily available in most supermarkets.

Oysters are available fresh, pickled or smoked. For elegant canapés, they are used fresh, direct from the shell.

OTHER INGREDIENTS

If we were to describe everything you can use as a delicious topping on bread, to mix with salads or to serve on a cold buffet, there wouldn't be enough room on these pages. Therefore, the following are only the essentials of cold cuisine.

Butter or margarine, whether used on bread or in dressings, must be fresh. Butter stays fresh at least ten days in a closed container in the refrigerator. Margarine will keep six weeks.

Eggs are a must in cold cuisine. Hard-cooked eggs are relatively neutral in flavor and are excellent combined with cold meat, ham, fish, shellfish and vegetables. In addition, raw eggs are an essential basis for mayonnaise. Use only fresh eggs for the best flavor.

Meat, fish and poultry are excellent cooked, then chilled for use in sandwiches, salads and other cold combinations.

Ham can be fresh-baked, smoked or boiled, as long as it is fully cooked before using.

Cheese varies from assertive or mellow Cheddar; moist, mild-flavored Monterey Jack; marvelous Swiss, such as Emmentaler, Gruyère, Appenzeller and Jarlsberg; white, salty and crumbly Greek feta; smooth, mellow Gouda and stronger Edam; delicately aromatic Brie with its silky texture and buttery color; to assertive blues—Roquefort, Danablu or Stilton. All of these can be used in sandwiches, canapés and salads. Cream cheese makes excellent sandwich and canapé toppings.

Smoked salmon is a delicacy, without which, cold cuisine would be only half as interesting. It includes *kippered salmon* which is mildly brined and smoke-cooked. *Scotch-smoked salmon* is a cold-smoked Atlantic salmon. When called merely *smoked salmon,* the product is cold-smoked

Roast-Beef & Asparagus Smorrebrod, page 147

HERBS

Cold cuisine is enhanced with the use of fresh and dried herbs. *Basil* is a spicy, peppery herb. Only the leaves are used in noodle, cheese, meat and fish dishes.

Both stems and leaves of aromatic, piquant *savory* can be used. It is good in all bean dishes, salads, legumes and meat. Both basil and savory can be used dried.

Fresh, young leaves and flowers of *borage* are tender. With age, they become coarse; dried, they lose flavor. Use fresh borage in cool summer drinks, desserts, salads and as an attractive garnish. Use finely cut leaves in cheese spreads.

Without *parsley*, cold cuisine would be pretty bland. It can be a seasoning and garnish at the same time.

Salad burnet has feather-like leaves that taste and smell like cucumber. It is delicious in salads and salad dressings, herb cheese and herb butter.

Fresh and dried *rosemary* is widely used. This member of the mint family is one of the oldest herbs known to man. The twigs, with their needle-shaped leaves, are used to season meat, fish, tomatoes and vegetable dishes. They are bitter, aromatic and pungent.

Dill is an annual herb with lacy foliage. It is popular for use in pickles, but is excellent in salads, cooked vegetables, fish, meat and sauces.

Tarragon is intensely aromatic and a little sweet. It is very good in salad dressings and herb butter.

Mustard cress, a member of the mustard family, generally grows in running water. Its leaves are used in salads, cold platters and soups. *Radish sprouts* are similar to mustard cress and can be used as a substitute.

Sage is used fresh, dried or frozen. Its full, spicy flavor makes it ideal for poultry or pork stuffings, sausage, cheese, egg dishes, salads, cooked vegetables and fish.

Sorrel imparts a delicate, tangy, somewhat citrus flavor. Use fresh or frozen leaves in cold sauces, soups or salads. It does not dry well.

Chives are thin, hollow, grass-like leaves. Their mild onion flavor is excellent in salads, vegetables and mild meats. Chives are available fresh or dried.

Use *celery leaves* in soups, salads, vegetables and as a garnish.

Use *bay leaves* in dishes that are simmered for a long time, in marinades and sauces. They are indispensable for fish dishes and for seasoning roasts that will be made into cold cuts. Be sure to remove bay leaves from the cooked product before it is served.

The leaves of *marjoram* are mainly used, fresh or dried, for meat dishes and stuffings.

Only the seeds of *coriander* are known as coriander. The highly spicy and aromatic leaves are called *cilantro* or *Chinese parsley*. Use only the young leaves in salads and in Chinese, Mexican and Mediterranean dishes.

There are more than 400 species of highly aromatic *thyme*. Sprigs and leaves are used in pork, lamb and game dishes; barbecue sauces; and salad dressings. Combine with marjoram, parsley and bay leaf to make *bouquet garni*.

Lemon mint is a tender, lemon-flavored herb, equally suitable for salads, herb sauces, butters and cheese. It is also used in alcoholic drinks.

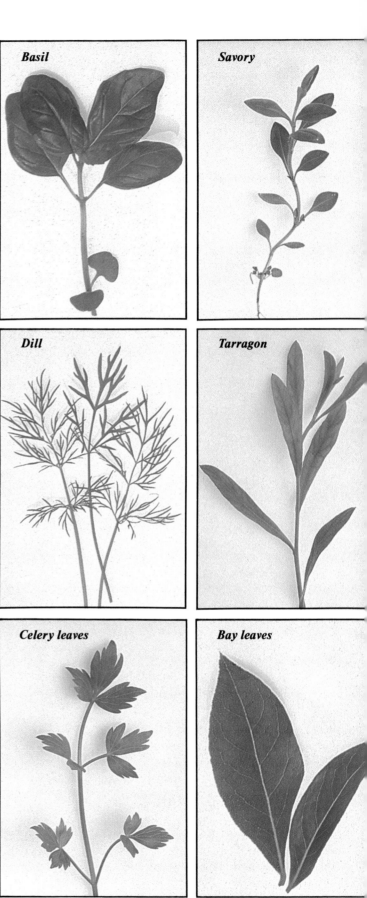

Basil

Savory

Dill

Tarragon

Celery leaves

Bay leaves

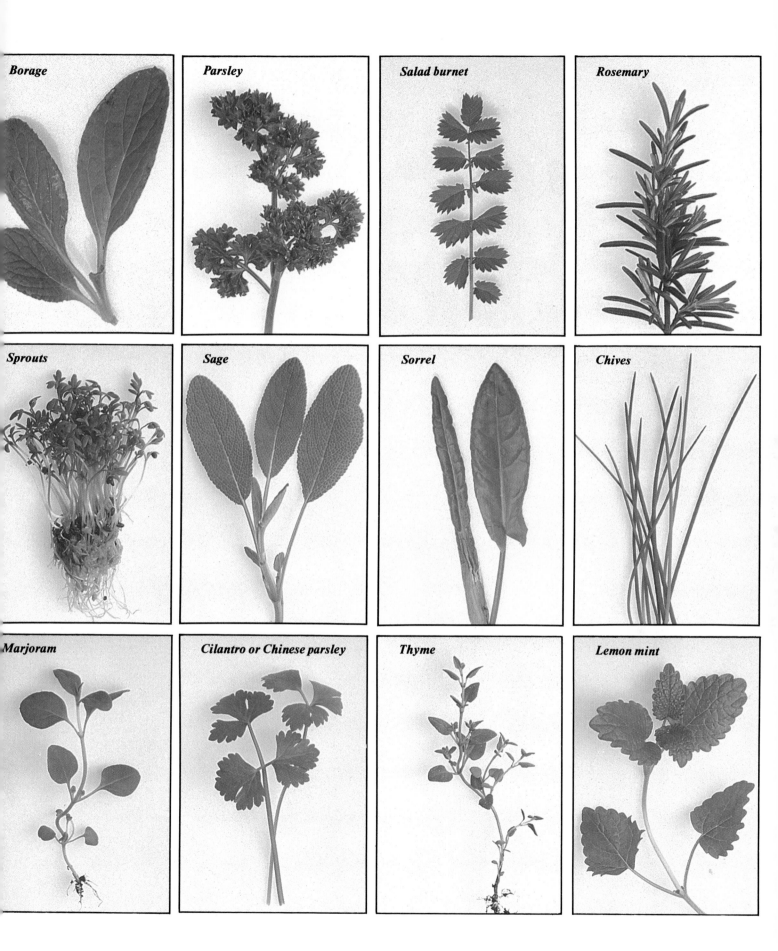

Borage

Parsley

Salad burnet

Rosemary

Sprouts

Sage

Sorrel

Chives

Marjoram

Cilantro or Chinese parsley

Thyme

Lemon mint

Guava

Dates

Prickly-Pear Cactus Fruit

Avocado

Kiwifruit

Kaki Fruit (Japanese Persimmon)

Lychee

Mango

Passion Fruit

Papaya

Lime

Kumquat

Watermelon

Honeydew, Cantaloupe & Crenshaw Melons

FRESH FRUIT

It is no longer a problem to get exotic fruit from around the world. Air transports and refrigerated ships make it possible to bring new and unusual fruits to our tables via well-stocked supermarkets.

Guava, for example, comes from tropical Middle and South America. It contains five times as much vitamin C as citrus fruits. Fresh *dates* are now readily available as well as dried dates.

Prickly-pear cactus fruit, sometimes called *cactus fig,* with its refreshing sweet flesh, originated in the south-west United States and South America. Today it is grown in the tropics and sub-tropics, as well. *Avocado,* originally from the tropics and hard to find in the supermarket, is now grown in the United States. It is readily available even in out-of-the-way places.

Kiwifruit originally came from New Zealand, but is now grown in California. The fuzzy brown fruit has a cool, green flesh with edible black seeds. Its delicate fruit is lovely in fruit salads.

Kaki fruit, also known as *Japanese Persimmon,* is native to Asia, but is grown in some Mediterranean countries today. It is very sweet and tastes faintly of apricots.

Pineapple

Lychee or *litchi,* from China and the United States, has a hard, brittle skin that is pebbled like a raspberry. When peeled, the inside has a sweet white flesh. When dried, lychees are called *lychee nuts.*

Mangoes have a pineapple-apricot flavor. Green mangoes are not ripe. Look for those with tinges of yellow and pink or red on the smooth skin. When ripe, its orange-yellow pulp is too soft to hold in your hand to eat, but is hard to cut away from the large flat seed in the center. Slice along the flat side, slightly off center, to miss the seed. Tropical *passion fruit,* or *granadilla,* comes from Mexico and Central America. Depending on the variety, the flesh may be white or gray. Its flavor is distinctive and penetrating, but is excellent in fruit salads when a small quantity is used. Because of its seeds, it is often used for juice.

Strongly aromatic *papaya* is a delight. Serve in slices or chop and use in salads. *Lime,* a type of citrus, gives more juice and is milder than lemon. *Kumquat* is a member of the citrus family. It has a slightly sweet edible skin and juicy, slightly bitter flesh. Slice thinly for use in salads.

What would cold cuisine be without *melons?* Today, some type of melon is available most of the year. They come in a variety of colors—red, orange, yellow and green. *Pineapple* comes from Puerto Rico, Mexico and Hawaii. Fresh pineapple is more acid than canned, but is sweet enough to blend well with other fresh fruit in salads. Use canned pineapple in gelatin, or cook fresh pineapple before using in gelatin. The papain in fresh, un-cooked pineapple keeps gelatin from setting up.

SALAD MAKINGS

Greens, whether used in salads, entree cocktails or in fruit salads, all belong to cold cuisine. The more care taken in their preparation, the more appetizing and deli-cious they will be. This also applies to other ingredients—whether vegetables, meats, fish, sausages, cheeses or fruits. If carefully and evenly sliced, they will be appetizing to the eye as well as the taste bud. Lettuce leaves, for example, should be torn into bite-size pieces, all about the same size. You may want to remove the coarse leaf ribs.

Endive and chicory, Chinese cabbage and iceberg let-tuce can be cut into even strips. Ingredients for raw vegetarian dishes, such as carrots, kohlrabi, celery, fennel or white radish, should be coarsely grated or chopped. Cucumbers, with or without skins, can be chopped or sliced with a knife, thickly or thinly, as desired. *Smorrebrod,* dainty Danish open-faced sandwiches, require very thinly sliced cucumbers.

Tomatoes are attractive cut into 8 or even 16 wedges. Always remove the stalk base or core before slicing tomatoes. *To skin a tomato,* dip it into gently boiling water, then immediately plunge into cold water. Peel off the skin. Cut the tomato into any desired shape.

Using a melon baller, cucumbers, melons and potatoes can be cut into balls. These are especially attractive. Or, you can use a serrated decorating knife to make decora-tive ridges on vegetables.

Sweet bell peppers can be sliced into rings, quarters or strips of the same length and thickness.

Vegetables for cold cuisine are not always raw. They can be, and sometimes must be, cooked. Peas and beans are usually cooked. Carrots, celery and kohlrabi are often served raw, but can be cooked and used in salads. Thick raw or cooked vegetable slices can be cut into shapes for garnishing, pages 215 to 217. Preferably, use a food for garnishing that is also used in the salad. An exception is hard-cooked eggs, which are chopped, sliced or cut in strips. They go well with most salads.

Other salad ingredients include meat, sausage, fish, seafood, poultry, cheese and fruit.

These few rules apply to all salad ingredients:
- Always mix salads in a large bowl to avoid crowding and bruising ingredients. Serve them in another bowl, if desired.
- If possible, cut all of one ingredient into the same shape—strips, cubes, slices, rings or balls. For variety, mix several different ingredients, each of a different shape.

- Meat is best cut into strips or thin slices. Sausage can be sliced or cubed. Cheese is best cut into small strips or cubes.
- Cooked fish does not cut well. It is best flaked.
- Most shellfish flakes nicely and looks very attractive. Leave shrimp, mussels and oysters whole. Crabmeat and lobster can be cut into relatively even pieces.
- Remove stones or pits from fruit, such as cherries or grapes.
- Cut apples and pears into strips or quarter them and cut into thin slices.
- Peel peaches. Cut peaches or nectarines into wedges.
- Section mandarins and oranges by cutting off the peel and white pith. Then cut on both sides of section membranes. Lift out the fruit.
- Peeled kiwifruit looks pretty in slices and cubes.
- Melons can be cubed or cut into balls with a melon baller.
- Use whole berries, except when strawberries are large. Then cut them into halves or thick slices.
- Cut crunchy jicama into cubes or strips for salads. Or cut into wedges or fingers for vegetable dippers.
- Cut whole onions into thin slices, rings, cubes or strips.
- Unless they are very tiny, cut mushrooms into vertical slices, halves or quarters.
- Celery is attractive cut into short diagonal pieces.
- Cut leeks into strips or slices.
- Cabbage is best cut into strips or shredded.
- Cut red or white radishes into slices, flowers or spirals.
- Cut asparagus into short sticks or pieces.
- Garnish delicate salads with bunches of herbs of the type used in the salad.
- Hard-cooked eggs look good in slices or wedges.
- Where they go well with the salad, use radish rosettes or cutouts from carrot slices.
- Cut pimento-stuffed green olives into slices or halves.

Kiwifruit, Citrus & Walnut Salad, page 75

SALAD DRESSINGS

Salad becomes something really special when its own special dressing is added. Spicy is nice, but it doesn't have to be so hot it burns your mouth. A dressing should have a special flavor that makes it unforgettable. It could be laced with a special vinegar flavored with fruit or herbs. Or, add a dash of cherry liqueur, brandy, wine or sherry. Even a special oil, such as piquant walnut oil, gives it an interesting touch. A dressing can be prepared from an oil-and-vinegar base, or it can have a crème-fraîche, sweet- or sour-cream, or a mayonnaise base. Flavored mayonnaise is very good on salads.

Vinegar and oil dressings are suggested for leafy salads or for salads made from fresh, tender vegetables. Dressings made from cream are also suitable. This includes all leafy vegetables, such as Chinese cabbage, iceberg lettuce and chicory.

A teaspoon of prepared mustard or grated horseradish is good in some dressings and marinades, as are chopped capers, pureed anchovies and pureed fruit chutney.

Spiced or *flavored vinegars* are available in some supermarkets and gourmet stores. Or, you can make your own. Start with a white-distilled, cider, red- or white-wine vinegar. Add whatever fruit, herb or spice you choose. Let the mixture stand long enough for flavors to blend, two to ten days. Depending on what was added, the vinegar mixture may need to be refrigerated. Most homemade vinegars should be used within three to six months. Use flavored vinegar sparingly. You can always add more later, if needed.

Flavored or *seasoned oils* are available commercially, but are easy to make. Combine a basic salad oil—sunflower, corn or soy—that has very little taste, with fruit, nuts, vegetables, herbs or spices. Let the mixture stand so the flavors can mingle.

You can also use *olive oil* with its interesting aroma. Commercial varieties may be plain or flavored. *Peanut oil* has a mild but special flavor. *Walnut oil* is tasty, but easily goes rancid. *Hazelnut oil* has a strong nutty flavor and must be used sparingly.

Crème fraîche, page 162, is made from whipping cream. It was served in France long before it was accepted in the United States. Crème fraîche is preferable for sweet fruit salads.

Lemon juice can be used as an alternative to vinegar or as a tasty ingredient in a dressing. Its flavor blends with mayonnaise and cream dressings and is often indispensable in crème fraîche dressings. But be careful. Lemon juice has a more intense flavor than most vinegars.

Spices are also important. Though *salt* is not a spice, at least a small amount is used in many dressings. White and black *pepper* belong in cold cuisine. Sometimes a pinch of red (cayenne) pepper gives the desired bite. Or, commercial spiced pepper and lemon pepper give added flavor. A pepper-and-garlic or salt-and-garlic mixture adds a Mediterranean flavor, while green pepper adds a very special flavor of its own. Some people like to add the inevitable pinch of *sugar* to a piquant marinade. Curry, paprika, ground ginger, and sometimes a pinch of cinnamon, are allowed. There is hardly a spice you can't experiment with in cold cuisine.

From top: Herbal Dressing, Rémoulade Sauce, Horseradish Cream, all on page 158; carafe holds Vinegar

Herbs can be combined with prepared or homemade dressings or mayonnaise to add some delightful flavors. When seafood or shellfish, meats, chicken, cheese or eggs will have a dressing on them, add a little basil, dill, saffron, savory, tarragon or thyme. Marjoram and oregano can be used in dressing for meats, chicken and vegetables.

Onion is another common salad-dressing ingredient. It can be chopped, finely chopped or grated, adding just the liquid from the grating.

Some people feel *garlic* is a must in their salad dressings while others absolutely avoid it.

POULTRY

Whether you're preparing duck, chicken, pheasant, Cornish hen, pigeon, turkey or goose, all should be handled the same. Frozen poultry is oven-ready. All you do is partially thaw and rinse them. Remove giblets, any pin feathers and excess fat. Then they are ready to season, stuff and bake.

Preparation is very different with fresh poultry. They must be carefully plucked to avoid damaging the skin. Burn off any down feathers that remain by holding over a flame. If there are still the remains of feather quills sticking out of the skin, pull them out with a pair of tweezers or needle-nose pliers. Remove the head, part of the neck and the feet before gutting the bird.

Now you can proceed as with an oven-ready bird. Rinse the bird inside and out, dry it, season the inside and stuff it. To prepare any poultry, follow steps 1 through 4, below. Then season the dressed bird on the outside. Cover tiny wings of pheasants and partridges with foil or bacon.

Carving Roasted Poultry:

5/Holding bird with a carving fork, use a carving knife to remove legs and thighs.

6/Cut off wings with a carving knife or poultry scissors.

Dressing Poultry:

1/Remove excess fat. Stuff with apple pieces or bread stuffing. Pin or sew opening closed.

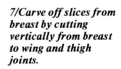

7/Carve off slices from breast by cutting vertically from breast to wing and thigh joints.

2/Tie drumsticks close to body.

8/Or, cut breast meat away from both sides of breast bone. Lay breast on a cutting board to slice.

3/Pull neck flap to back. Tie in place. Prick duck skin all over to let fat drain during roasting.

9/Cut breast meat into thick slices. Remove remaining meat from bones. Cut into pieces.

4/Place breast-side up on a rack in a shallow roasting pan. Add about 1 cup water. Roast 2 hours at 350F (175C) or to 180F to 185F (80C to 85C) or until juices run clear.

10/Serve as legs, thighs, wings and breast slices. Cut small birds into quarters. Serve pigeons or Cornish hens whole.

FISH

No food product is more perishable than fish and shellfish. Cold temperatures help to slow deterioration, but fresh or frozen fish and shellfish should be eaten as soon as possible after catching or purchasing. They can be purchased fresh, frozen and canned. If at all possible, purchase fish the day it will be served.

When purchasing frozen fish, choose undamaged, solidly frozen packages without discoloration, signs of drying or off odor. Unless frozen fish will be breaded, deep-fried or stuffed, do not let it thaw completely. When completely thawed, the flesh may loose much of its moisture and result in a dry cooked product. Thaw frozen fish and shellfish in the refrigerator. Or, wrap airtight in plastic and immerse in cold water. Or, partially thawed in a microwave oven following the manufacturer's instructions.

Fish markets usually sell fresh fish already gutted, portioned and even filleted. However, by purchasing a whole fish, you can use the bones and trimmings for fish stock. Photos on this page show how fish are cleaned and filleted. To begin, rinse the fish quickly under running cold water. *Do not let fish soak in water.* Pat them dry with paper towels. Sprinkle fish with vinegar or lemon juice to make the flesh firm. Lightly salt fish shortly before placing it in the pot or frying pan. Never let a salted fish stand. Salt draws water from the fish, making it dry.

Large fish, such as sole, or fish with inedible tough skins, such as catfish, must be skinned.

4/With long, smooth strokes, separate upper fillet from backbone. Remove rib bones from fillet.

5/To remove skin, separate skin from fillet at tail end. Pull up slightly, then peel off skin from tail to head.

Skinning & Filleting Flatfish:

6/Place dark-side up. Just above tail, cut through skin but not into flesh. Cover tail with paper towels; hold firmly. Peel off skin from tail to head. Turn and pull off skin from belly.

Cleaning & Filleting Roundfish:

1/If skin will be left on, use a knife to scrape fish from tail to head to remove scales. Split open belly. Use a knife or scissors to cut off fins.

7/Cut midway between dorsal and anal fins, deep enough to expose backbone.

2/Cut off head. Remove and discard viscera. Head can be used to make stock.

8/Starting at head, use long, smooth strokes to separate flesh from bones.

3/Cut fish along center back from head to tail, deep enough to expose backbone.

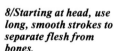

9/Carefully cut off 2 fillets from back and 2 fillets from belly.

SHELLFISH

There are two basic types of shellfish for cooking: *mollusks* and *crustaceans*. Mollusks have soft bodies fully or partially enclosed in shells. They include abalone, clams, oysters, scallops and squid. Crustaceans have long, segmented bodies inside jointed shells. Crab, crayfish, langostinos, lobster and shrimp are crustaceans.

Shells of live clams, oysters and scallops should be tightly closed, or they should close tightly when you tap on the shell. Soft-shell clams are the exception. Live crab, crayfish and lobster should be active and heavy for their size. For safety, use tongs to handle them.

Lobster—After lobster is cooked and chilled, combine it with sauces to use in cocktails or toppings for special canapés. Some fish markets offer live lobsters as well as cooked and frozen.

If you buy cooked lobster, the tail should be tucked tightly under the body. This is an indication the lobster was alive and fresh when cooked.

Two kinds of lobsters are commonly available in the United States and Canada—American or Maine and spiny lobsters. American or Maine lobsters are caught in the Northwest Atlantic. They are the traditional lobsters with large, meaty claws. Because of the cold waters, their flesh is succulent and highly prized. Spiny lobsters are found in warmer waters off Florida, Southern California, Mexico, Australia, New Zealand and South Africa. There is little meat in their small claws, but the tail is meaty.

Live lobsters have strong claws that can crack right through a persons small finger. Therefore, do not remove the strong bands that bind the claws until after the lobster has been cooked. The more active the live lobster, the more recently it was caught and the fresher it is.

Fresh lobsters can be stored in the refrigerator up to 12 hours. Keep them in a loose plastic bag or in salted water. Fresh water will kill them. If a lobster dies, cook it immediately. Lobsters used in cold cuisine are cooked by boiling, opposite.

3/Using a sharp knife or kitchen scissors, cut lobster shell open from tail to head. Cut lobster body in half.

4/Remove eyes and small stomach sac near eyes. Pull out intestinal vein running down tail.

5/Holding shell firmly, pull out meat.

6/Use a lobster cracker, nut cracker or small hammer to crack centers of claws.

Cleaning & Cracking Cooked Lobster:

1/Lay lobster on its back; twist off legs.

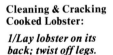

2/Using your hands, twist off and remove claws at joints. If necessary, cut through joints with point of a knife.

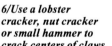

7/Pull off upper pointed claw shell, leaving tender meat.

8/Twist off lower joint of claw; remove meat before serving. Slice tail meat to serve.

To cook lobsters, pour 6 to 8 inches of water into a deep kettle. Add 1 to 2 teaspoons salt, if desired. Plunge lobsters, 1 at a time, head first into the boiling water. Partially cover the kettle. Bring the water back to a simmer before beginning timing. Cook 1-pound lobsters 6 to 8 minutes. Add 2 to 3 minutes for each additional pound. Use tongs to remove cooked lobsters from the kettle. Plunge into cold water to cool and prevent overcooking. Lobster shells become cardinal red when boiled.

Crayfish—Like lobsters, crayfish should be active and heavy for their size. Cook by immersing in water flavored with spices and herbs. Plunge them head first into the boiling liquid. When the liquid comes back to a boil, cook the crayfish 4 to 8 minutes, depending on their size. Like lobsters, they will turn bright red when cooked. They are a little more difficult to eat than lobster.

To eat crayfish, using your hands, break the tail away from the body with a twisting motion. Most of the meat is in the tail. Break off claws at the joints. The claws take time to crack and don't yield much meat, but the meat is especially sweet. Use a lobster fork to remove the meat. Bend the head back and pull out the breast shell. Scoop out the meat with a small spoon or lobster fork.

Crab—Crab is available fresh, cooked or canned. Cook fresh crab in boiling salted water 20 minutes. It will turn red when cooked. To use the cooked flesh, pull off the top or back shell. Cut off the face. Pull out and discard the bile sac. Turn the crab on its back. Pull off the rough triangle of shell called the *apron.* Pull out and discard the feathery gills. Save the creamy *butter* from the cavity, if desired. Use it as a dip or spread. Rinse out the cavity and remove the small white intestine. Twist off the legs; crack the legs and claws and remove the meat. Crabmeat must be cooked to use in cold foods.

Oysters—Available fresh in-the-shell, shucked and canned, oysters are available year-round. They are best for serving on-the-half-shell during the fall and winter. See photos 2 to 4, right, on shucking an oyster.

Mussels—Once called *poor man's oysters,* mussels have finally achieved the recognition they deserve. They can be eaten boiled, stuffed, grilled and combined with other ingredients. See photo 1 on right.

Snails or Escargots—Snails are considered a delicacy. They are sometimes available fresh, but most often are canned. They are baked in a special indented snail pan or on a bed of rock salt. They can also be cooked and eaten without the shells. Natural shells are difficult to sterilize for reuse. Ceramic shells are available in cookware shops.

To prepare snails, remove snails from shells, if necessary. Blanch in boiling water 30 seconds. Drain on paper towels. Cream 1/2 cup butter, 2 crushed garlic cloves, 1 minced green onion, 1 teaspoon finely chopped parsley, 1 drop hot-pepper sauce and 2 tablespoons dry white wine. Season with salt and pepper. Place about 1/2 teaspoon butter mixture into each shell or into each indentation in pan. Insert snail into each shell or place on butter. Spoon about 1 teaspoon butter mixture into each shell or over snails. Bake at 350F (175C) 8 to 10 minutes.

To eat snails, pour melted butter mixture into a small bowl. Use a small fork to remove snails from shells. Dip French bread into melted butter mixture; eat with snails.

Shucking Mussels:

1/Insert a thin knife between shells. Run knife blade around shell to sever muscles holding mussel to shells. If desired, remove mussels from shells by using an empty mussel shell as pincers.

Shucking Oysters:

2/Lay oyster on a kitchen towel with deep-shell side down. Cover with cloth; hold firmly. Use an oyster knife or punch-type can opener to open shell.

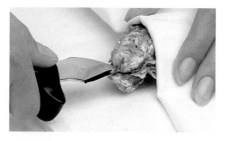

3/Gradually open shell by moving knife gently to and fro until upper shell loosens.

4/Ease knife around top shell to sever muscle holding shells together. Use knife or your thumb to separate oyster from bottom shell. Eat raw oysters on-the-half-shell, or cook oysters, both page 105.

Cooking & Eating Snails:

5/Cook as directed, opposite. Holding filled shell with snail tongs, pour out butter into a spoon or bowl for sopping up with bread.

6/Using snail tongs and a lobster or snail fork, remove snail from shell.

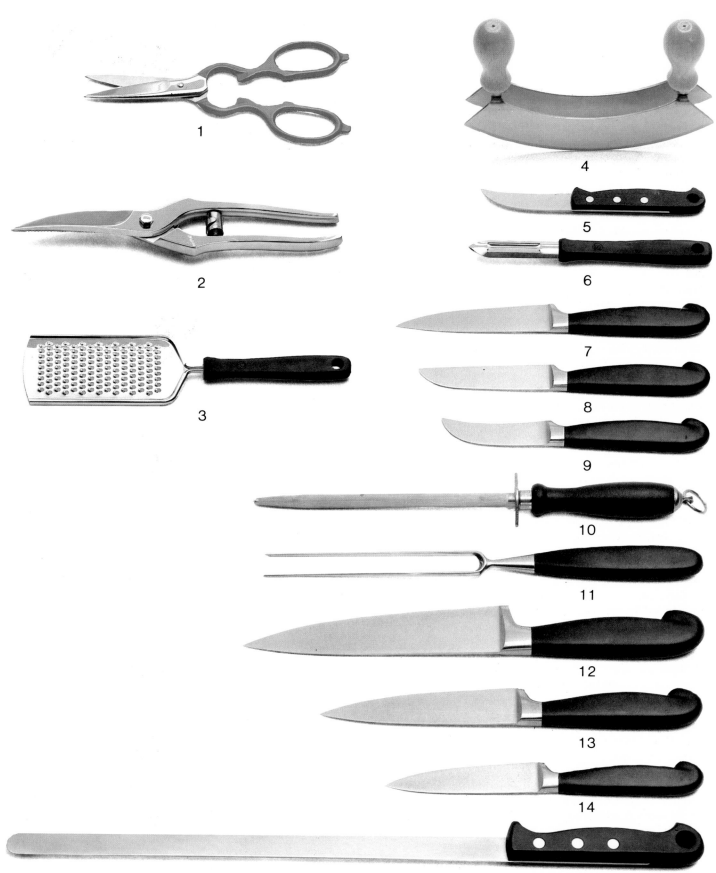

1

2

3

4

5

6

7

8

9

10

11

12

13

14

15

USE ONLY THE BEST TOOLS

All the delicious recipes in this book are prepared easily when you have the right equipment. They don't have to be new or handsome, but should be of good quality. If you don't already have them, consider purchasing an electric mixer, food processor or blender, toaster, wire whisk and an assortment of sharp knives. With these basic tools, you can do just about anything with cold cuisine. Make sure your equipment is in good working order and that your knives are *sharp*. Without sharp knives, you are working with a distinct handicap. Let's take a look at what tools your well-equipped kitchen should contain:

Kitchen scissors (1) are an all-purpose utensil. With them, you can cut open packages, cut up tiny herbs or remove fish fins. Stubborn screw-type bottle tops and some corks can be opened with the indentation behind the blades.

The strong sharp blades of *poultry scissors* (2) help you cut raw and cooked poultry. They are strong enough to cut through bones.

A *grater or shredder* (3) is ideal for grating or shedding small amounts of cheese or other soft or crisp ingredients.

The *mincing knife* (4), with its two curved blades and handles, is used for chopping herbs, vegetables and meat.

Paring knives (5, 7, 8, 9) are used for peeling and cleaning fruit and vegetables. Larger paring knives, such as the *chef's knife* (7), are used to slice large vegetables, small roasts or other pieces of meat.

Use a *vegetable peeler* (6) to peel fruits and vegetables and to cut vegetable curls. Peelers come in a variety of shapes. Be sure yours is sharp.

The *whet steel knife sharpener,* (10) used to sharpen knives with smooth blades, is indispensable in any kitchen. Knives with scalloped or serrated edges can also be sharpened with a steel sharpener, but it is best to have them sharpened professionally. There are also mechanical and electric knife sharpeners available for sharpening smooth bladed knives.

Carving forks (11) have two long prongs; some have longer prongs than others. Use the fork to hold meat while slicing it with a long sharp knife. Carving forks are indispensable for carving large roasts and poultry.

Slicing and *carving knives* (12, 13, 14) include the *French chef's knife* (12). Its curved blade lets you use a rocking motion as you chop. Use a French knife and shorter versions to cut raw or cooked meat, herbs, vegetables and fruit. Some knives have thin blades, making it easy to cut thin slices.

Most *bread knives* (15) have serrated blades that easily cut through soft or hard bread crusts without crushing the bread. Some bread knives have a smooth cutting edge.

The *garlic press* (16) is a super invention. Although the garlic clove must be peeled, the press crushes it so your hands don't smell like garlic.

An *orange peeler* (17) helps to peel juicy citrus fruit, removing both the peel and white inner skin or *pith*.

There are many *garnishing tools* (18) on the market. This one lets you shape cold butter into swirls and balls. It will also cut grooved slices from butter.

This *egg cutter* (19) cuts hard-cooked eggs into six wedges. Another type of egg cutter cuts eggs into even slices. Use either of the cutters to cut big thick mushrooms into wedges or slices.

For decorating, a *pastry bag* (20) and its variety of *tips* are indispensable. Also use it to pipe cheeses, whipped cream, mayonnaise and butter fillings.

Hors d'oeuvres or *garnish cutters* (21) help you create beautiful shapes from raw or cooked carrots, kohlrabi, cucumbers, celery, apples and beets.

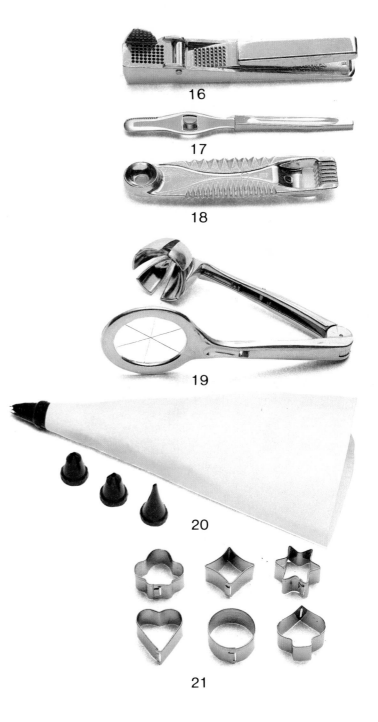

16

17

18

19

20

21

Equivalency Chart

Food Item	Market Unit	Household Measurement
Apple	1 medium	1 cup chopped
Bacon	1 lb.	24 slices
crisply fried, crumbled	1 lb.	3 cups
	8 slices	1 cup
Butter or margarine	1 lb.	2 cups
	1/4 lb.	1/2 cup
Cereal, cold flaked	15 oz.	about 11 cups
Cheese		
Cheddar-type, shredded	1 lb.	4 cups
cottage cheese	1 lb.	2 cups
cream cheese	3 oz.	6 tablespoons
	8 oz.	1 cup
Chocolate		
pieces (chips)	6 oz.	about 1 cup
unsweetened baking	8 oz.	8 squares
	1 oz.	1 wrapped square
Cocoa powder, unsweetened	8 oz.	2 cups
Coconut, shredded or flaked	4 oz.	1-1/3 cups
Corn syrup	16 oz.	2 cups
Cream		
sour	1 lb.	2 cups
whipping cream	1/2 pint	1 cup
whipped	1/2 pint	2 cups
Egg whites	12 eggs	1-1/4 cups
	1 egg	5 tablespoons
Egg yolks	12 eggs	3/4 cup
	1 egg	about 4 teaspoons
Flour		
all-purpose	5 lbs.	about 20 cups
	1 lb.	3-1/2 to 4 cups
instant	13.5 oz.	about 3 cups
whole-wheat	5 lbs.	about 18-1/3 cups
Gelatin		
unflavored	1 oz.	1/4 cup
flavored	3 oz.	7 tablespoons
Graham crackers	1 lb.	about 4 cups crumbs
Lemon juice	1 lemon	3 to 4 tablespoons
Lemon peel, grated	1 lemon	about 2 teaspoons
Milk, instant nonfat powder	1 lb.	about 6 cups
Nuts, shelled		
almonds	1 lb.	3 cups
peanuts	1 lb.	3 cups
pecans		
halves	1 lb.	4 cups
chopped	1 lb.	3-1/2 to 4 cups
pistachios	1 lb.	3-1/4 to 4 cups
walnuts		
halves	1 lb.	3-1/2 cups
chopped	1 lb.	3-1/2 cups
Oats, rolled	18 oz.	about 6 cups
Onion	1 whole	3/4 to 1 cup chopped
chopped fresh	1/4 cup	1 tablespoon dried
Orange juice	1 orange	6 to 8 tablespoons
Orange peel	1 orange	3 to 4 teaspoons
Shortening	1 lb.	2 cups
Sugar		
brown, packed	1 lb.	2-1/4 cups
granulated	5 lbs.	about 15 cups
	1 lb.	3 cups
powdered, unsifted	1 lb.	3 to 4 cups
sifted	1 lb.	about 4-1/2 cups
Yeast		
active dry	1/4 oz.	scant 1 tablespoon
compressed	0.60 oz.	4 teaspoons

Metric Chart

Comparison to Metric Measure

When You Know	Symbol	Multiply By	To Find	Symbol
teaspoons	tsp	5.0	milliliters	ml
tablespoons	tbsp	15.0	milliliters	ml
fluid ounces	fl. oz.	30.0	milliliters	ml
cups	c	0.24	liters	l
pints	pt.	0.47	liters	l
quarts	qt.	0.95	liters	l
ounces	oz.	28.0	grams	g
pounds	lb.	0.45	kilograms	kg
Fahrenheit	F	5/9 (after subtracting 32)	Celsius	C

Fahrenheit to Celsius

F	C
200—205	95
220—225	105
245—250	120
275	135
300—305	150
325—330	165
345—350	175
370—375	190
400—405	205
425—430	220
445—450	230
470—475	245
500	260

Liquid Measure to Milliliters

1/4 teaspoon	=	1.25 milliliters
1/2 teaspoon	=	2.5 milliliters
3/4 teaspoon	=	3.75 milliliters
1 teaspoon	=	5.0 milliliters
1-1/4 teaspoons	=	6.25 milliliters
1-1/2 teaspoons	=	7.5 milliliters
1-3/4 teaspoons	=	8.75 milliliters
2 teaspoons	=	10.0 milliliters
1 tablespoon	=	15.0 milliliters
2 tablespoons	=	30.0 milliliters

Liquid Measure to Liters

1/4 cup	=	0.06 liters
1/2 cup	=	0.12 liters
3/4 cup	=	0.18 liters
1 cup	=	0.24 liters
1-1/4 cups	=	0.3 liters
1-1/2 cups	=	0.36 liters
2 cups	=	0.48 liters
2-1/2 cups	=	0.6 liters
3 cups	=	0.72 liters
3-1/2 cups	=	0.84 liters
4 cups	=	0.96 liters
4-1/2 cups	=	1.08 liters
5 cups	=	1.2 liters
5-1/2 cups	=	1.32 liters

Index

238 **Index**